The Mathematics of Sex

The Mathematics Of Sex

How Biology and Society Conspire to Limit Talented Women and Girls

Stephen J. Ceci

and

Wendy M. Williams

OXFORD
UNIVERSITY PRESS

2010

OXFORD
UNIVERSITY PRESS

Oxford University Press, Inc., publishes works that further
Oxford University's objective of excellence
in research, scholarship, and education.

Oxford   New York
Auckland   Cape Town   Dar es Salaam   Hong Kong   Karachi
Kuala Lumpur   Madrid   Melbourne   Mexico City   Nairobi
New Delhi   Shanghai   Taipei   Toronto

With offices in
Argentina   Austria   Brazil   Chile   Czech Republic   France   Greece
Guatemala   Hungary   Italy   Japan   Poland   Portugal   Singapore
South Korea   Switzerland   Thailand   Turkey   Ukraine   Vietnam

Copyright © 2010, by Stephen J. Ceci & Wendy M. Williams

Published by Oxford University Press, Inc.
198 Madison Avenue, New York, New York 10016

www.oup.com

Oxford is a registered trademark of Oxford University Press

Library of Congress Cataloging-in-Publication Data

Ceci, Stephen J.
The mathematics of sex : how biology and society conspire to limit talented
women and girls / Stephen J. Ceci and Wendy M. Williams.
    p.   cm.
Includes bibliographical references.
ISBN 978-0-19-538939-5
1. Women in mathematics—Social aspects.   2. Women in science—Social aspects.
I. Williams, Wendy M. (Wendy Melissa), 1960–   II. Title.
HQ1397.C43 2009
305.43'5—dc22
2009006415

1   3   5   7   9   8   6   4   2

Printed in the United States of America
on acid-free paper

To our daughters, Wynne, Sterling and Nicole—who have made
our interest in writing this book more than academic

Contents

Preface: Setting the Stage

"If women had wives to keep house for them, to stay home with vomiting children, to get the car fixed, fight with the painters, run to the supermarket, . . . listen to everyone's problems, . . . just imagine the number of books that would be written, companies started, professorships filled, pubic offices that would be held, by women."

—Gail Sheehy, *Passages*, 1976

Honors Math 55 at Harvard University (called Advanced Calculus and Linear Algebra) is advertised in the course catalog as "probably the most difficult undergraduate math class in the country." It is legendary among high school math prodigies, who hear terrifying stories about it at their computer camps and Math Olympiads. Some go to Harvard just to have the opportunity to enroll in Honors Math 55. The year-long freshman course meets for 3 hours a week, but the catalog warns that completing the assigned homework takes between 24 and 60 hours a week!

The philosopher Christina Huff Sommers commented recently, "Math 55 does not look like America. Each year as many as 50 students sign up, but at least half drop out within a few weeks. As one former student told *The Crimson* newspaper in 2006, 'We had 51 students the first day, 31 students the second day, 24 for the next four days, 23 for two more weeks, and then 21 for the rest of the first semester.' Said another student, 'I guess you can say it's an episode of *Survivor* with people voting themselves off.' The final class roster, according to *The Crimson:* '45 percent Jewish, 18 percent Asian, 100 percent male.' "[1]

This book is about the reasons males are overrepresented in mathematics and mathematically intensive scientific professions such as physics, computer science, chemistry, operations research, mathematics, and engineering. Sometimes (but not always) sex differences in math and related aptitudes (like spatial reasoning) show up early in childhood, but usually they begin to show up later—around puberty, and the size of the male advantage accelerates greatly during junior high and high school. By the end of high school, boys excel on math aptitude tests and are more likely to be part of what is called the "right tail of the distribution"—the top 10%, 5%, 1%, 0.1%, and 0.01% of scorers on tests such as the Scholastic Assessment Test-Mathematics (SAT-M). The farther out on the right tail one goes (toward the top 0.01%, or 1 in 10,000), the fewer females there are. Males are often overrepresented in the top 1% by 2 to 1, and in the top 0.1%, they are sometimes overrepresented by a factor of 7 or more to 1.

According to some, male overrepresentation at the right tail of math ability is the reason so few women are to be found working in math-intensive fields. These fields allegedly draw on the top 1% of math talent, or an even higher-scoring group such as the top 0.1%, or even the top 0.01%—and there are fewer women at this level. In this book we shall examine this claim and related claims, such as that there are fewer women at the top of the spatial ability distribution, and that spatial ability undergirds competence in mathematically intensive fields. As we will show, a score of 650 on the SAT-M captures nearly twice as many boys (19%) as girls (10%); twice as many boys score above a 700 on the SAT-M test as do girls (10% versus 5%). Similarly, the farther out on the right tail one looks, the greater the ratio of boys to girls, as will be seen in Chapter 4. As a final example, in the latest year for which national SAT-M data exist (2007), there were 23,281 boys who scored 750 or above; in contrast, there were only 11,852 girls. Thus, boys outnumbered girls 2 to 1 in this range which some claim is the math ability level of the average physical scientists, engineers, or mathematicians.

Some argue, however, that tests such as the SAT-M do not measure the kind of intense, highly creative thinking required of mathematicians. The Putnam Mathematical Competition is a 6-hour intercollegiate examination administered by the Mathematics Association of America. The test is taken by U.S. and Canadian students on the first Saturday of every December. Putnam winners are regarded as the top mathematics talent; many have gone on to lead distinguished careers in mathematics, and several have become Nobelists and Fields medalists. Any student can sign up to enter the Putnam competition, although men are far more likely to register.

In recent years the exam has been taken annually by 3,500–3,750 undergraduate mathematics students. Attesting to the extreme difficulty of the questions, most of these math-talented students are unable to solve even a single one of the 12 problems. The top 25 scorers usually solve five or more of the problems; the top five scorers, designated Putnam Fellows, typically solve 8 to 11. Women are vastly underrepresented among Fellows; for example, in the last decade, only three women were named Putnam Fellows out of 51 recipients. A similar gender imbalance can be found among members of U.S. Math Olympiad teams.

Despite these pronounced right-tail differences on math and spatial aptitude tests, girls and women outperform boys and men in math and science classes. In other words, on average girls and women get significantly better grades in math and science classes in high school and college. In fact, girls and women outperform boys and men in virtually all classes. This fundamental observation has led to debates over the validity of aptitude tests. Debate has centered on the question of whether these tests *underpredict* women's performance in college math classes (because women end up getting better grades than would be expected on the basis of their SAT-M scores) or, conversely, whether college grading discriminates against men because they end up getting lower grades than would be expected on the basis of their SAT-M scores. For example, a man with the same SAT-M score as a woman seated next to him earns a grade nearly two letter grades lower than hers in a mathematics course—he gets a C/D versus her B.

Despite the findings of female dominance in classroom grades, the ranks of professionals in math-intensive fields are lopsidedly male. Anywhere from 64% to 93% of the professors on tenure track in these fields are men, and among full professors, the percentage of women is usually under 5%. Although women have made great strides in entering these fields in the past 25 years, they show no signs of reaching parity with men in the coming decades. Even if women suddenly entered math-intensive fields at rates comparable to men, and even if they completed their PhDs at rates comparable to men—neither of which seem likely to happen any time soon—they do not hold tenure-track jobs at rates comparable to men. This is due to myriad reasons we shall discuss, such as women disproportionately taking part-time jobs while they launch families, or preferring careers that are more people oriented or offer greater flexibility. Part-time positions do not lead to tenure or high-paying jobs; they tend to be teaching-intensive posts that must be renewed periodically, are remunerated at lower rates than tenure-track positions, and are the first to be cut in time of economic downturns. Importantly, part-time positions do not allow for research or professional development, so those in them have a hard time transitioning to better-paid and more secure jobs because the latter depend on a candidate's publication record, whereas those in part-time jobs are hired to teach, rather than do research, and little or no support is provided to conduct research.

THREE ALLEGED CAUSES OF WOMEN'S UNDERREPRESENTATION

Three classes of explanations have been offered to explain the underrepresentation of women in math-intensive fields, and we discuss each of these in the following chapters. The first concerns innate ability, and as will be seen, it is claimed that mathematical and spatial ability favor boys and men. The argument is that male brains are optimized for acquiring the ability to perform complex, abstract math and spatial visualization in math-intensive domains, and the dearth of women in math-intensive fields can be tied to their underrepresentation among the very highest-ability mathematics and spatial reasoning students—such as Putnam Fellows, members of the Math Olympiads, and those who succeed in Harvard's Math 55 course—who, it is alleged, go on to become successful in math-intensive fields. When engineering programs have initiated courses to enhance the spatial ability of freshmen women, their grade point averages and retention rates have improved, lending some credence to the argument that it is spatial and mathematical ability rather than gender per se that leads to the sex imbalance in these fields.

innate ability

A second class of explanations we shall delve into argues that the underrepresentation of women in math-intensive fields is not the result of women's lower ability in mathematics and spatial reasoning, but rather results from social and cultural biases and barriers that prevent women from maximizing their potential in these domains. These biases are said to include stereotypes and cultural expectations that channel women into fields that are less prestigious, less secure, and less well remunerated than math-intensive fields. According to such arguments, if the gender composition of math-intensive careers was divvied up according to actual mathematical and spatial ability, there would be far more women in them; their underrepresentation far exceeds that which can be accounted for by sex differences in math and spatial ability.

cultural bias

Finally, a third argument explaining the reason for the sex asymmetry in these professions alleges that women are simply less interested in math-intensive careers than men. This argument supposes that even when they have math aptitude comparable to men, women prefer people-oriented careers. Further, it is claimed from survey data that women are far more likely than men to prefer jobs that can be adapted to personal and family needs, and this leads to their underrepresentation among mathematical scientists. We will review evidence supporting this view, although, as is true of the other two views, it cannot fully account for the dearth of women in mathematically intensive careers.

motivation

In this book we describe and dissect the evidence for each of these three classes of explanations, each of which contains a layered set of interrelated arguments. To foreshadow our conclusion, we believe that the evidence, when taken in its totality, points to nonbiological/ability factors as the *major* causes of the underrepresentation of women in mathematically intensive careers. These include sex differences in occupational preferences and work–family conflicts that limit women's entry into these professions far more often than they do men's: Women with high mathematical talent prefer to enter nonmath fields such as medicine, veterinary medicine, law, and biological sciences, while men with high math talent are more likely to prefer math-intensive fields such as engineering and physics. Women are also far more likely to be equally talented in *both* math and verbal domains simultaneously, giving them more options to enter nonmath fields than are available to men. And women pay a child penalty that is greater than men's; they are less likely to be promoted in some physical sciences if they have a young child than are comparable men. A number of *secondary* factors that emerge as possible influences include cognitive ability differences between men and women and biological factors such as hormones and brain organization, as well as biases and barriers, although the latter have declined in importance in recent years and now seem fairly weak as an explanation for women's current underrepresentation.

A resolution of the debate over the putative causes of women's underrepresentation in mathematically intensive careers has been hindered by the breadth of fields involved. A comprehensive analysis of all possible causes necessitates evaluating evidence beyond any single scholar's area of training and expertise. As readers will see, the relevant data come from at least seven different fields: endocrinology, economics, sociology, education, genetics, cognitive neuroscience, and psychology. Excellent reviews of pertinent research exist within each of these specific fields, but they do not make contact with the data and arguments of researchers in most of the other fields. We strove to change this; in writing this book we went well beyond our own field of psychology and evaluated the key evidence from all seven fields. So this book is the culmination of many years of focused reading, research, and discussion with colleagues. At various turns, we relied on those with expertise in fields outside our own to critique our interpretations and conclusions. For example, we asked experts in behavioral endocrinology to critique our analysis of the massive body of data on the relationship between male hormones and spatial and mathematical ability. Similarly, we relied on colleagues in sociology and economics to alert us whenever they felt our interpretations of the scientific literature in their fields were off the mark. Ultimately, however, this is our book and we accept full responsibility for its accuracy and its conclusions.

The detailed scientific basis that underpins this book's conclusions can be found in our recent extensive review and synthesis of over 400 publications, entitled "Women's Underrepresentation in Science: Sociocultural and Biological Considerations."[2] Readers interested in the technical details surrounding our analyses of the evidence from the seven fields can find it there (along with 84 pages of supplemental graphs, tables, and text that accompany the article online). That article was the result of 3 years of research by the two of us, along with our colleague and friend, Susan M. Barnett, and it was easily the most arduous research we have done in our long careers. When the article was reviewed by the journal *Psychological Bulletin*—the premier review journal in psychology—reviewers across the nature–nurture divide gave it high marks. This very lengthy scientific journal article provided the evidentiary basis for many of the arguments in the present volume.

Because the topic of women's underrepresentation is emotionally laden, few individuals, including academic researchers, are truly neutral. Most of our colleagues have agendas—some to prove that women do not lack any ability that would preclude them from success in math-intensive careers, and others seeking to prove the opposite. We had only one agenda in writing this book: to present the fairest, most dispassionate analysis warranted by the data. Of course, this sounds quite self-serving, but as evidence of our lack of a political agenda, we can point to the frequency with which we have changed our views on this topic over the past 3 years of synthesizing this large research corpus. We began this project with *markedly* different positions than we ended up with; in fact, during the first 2 years of researching and writing, we engaged in a considerable degree of (often heated) debate among ourselves. Over time, all of our views changed in response to arguments among ourselves and upon considering new evidence. We have ended up with a position that is in some respects opposite to where we began. We mention this in the context of discussing why we are confident that our conclusions will be seen as an honest synthesis of research up to this point. Although we had our own theories about women's underrepresentation in math-intensive fields, we were not so entrenched that we refused to budge. We attribute this to our willingness to go with the data, rather than fight it relentlessly as some ardent proponents on each side of the debate seem to do. This dispassionate stance might have been unlikely had we come to this book defending a career-long record of endorsing one side in this debate. But we had not worked on this topic until late in our careers, so we had nothing to defend. Yet, our training across a number of subfields of psychology (developmental, cognitive, and educational) served us well when synthesizing the seven classes of research on which we base our conclusions.

Finally, it may be obvious, but is nonetheless worth stating, that not everyone will agree with our conclusions. Full agreement is unattainable in such a contentious area, much like any treatise on an emotionally charged topic. Ardent supporters on both sides of the nature–nurture divide who have spent some or all of their careers defending their positions are unlikely to "roll over" upon reading our analysis and admit they got it wrong. In fact, we have no doubt that some will ferociously attack our conclusions. However, in the court of expert opinion, we believe that our analysis will withstand the test of time, even if some pockets of individuals disagree.

In the following pages we examine the most relevant evidence from the seven scientific fields mentioned earlier and, in doing so, show why some of these issues in the debate over women's underrepresentation have proved so difficult to settle. We clarify the issues necessary to resolve areas of disagreement, basing our conclusions mainly on the past three decades of analyses and arguments about patterns of sex differences in achievement and behavior. As already noted, our conclusions are based on more than 400 studies that span biological sex differences (such as hormones, brain organization, and evolutionary pressures) and gender differences in childrearing and personal preferences/career aspirations, to studies of the determinants of mathematical aptitude (like spatial cognition), to a growing literature on stereotypes and institutional biases that impede women's progress. Upon reaching the final chapter, readers will discover that we find the evidence debunks a number of claims made by scholars and policy makers; fortunately, it also supports a number of equally important claims.

The Mathematics of Sex

Introduction: Why care about women in science?

"There are issues of intrinsic aptitude."

—Lawrence Summers, 2005

"Mathematical and scientific reasoning develop from a set of biologically based cognitive capacities that males and females share. These capacities lead men and women to develop equal talent for mathematics and science."

—Elizabeth Spelke, Harvard University, 2005

"I have frequently been questioned, especially by women, of how I could reconcile family life with a scientific career. Well, it has not been easy."

—Marie Curie, 1897–1956

The plight of women who opt out of work because of family needs is an old one, and it has received a great deal of press attention. In a special report for the *American Prospect Magazine* in March 2007, Joan Williams, professor of Law at the University of California Hastings College of Law and director of the Center for WorkLife Law, reviewed 119 news stories appearing between 1980 and 2006. These stories described the circumstances of women who felt pressured to leave jobs because of inflexible working conditions and unaffordable childcare. The women didn't generally want to leave their jobs, and felt frustrated and economically vulnerable doing so. Williams argued that the idea that these women opted out of their jobs is misleading; rather, they were forced out due to a lack of options. Their jobs required that they work full time (for professional women this means at least 40 hours a week, often more), and there is a penalty for those who interrupt their careers. Future employers see gaps in employment as a lack of commitment. As one of the women in Williams's study put it: "Be prepared for the realization that in the business world your stepping out time *counts for less than*

3

zero ... [and] may make potential employers think you are not as reliable as other applicants."[1]

Our interest is in the subset of women who are capable of earning higher degrees in mathematically intensive fields (such as computer science, chemistry, physics, economics, accounting, statistics, engineering, mathematics, and operations research) but who either do not do so for a variety of reasons we will describe, or do earn advanced degrees in these fields but end up making less progress as professionals in them than do men who earn comparable degrees—again, for a variety of reasons. We do not discuss women who work in clerical or support positions and feel pressured to balance the demands of their jobs and families; the focus of this book is squarely on women with math-intensive capabilities. These women present a particularly intriguing scientific and public policy challenge, as will be seen. They are especially underrepresented among professionals in math-intensive fields, occupying less than one-third of tenure-track positions, and often less than one-eighth of them. And even these numbers misrepresent the presence of *American* women in these fields because the majority of the women in some of them are foreign born. For example, according to a recent report, only 20% of the female faculty in the top five mathematics departments are born in the United States. Of the 80% born elsewhere, many are immigrants from countries in which girls are frequently members of International Math Olympiad teams.[2]

In Table 4 of their article in *Notices of the American Mathematical Society*, Andreescu et al. provide data on the top 15 countries as far as performance in the International Math Olympiad competition. This is a 9-hour essay-style examination given annually to teams from approximately 95 countries. Romania, Russia, Hungary, Korea, China, Taiwan, Viet Nam, and Bulgaria have a high percentage of girls on their math Olympiad teams, and these are the same countries that provide a disproportionate number of women to math-intensive fields, both in their countries and in academic departments in the United States when they immigrate. No country from Western Europe makes this top 15 list, and although the United States did make it, half of its girls were either immigrants or children of immigrants from Asia or Eastern Europe. Andreescu et al. argue that the prevalence of girls on the Math Olympiad teams is cultural rather than genetic because there are significant disparities in the prevalence of girls in neighboring countries that are ethnically similar (for instance, between East and West Germany, between Korea and Japan, or between Slovakia and the Czech Republic) as well as marked changes in the prevalence of girls within the same country over time. In the United States, ethnic Jewish and Asian boys are 10- to 20-fold more likely to be members of these Olympiad teams than other ethnic groups.

Women's underrepresentation does not end on Math Olympiad teams or in academia; they are also underrepresented in leadership posts in business and industry. Numerous policy makers have commented on the need to utilize all of our intellectual resources, particularly in the aftermath of 9/11 when we saw a reduction in the admission of foreign graduate students to the United States to do doctoral training in math-intensive fields. Any lacuna created by a reduction in foreign graduate students can only be filled by bringing more U.S. men and women into these careers.

OVERVIEW OF THE PROBLEM

Roughly half the population is female, and by most measures they are faring well academically. Consider that by age 25, over one-third of women have completed college (versus 29% of males); women outperform men in grades in nearly all high school and college courses, including mathematics[3]; women now comprise 48% of all college math majors[4]; and women enter graduate and professional schools in numbers equal to or greater than men in most, but not all, fields (currently women comprise 50% of MDs, 75% of veterinary medicine doctorates, 48% of life science PhDs, and 68% of psychology PhDs).

However, in mathematically intensive STEM (science, technology, engineering, and mathematics) fields, women are highly underrepresented as faculty members at 2- and 4-year colleges, as seen in Figure I.1. Although this

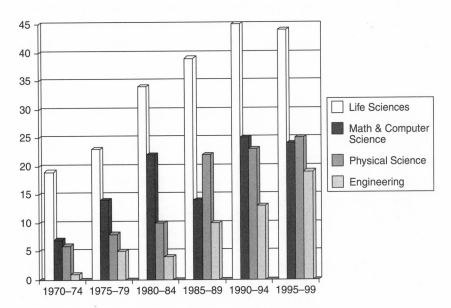

FIGURE **I.1.** Percentage of women science faculty employed at 2- and 4-year colleges and universities by field of study and year of PhD completion. Source: NSF Survey of Doctoral Recipients.

figure shows the enormous gains made by women in the last three decades—for example, in the 10 years between 1989 and 1999, women nearly doubled their presence among engineering faculty, from 10% to 19%—women still comprise only a quarter or less of the faculty in math-intensive fields, in contrast to the biological sciences in which they occupied 44% of faculty posts in the year these data were compiled (and now occupy 48%). The dearth of women is even more pronounced if we look at their numbers among the highest faculty ranks—full professors, directors, chairs, and deans. At the top 50 U.S. universities, the proportion of full professorships in math-intensive STEM fields held by women ranges only from 3.7% to 15%, as can be seen in Figure I.2, which is based on 2005 National Science Foundation Science Indicators data (National Science Board, 2006).

Is the underrepresentation of women just a temporary glitch? Will the bumper crop of recent female PhDs work its way through the professional ranks until the proportion of female full professors, deans, and center directors is reflective of the proportion of female PhDs in each field? Probably not, for two reasons. First, the proportion of women hired as assistant professors in some scientific fields is still lower than the number of women receiving PhDs in them, and in some fields it is considerably lower. In biological sciences, although 46.3% of the PhDs awarded between 1996 and 2005 were to women, they were hired for only 35% of the assistant professorships at research universities. Similarly, in chemistry although 32.4% of PhDs were awarded to women, only 21.2% were hired as assistant professors at research universities. On the other hand, in civil, mechanical and chemical engineering, physics, and astronomy the numbers of women hired as assistant professors

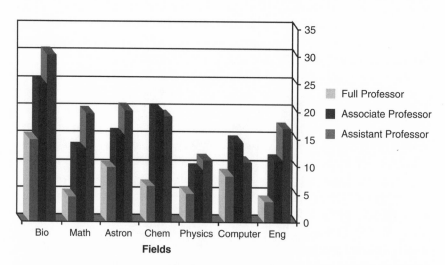

FIGURE **I.2.** Percentage of women faculty by rank at 2- and 4-year colleges (2002). Source: NSF Survey of Doctoral Recipients.

actually exceeds their base rate among PhD recipients; for example, women comprised only 8.4% of PhD recipients in mechanical engineering but were hired for 18% of its assistant professor positions—see Donna Nelson, 2007, Table 11. The second reason is that in the fields that have hired women at higher rates than their PhD participation, the overall numbers of women are very small. Only 8.4% of mechanical engineering PhDs are women, only 14.3% of physics PhDs are women, only 21% of computer science PhDs are women, and only 12.3% of electrical engineering PhDs are women. It would take a very long for such low base rates to reach parity with men. In a nutshell, in the mathematically intensive STEM fields, women are less likely to matriculate in mathematical fields and less likely to complete graduate work, and when they do, they are sometimes but not always less likely to be hired as assistant professors, especially in tenure-track posts. These are the premier jobs in the academy, with a route to job permanence and benefits.

Some have argued that women are even less likely to prosper once they are hired. Economist Anne Preston did an analysis in 1994 that is still valid. She showed that women, once hired, exit science and engineering careers at higher rates than do men, and this is true at every stage of their careers—from starting scientists to senior scientists. Interestingly, this is also true among women without children. So the reason women exit STEM careers cannot solely be attributed to family needs, although as we shall see some portion of it can. But the fact is that women are far more likely to abandon such careers than men are, and women are more likely to abandon careers in math-intensive fields than they are in less math-intensive areas. For example, women are 2.8 times more likely than men to exit STEM careers for other occupations, and 13 times more likely to quit the labor force completely. (One caution: A 13-to-1 ratio sounds dramatic, but very few men or women quit the labor force completely, although of the minority who do, women predominate.)

Inquiring Minds Want to Know

Do more women belong in these mathematically intensive fields than are being trained and hired at the entry level into their professions? Is their underrepresentation in these fields a consequence of their having less ability (and, presumably, recognizing this only after having advanced in their fields to a certain stage)? Or are nonability factors the culprit, such as less interest in being an engineer or a physicist than, say, a psychologist or veterinarian? Or is the shortage of women in math-intensive STEM fields the consequence of societal/institutional biases, beginning with lack of parental encouragement during childhood and gender stereotypes that handicap women's test performance and deter them from taking future math and science coursework or prompting them to exaggerate the level of performance needed to succeed—leading women to disproportionately sacrifice their careers to raise families or care for elderly parents—and ending with discriminatory hiring and promotion practices, as some studies have claimed?

And even if they don't face overt discrimination, do women just get tired of dealing with the predominance of socially awkward, highly competitive men they encounter in math departments or engineering firms, as suggested by one ex-physicist who left her field? If ability differences are responsible for part of the dearth of women in math-intensive STEM fields, what are the specific abilities women lack? Are these differences innate? Put another way, is our society holding girls and women back, or are girls and women simply not as interested or equipped as men to succeed in math-intensive fields? And *if* society could change the number of women entering math-intensive STEM fields, *should* it do so—and what level of resources should society invest to bring about such a change? What are the opportunity costs to women if they are urged into these fields, possibly at the expense of entering other fields in which they would thrive and find greater satisfaction? These are some of the questions we attempt to answer in the coming pages. Answers will require connecting the dots across myriad bodies of research.

Throughout this book we use the acronym STEM to refer to those scientific fields that are heavily math intensive, such as mathematics, physics, engineering, chemistry, operations research, economics, accounting, materials science, and computer science. We explicitly exclude other STEM fields such as psychology, biology, and sociology, which are generally less mathematical, except where noted otherwise. We acknowledge exceptions to this division of disciplines, with some STEM subspecialities being less math intensive and others being heavily mathematical. For example, one of our daughters completed graduate work in the field of environmental (civil) engineering, which although heavily mathematical, may be no more so than some of the heaviest math-laden specializations in certain social sciences, such as quantitative psychology, economics, and sociology. Notwithstanding these exceptions, on average, the fields listed previously are regarded by those who work in this area as the most math intensive, and they are also the ones with the greatest gender gap among professionals, including academic professionals.

Beyond "Beyond Bias and Barriers"

Many individuals and organizations have tried to answer the questions we raised previously.[5] Indeed, many have thought they have done so, and have gone on to recommend solutions to the problems they identified. However, agreement has proven to be elusive. A case in point is the furor surrounding the fall 2006 National Academy of Sciences report, spearheaded by Donna Shalala, former secretary of the Department of Health and Human Services, on the issue of the underrepresentation of women in some STEM fields. Her august 18-member Committee on Science, Engineering, and Public Policy of the National Academy of Sciences (NAS) issued the results of its year-long deliberations[6] with a title that signaled its conclusions: *Beyond Bias and Barriers: Fulfilling the Potential of Women in Academic Science and Engineering.*

The report was hard-hitting, arguing against aptitude differences in mathematical ability as an explanation for the shortage of women in mathematically intensive fields. The report concluded: "It is not lack of talent, but unintentional biases and outmoded institutional structures that are hindering the access and advancement of women.... Women are capable of contributing to the nation's scientific and engineering enterprise but are impeded in doing so because of gender and racial/ethnic bias and outmoded 'rules' governing academic success."[7] The authors of the NAS report recommended a call to action: "Faculty, university leaders, professional and scientific societies, federal agencies and the federal government must unite to ensure that all our nation's people are welcomed and encouraged to excel in science and engineering in our research universities." This call to action was accompanied by a set of specific steps institutions were urged to take.

Although this report was intended to end the debate once and for all about the roots of gender inequality in math-intensive STEM fields, representing as it did the consensus opinion of a very distinguished group of 18 scholars and administrators, the outcome was rather different. Critics inveighed against its science, calling the report a "political tract"[8] and stating that it "upheld an orthodoxy of female victimization."[9] Editorial writers across the country lined up to take sides. On one side were the supporters of the report's conclusion that cognitive sex differences, to the extent that they exist at all, are the consequence of biases and various cultural assumptions and stereotypes, but not the cause of women's underrepresentation in STEM sciences.

For example, Maxine Singer, president emeritus of the Carnegie Institution, wrote in a lead editorial in the journal *Science* that universities are wasting the skills and talents of many women by discouraging and inhibiting them from fulfilling their potential in academic science and engineering. She endorsed the NAS report's conclusions that biases, not differences in aptitude, were at the root of the problem: "The new report...is an exhaustive and critical review of relevant published research and analyses, as might be expected given the distinguished authoring panel of scientists and engineers.... Societal assumptions and their cultural consequences can account for most of the actually minor cognitive differences measured between the sexes."[10] Other commentators, however, were notably less sanguine about the report's balance. Consider:

> A committee of experts looked at all the possible excuses—biological differences in ability, hormonal influences, childrearing demands, and even differences in ambition—and found no good explanation for why women are being locked out. [However] the panel included a number of strong proponents of the belief that women in science are held back primarily by sexism and that aggressive remedies to these biases are needed. Noticeably absent were proponents of other viewpoints who argue that biological sex differences influence cognitive skills in some areas. Ultimately, the report is a missed opportunity. It could have addressed the personal and family choices women could make to maximize their career potential, or looked at the factors in the high achievement of Asian-American women in science. Instead, it upheld an orthodoxy of female victimization. Women, and science, deserve better.[11]

> The report says that women are discouraged from going into science because of social pressure and 'unintentional' and 'unconscious' biases—which may well exist. But Shalala's committee is so determined to blame everything on discrimination that it dismisses other factors without giving them a fair hearing.[12]

Clearly the NAS report did not resolve the issue of why so few women are thriving in mathematically intensive fields—nor have the national symposia and debates that were convened in the wake of its release, such as the one by the American Enterprise Institute in fall 2007, or special issues of journals that have been devoted to this question.[13] Why does the debate over women in science continue? What is it that makes this issue so difficult to resolve?

We recognize that we are trying to explain social phenomena using raw data that are, in most cases, several steps removed from the final outcome being explained. For example, on the one hand, the relationships between preschool children's activities that are allegedly related to their emerging mathematical and spatial skills—such as block building, Lego assembly, erector set activities, and jigsaw puzzle assembly—and on the other hand, the tenure and promotion of middle-aged female academics in math-intensive STEM fields. As social scientists, we are trained to build a case by analyzing and triangulating data and testing alternative hypotheses to surmount data limitations when they occur. This is by no means a guaranteed recipe for discovering truth, but it is better than reliance on subjective individual testimonials, ideological positions, or dependence on only a subset of the relevant data.

BACKGROUND TO THE CONTROVERSY

The underrepresentation of women in mathematically intensive STEM fields is a key controversy of our time, one sparking debates on campuses across the United States. In 2005, an editorial in *Science Magazine* commented that Lawrence Summers, former president of Harvard University and chief economic consultant in the Obama administration, "put the issue of women in science on the front burner." While trying to explain the lack of women at the top of their professions in science and engineering, Summers attributed some of women's lower success rate in these math-intensive fields to a lack of innate ability ("There are issues of intrinsic aptitude"), although he also acknowledged other sources of sex differences that we describe later. Yet when the National Center for Education Statistics issued its long-awaited updated report, *Trends in Educational Equity of Girls and Women: 2004,*[14] based on its analysis of extensive data sets, the report concluded: "While females' performance in mathematics is often perceived to be lower than that of males, NAEP [National Assessment of Educational Progress] results have shown few consistent gender differences over the years, partic- *NAE?* ularly among younger students. Twelfth-grade NAEP assessments in mathematics and science show no significant gender differences in achievement scores."[15]

If 12th graders don't show sex differences on the NAEP math test, then what is causing the dearth of women scientists, mathematicians, and engineers? Is it due to a lack of intrinsic aptitude that shows up on mathematics tests that do not assess what has been directly taught, as does the NAEP, but rather require creative solution of novel problems, as some aptitude tests claim to do? Or do sex differences in mathematics show up after high school, as mathematics becomes more complex? Or is it something else? If women are intrinsically less capable, how do they do so well not only on the NAEP mathematics test in high school but also in college math courses, where they tend to outperform males? Are their superior grades due to noncognitive factors such as being better prepared for tests, doing homework assignments, and participating more actively in class?

Some scholars on this topic have cautioned that the focus should not be on *mean* differences between men and women—that is, in average grades, average test scores, or average passing rates. Rather, some believe we should focus on differences at the *extreme right tail of the ability distribution,* for example, in the proportion of men and women who score in the top 1% or even the top 0.1%, .01%, or 0.001%, as with the Putnam Fellows, who are alleged to be 1 in a million.[16] In other words, it might be irrelevant that men and women have similar average math grades or NAEP scores if they differ in their frequency of scoring among the top, say, 1 in 1,000, if in fact this is the rarified segment of the ability distribution from which STEM scientists hail. By analogy, if we were interested in understanding why more African Americans were in the starting lineups for the NBA All-Star game, we would not be interested in whether the *average* ability of white males and black males was similar.

We'd want to know whether more African Americans performed in the top 1 in 100 or perhaps even the top 1 in 1,000 or 1 in 10,000, because this is the segment of the basketball-playing population that is successful in the NBA. We will return to this point later when we examine conflicting evidence on the ratio of men to women in the very top range of mathematical ability.

By suggesting that a gender difference in intrinsic mathematical ability is the basis for the dearth of female scientists, engineers, and mathematicians, proponents relegate rival explanations to secondary status. So biased hiring, discriminatory tenure and promotion practices, negative stereotypes about women's ability, and socialization and other experiential differences are downplayed. Some suggest that the underrepresentation of women in math-intensive fields only secondarily results from gender differences in career interests or female-unfriendly (or parent-unfriendly) institutional policies, a position we will directly address later.

The insinuation of biologically based sex differences in cognitive ability has been radioactive on college campuses, provoking debates across the nation as well as an outpouring of editorials and commentaries in the national print media,[17] letters from groups of eminent science administrators,[18] and edited volumes and entire issues of journals devoted to this issue.[19] There has also been a host of policy summits on the topic, including the commissioning of the year-long effort by the National Academy of Science's Committee on Science, Engineering, and Public Policy (culminating in the 2006 Shalala report mentioned earlier) and an open convocation entitled "Maximizing the Potential of Women in Academe: Biological, Social, and Organizational Contributions to Science and Engineering Success," held at the National Academy of Sciences.[20] There were also full-day and multi-day symposia and debates at think tanks such as the one at the American Enterprise Institute mentioned earlier.

Perhaps one could argue that scientists and public figures such as Lawrence Summers should refrain from this debate. However, we favor free speech in science; one ought not to be vilified for speaking or publishing opinions that are accurate depictions of scientific data unless such statements fail to consider counterevidence that persuasively refutes them. If other data can be invoked to refute the claims of proponents of gender differences in intrinsic ability, then that is how scientific knowledge accumulates to solve important problems, and that is precisely how many important consensuses have come about. Instead of making attributions about the putatively flawed character of proponents of a certain view, we as a community should focus on attempting to refute the evidentiary basis for it. Perhaps we can do this, and if so it will advance our understanding far better than silencing proponents who have arrived at opinions to which we object.

QUESTIONS AND ANSWERS

Numerous efforts have addressed the question: What is the cause of the pronounced difference in the number of men and women in STEM fields, particularly those that are mathematically intensive? Proffered explanations have included all of the following:

- Male brains are genetically more efficient at doing complex mathematics (they are optimized for certain forms of spatial cognition that underpin certain types of advanced mathematics), and even in infancy boys excel at spatial skill.
- The environment—society, schools, parents, peers, and so forth—creates performance and "ability" differences in the absence of innate differences, and it does this through the transmission of cultural beliefs and stereotypes that impede girls with high mathematical aptitude.
- Society discriminates between equally capable individuals on the basis of their gender, giving preferential hiring, publications, and grants to men over women who have identical capability, backgrounds, and productivity.
- Mathematically capable women "choose" not to reach the top in these fields, typically because they opt to become parents, defer to their partners' aspirational paths at the expense of pursuing their own, care for elderly relatives, or prefer to pursue careers that are more people oriented, such as medicine, psychology, dentistry, veterinary medicine, and law.
- The rigidities of the academic career path render it disproportionately difficult for women to have both a family and a successful career, and this trade-off is exacerbated in those STEM fields in which women are most underrepresented.
- Hormones (both prenatal organizational ones as well as postnatal activating ones) mediate math ability via skill at rotating three-dimensional objects in space; when women are given male hormones, their ability to do mental rotation and math improves.

To resolve these competing claims, it is first necessary to understand the data upon which they are based, including those concerning the precursor performance or behavioral differences that purportedly lead to differential career progress in math-intensive fields. Next, areas of disagreement can be pinned down and analyzed. The following chapters of this book will take the reader on an excursion through studies used to support the aforementioned claims. We refrain from providing archival accounts of these studies, however, because we have done that elsewhere,[21] as mentioned in the *Preface* and we approach the data without presuming that readers had training in quantitative social science methods. Instead, we present the evidence from these studies in a narrative form that requires little statistical knowledge. We discuss five dimensions along which the evidentiary base may be organized:

(1) an examination of the measures used to document sex differences in cognitive abilities, *(2)* comparative trans-national data on achievement differences between the sexes, *(3)* the particular groups of males and females that have been studied, *(4)* aspects of assessment, such as test content and context, and performance-evaluation procedures that can influence sex differences in scores, and *(5)* temporal factors related to sex differences, such as cohort effects and historical epochs under study. We hope this five-category organization proves helpful to readers.

One might imagine that the resolution to the debate over the nature and cause of gender differences in cognition would be a straightforward task—just take the essentials of each analysis and test rival claims using meta-analytic (or research synthesis) techniques. However, matters as complex as this cannot be resolved by tallying the pros and cons on a point-by-point basis, and the many meta-analyses on this topic to date, though they are very important, have not ended the debate. As we show, many of the arguments and counterarguments do not align perfectly; thus, one argument cannot be invoked to nullify another.

But even more important (and problematic), the various sides in the debate often draw on the very same evidence. In other words, it is often the case that the evidence invoked by one side in this multisided debate can be interpreted in a way that renders it compatible with the views of opposing sides, as we describe later. Furthermore, protagonists in this debate come from many different fields, publish in different journals and speak at different conferences, and are sometimes uninformed about evidence and findings from other disciplines or subdisciplines. To resolve these disputes, an integrative approach is helpful, one spanning multiple fields, methods, historical epochs, and developmental levels.

Our primary objective is to juxtapose the plethora of conflicting evidence across a number of scientific disciplines in service of our main goal of synthesizing and interpreting the most relevant data and arguments on each side. Although we analyzed over 400 primary sources, we made a strategic decision to exclude hundreds of additional studies because they were duplicative, flawed, or in our opinion unimportant. No single critical review of this type can hope to quiet the strident debate that has raged on this topic, but we set for ourselves the more modest goal of propelling the debate forward by presenting a fair and dispassionate analysis of the evidence, and organizing it in a way that we hope will have heuristic value for readers and will guide recommendations about gender-related policies.

Will this alleged objectivity and narrowed scope make all readers happy with our conclusions? Definitely not. We have learned from past experiences that the field is so contentious that every point one camp embraces produces an allergic reaction in another camp. The entrenched and ardent zealousness of each side presented significant hurdles for us to climb in the course of revising our work until reviewers of all stripes gave it the green light. Some never did. But we stand by our conclusions and challenge those with different views to present evidence that they believe we ignored or misinterpreted.

A multidimensional problem

"Nobody objects to a woman being a good writer or sculptor or geneticist if at the same time she manages to be a good wife, good mother, good looking, good tempered, well groomed and unaggressive."

—Leslie M. McIntyre

In this chapter we lay out a set of interrelated phenomena: Women are underrepresented in math-intensive STEM fields; they are also underrepresented at the extremes of the spatial cognition and mathematic aptitude distributions; and there is some evidence that spatial cognition is a causal agent in mastering complex math. Finally, there is evidence that those who succeed in math-intensive fields come from the outer right tails of the mathematics and spatial cognition distributions—the top 1% or higher. Putting these pieces together has led some scholars to the following causal interpretation: *Women are underrepresented in prestigious math-intensive careers because of a math/spatial ability shortfall: The shortage of women in the very top ability group translates into fewer women in the pool from which graduate students are chosen and, later, from the pool in which professors are hired.*

WOMEN'S GROWTH IN STEM FIELDS

The first fact of note is that the so-called Nation's Report Card, the National Assessment of Educational Progress (NAEP), shows that there are no longer gender differences in the number of demanding mathematics courses taken in high school. Furthermore, girls do better, on average, than do boys in these courses, earning consistently higher scores.[1] Second, without interruption, in every year since 1966, the proportion of women earning bachelor's degrees in scientific and engineering fields has increased. By 2001, the number of women earning bachelor's of science degrees actually exceeded the number of men earning degrees in some STEM fields, as we detail later.

Figure 1.1 shows this graphically. Over 28% of all STEM degrees awarded in 2004 went to women. However, this figure combines bachelor's degrees in math-intensive STEM sciences such as physics and engineering (where the percentages of women are far lower) with less math-intensive fields such as psychology, biology, and sociology (where the percentages of women are much higher). Men and women earn equal grades in college math classes that are of comparable difficulty, and this has been true for a long time.[2] Finally, as noted in the Preface, women major in mathematics in nearly equal numbers to men. In recent years, for example, women earned 48% of bachelor's degrees in mathematics. Such facts have led Harvard psychologist Elizabeth Spelke to argue, "By the most meaningful measure—the ability to master new, challenging mathematical material over extended periods of time—college men and women show equal aptitude for mathematics."[3]

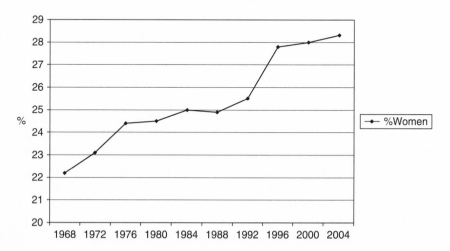

FIGURE 1.1. The percentage of STEM bachelor's degrees awarded to women over time from 1968 to 2004. Source: Data abstracted from: National Science Foundation/Division of Science Resources Statistics; Data from Department of Education/Center for Education Statistics/Integrated with Post-Secondary Education Data Systems Completions Survey.

In addition to their impressive performance on high school NAEP mathematics tests and their gains in undergraduate math and science degrees, women are also attaining doctoral degrees in scientific and engineering fields in growing numbers: By 2001, women earned 37% of PhDs in scientific and engineering fields, up from just 8% in 1966.[4] However, as was true for bachelor's degrees, disproportionately more of these PhDs were earned in non-math-intensive STEM fields such as biology and the social sciences.

Nevertheless, women have made impressive gains even in the most math-intensive fields: They are currently obtaining 29% of the PhDs in mathematics, 17% in combined engineering, and 22% in computer/information sciences. And as mentioned earlier, women's successes have been even greater in some other scientific fields that are not considered math intensive but nevertheless require mathematical competence: Women currently obtain 50% of the MD degrees from medical schools, almost 75% of the DVMs from veterinary schools, and 48% of PhDs in biology/life sciences. A generation ago, the corresponding percentages were far lower in all of these fields. It is worth keeping these statistics in mind when we delve later into sex differences in mathematical and spatial skill, because to whatever degree such differences exist, they obviously have not precluded growing numbers of women from achieving highly. It is also important to bear in mind that had we written this book in the late 1960s, when women were awarded less than 10% of the PhDs in scientific and engineering fields, it would have been easy to have been seduced into imagining that this was their natural limit given their underrepresentation among the top math and spatial scorers. As is already obvious, this is not the case, and women have quadrupled their PhDs in the last 40 years in virtually all fields of science and mathematics.

Notwithstanding the impressive progress women have made in pursuing coursework and degrees in science and mathematics, the increased representation of women among doctoral recipients has not coincided with their increased representation in the most mathematically intensive fields of faculty. As we saw in the Introductory chapter, the hiring of new assistant professors in some of these fields has not been proportional to the size of the new PhD pools or even to the size of the postdoctoral pools. Recall that in chemistry women were hired to fill only 21.2% of the available assistant professorships, even though they comprised 32.4% of all chemistry PhD recipients in the prior decade. In the biological sciences, the drop-off between doctoral and assistant professor stages is similar: in the most recent ten year period women were hired for only 35% of the assistant professorships, even though they earned 46.3% of the PhDs leading up to this point. Similar trends exist for computer science, earth sciences, and mathematics. Comparable drop-offs have been observed even when the hiring of assistant professorships is statistically conditioned on the postdoctoral talent pool rather than on the graduate school pool, to control for women who opted out of careers upon receipt of their PhDs to start families rather than segue to academic jobs.

So what happened to the rest of these talented women after they earned their doctorates but did not transition into assistant professorships? Did they fail to be hired as assistant professors in their fields because of discrimination, or was it because they chose not to apply for these positions at levels commensurate with their numbers? Of course, one need not resort to claims of gender discrimination to explain such drop-offs between women with PhDs and job hires. Perhaps women with PhDs are more inclined or pressured to pursue family responsibilities, opting out of tenure track faculty positions for adjunct teaching positions (especially part time), or perhaps they prefer positions in industry or consulting that can be worked flexibly, even from home, or perhaps they migrate toward non-research posts rather than the better paid and more prestigious research university positions. We will discuss such possibilities in detail later, but first we address issues related to sex differences in mathematical ability.

THE EXTENT OF MATH TALENT

One potential problem exists, however, in assuming that the number of men and women who receive bachelor's degrees and PhDs is a control for expertise in mathematics and science. Perhaps achieving a PhD is *not* a good measure of the extremely high math potential needed to successfully compete for and retain a tenure-track assistant professorship in a math-intensive field. This may seem counterintuitive because majoring in mathematics would seem to be the very definition of high potential in mathematics; certainly someone capable of doing doctoral work in mathematics would seem to be outstandingly gifted in mathematics. And compared to the rest of us, this is undoubtedly true.

However, as we alluded to in the Introduction, some have argued that this type of reasoning is akin to using the size of the pool of college varsity basketball players to make inferences about the underselection of white males by NBA teams. Again, what if college varsity basketball players are in the top 1% of the athletic distribution for their sport, but the NBA takes only the top one-hundredth of the top 1% of varsity players (that is, the top 0.01%, or the top 1 in 10,000)? So, if every one of the male varsity basketball players was invited to try out for the NBA, would they fare equally well? Probably not. Advancing to the college varsity level is undoubtedly evidence of outstanding ability compared to the rest of us; but not all players at that level are equally capable of excelling on an even higher level, and this could also be the case for achieving a tenure-track appointment in a math-intensive field.

Perhaps only a portion of those with PhDs in math-intensive fields can be successful professors in those fields, and an even smaller fraction of those with undergraduate degrees in mathematics can be. This is an empirical question.

As the basketball analogy suggests, we lack data on who becomes successful as STEM scientists in math-intensive fields and where in the distribution of mathematical talent they fell as college students or graduate students. Of the 48% undergraduate mathematics majors who are female, what portion of them is in the talent range of those who go on to become successful mathematicians, computer scientists, engineers, and physicists? We simply do not know because, as we will show, there is a debate over how to measure such talent and also how rarified the mathematical competence is of those who succeed as professionals in these fields (men or women). Where there is no debate is that women's grades in college math classes are as good as those of men who take comparable courses in mathematics. But whether equivalent grades are evidence of equivalent mathematics aptitude for the subset of people who go on to become successful STEM scientists is a point of controversy.

Some researchers, as readers will see in the coming chapters, have argued that fewer of the female math majors achieve scores in the upper reaches of math ability, and this is why women are less likely to be found among STEM professionals than men. Others argue that STEM professors' math ability is not very different from that of the typical humanities major, and therefore this cannot account for the dearth of women in these fields. The latter is a pretty surprising claim, but numerous scholars have made it. Later we will call into question their reasoning related this claim. By combining the best data sources, it seems fairly clear that graduate students in math-intensive fields possess, on average, math ability that is far higher than individuals in the humanities.

The foregoing claims and counterclaims demonstrate some of the complexity of understanding sex differences in cognition. Sex differences are both more and less than what one usually thinks, and they are both more and less tractable. As Maccoby and Jacklin[5] concluded 35 years ago in their landmark book on the psychology of sex differences, although social and emotional sex differences often show large-magnitude differences (sex differences for aggressive play, gross motor behavior, throwing velocity, and masturbation often are very large), only a few cognitive skills are associated with large sex differences, and in the following chapters we will review those that have been linked to women's underrepresentation in STEM careers.

GAUGING THE SIZE OF SEX DIFFERENCES

Before discussing sex differences any further, it is important to quantify what we mean when we say that various differences between men and women are small, moderate, or large. Throughout this book we adhere to the conventions for effect sizes used by Hyde[6] and others to quantify the magnitude of the differences between men and women, that is, Cohen's 1988 d statistic, simplified as:

$$d = \frac{M_M - M_F}{s_W}$$

where d is the magnitude of the difference and s_W is a range of variability among same-sex scores—the so-called pooled within-sex standard deviation, and if we wanted to be complete, we would also add the male and female fractions of the sample to this, but for the sake of simplicity the above equation is fine. Most sex-differences researchers adhere to Cohen's original recommendations that a d score of ≤ 0.20 is considered a small effect, a score between 0.50 and 0.79 is considered a medium-sized effect, and a score ≥ 0.80 is viewed as a large effect. Effect sizes can be converted directly into other useful statistics, such as Cohen's U statistic, used to quantify the percentage of overlap between male and female distributions. Throughout this discussion we will take advantage of such conversions to put findings into more accessible terms without burdening readers with the statistical steps involved in doing so. For example, a d equal to 0.20 can be translated into a U of 15%; that is, 85% of the areas of the male and female distributions overlap, making the differences between the two groups (or d) small; or it can be translated into 54% of one group of individuals exceeding the 50th percentile of another group, or, alternately, into a Pearson's correlation of $r = 0.10$.

One thing worth noting about d scores is that even small scores can nevertheless be practically important. For example, the magnitudes of such critical public health findings as the link between passive smoking and lung cancer, or the link between viewing media violence and childhood aggression, are very small by conventional standards, and yet everyone acknowledges that these are important relationships.[7] And there is some evidence to be described later showing that a very small effect resulting from asking a test taker to indicate her gender before she takes the Advanced Placement Calculus AB test, as opposed to checking it off after she has completed the test ($d < 0.10$), results in over 4,000 fewer women starting college each year with advanced credit for calculus AB. (This is because making gender salient at the start of the exam raises doubts in some women's minds about their competence, generating a so-called "stereotype threat," and the result is that they score lower than peers who are asked to indicate their gender after the test is over.) Moreover, a small effect size that gets repeated over time will produce surprisingly large changes as we show later. This would occur in a situation, for example, in which a small bias in favor of men getting their articles published or their grants funded occurred not once but repeatedly. (Note that we are not claiming this happens; others, however, have made such arguments and we will analyze their claims later.)

Although the d's for aggressive play, gross motor behavior, throwing velocity, and masturbation are very large, often exceeding 1.0, only a few cognitive skills show large sex differences (spatial targeting and mental rotation being two of the most frequently studied). Janet Hyde,[8] a well-known and respected sex-differences researcher at the University of Wisconsin, recently examined 128 effect sizes and concluded that overall, men and women were much more alike than different, although she did report fairly large effects for mental rotation and mechanical reasoning in favor of men (d's ranging between 0.56 and 0.76), and others have reported even larger effect sizes. Are these two areas of male advantage a result of a long chain of environmental factors that begins with girls' greater initial interest in people and boys' greater initial interest in mechanical things, which become amplified as a consequence of later sex differences in play (Legos, blocks, and erector sets versus dolls and dress-up)? Is either mental rotation or mechanical reasoning necessary for successful training and subsequent careers in mathematically intensive fields? If so, are there known brain regions that subserve them? How malleable are they, and what environmental manipulations would maximize skill development in these areas? The data relevant to answering these questions are described next.

SPATIAL ABILITY

A number of researchers have argued that spatial ability forms the basis of later mathematical ability.[9] Friedman (1995) reported a meta-analysis of the link between spatial and mathematical ability. Although the correlations are in general not high, Friedman reported that the correlations between math and spatial ability are higher in females than in males. Moreover, these sex differences become larger with greater selectivity of sample (college-bound, gifted). So, we can start by examining the antecedents of male superiority in spatial ability.

Starting in infancy, male 4- to 6-month-olds demonstrate a superior ability to mentally rotate objects, a finding reported by independent labs.[10] Putting aside Friedman's demonstration of concurrent correlations between spatial and mathematical ability, there is some evidence that very early spatial skills predict much later math skills. For example, Kurdek and Sinclair[11] noted that kindergartners' perception and discrimination of various shapes and geometric forms predict differences in their fourth-grade math performance, and Kulp[12] showed that visual integration ability of kindergartners predicts their math grades 4 years later. Analyzing data from the Wechsler Preschool and Primary Test of Intelligence-Revised, LoBello and Gulgoz[13] showed that math performance "loads" 0.4 on the perceptual organization factor for every age group in the sample. This means that the same underlying processes that foster visual spatial ability are involved in mathematics performance.

Most of the aforementioned studies did not employ measures of 3-D mental rotation, the most popular construct invoked by researchers as the basis for sex differences in advanced mathematics. Instead, these studies have often employed other spatial measures that have not been commonly linked to math ability, such as 2-D mental rotation, spatial memory, visual integration, and perceptual discrimination. These studies did not link early spatial skills to the advanced mathematics associated with sex differences on the SAT-M, though the two that studied infants did look at mental rotation and found male babies superior at it. Finally, it is unsurprising that correlations between spatial ability and math performance are not larger in childhood given that sex differences in early math are neither large nor consistently in favor of boys. Consider the K through third-grade longitudinal study by Lachance and Mazzocco,[14] which reports very small effect sizes for sex differences in early mathematics—more often than not in favor of *girls*. So, the aforementioned studies predicting math ability in fourth grade on the basis of spatial performance in kindergarten are notable. Notwithstanding these caveats, the evidence showing that elementary school math can be predicted by kindergarten spatial skills together with the correlations between spatial skills and math ability among college-bound and gifted students does suggest a possible role for early spatial cognition in explaining sex differences in later math performance.

Another type of evidence suggesting a role for spatial ability in advanced mathematics comes from studies of the SAT-M. As a thought experiment, ask yourself what would happen if you examined the SAT-M scores of men and women who were matched on mental rotation ability—would the SAT-M scores still differ between men and women with identical mental rotation ability? A number of investigators have controlled for differences in mental rotation ability (this is evidenced on tasks such as trying to figure out what a two- or three-dimensional object looks like when it is rotated various degrees or trying to determine what a paper object looks like when it is unfolded). Using both high-ability and low-ability samples, researchers found that when mental rotation scores are statistically controlled or held constant, the male advantage on the SAT-M disappears.[15] Conversely, when math aptitude scores are controlled (or what is statistically termed "co-varied" out of mental rotation scores), the significant male advantage in mental rotation ability still remains.

In other words, sex differences in mathematics on the SAT appear in part to result from sex differences in mental rotation ability, such that when the latter is equated for both sexes, no sex differences remain in their SAT-M scores. And this is true for all ability levels studied. Such findings have led some to conclude that sex differences in mental rotation (especially three-dimensional mental rotation) mediate sex differences in math aptitude, such that once this form of spatial ability is taken into account, there is no longer any difference in math scores.[16] This is the closest to a construct validation in the scientific literature on this topic, one that elevates mental rotation to an important role in explaining sex differences in later math aptitude and ultimately to careers in science. But it depends on a series of assumptions about hypothetical data that are presently unavailable, as we will show.

Finally, spatial ability can be measured in many ways, and this is especially true of mental rotation ability. Figures 1.2 through 1.8 illustrate a number of common methods for assessing mental rotation and other spatial abilities, such as when pairs of perspective drawings are shown and the task is to decide whether they are the same or mirror reversals. (For children, a familiar item must be matched with a pair of rotated items.) Many other mental rotation and disembedding measures are used by researchers.[17]

Somewhat unfortunately for our purposes, the results from these different methods of assessing mental rotation ability are sometimes inconsistent, a point first noted by Linn and Petersen in their 1985 meta-analysis. Scores on the various mental rotation tests often are not highly correlated with each other. Minor adjustments to the test administration procedures such as extending the time limits, or adding items, can alter results significantly.[18] David Geary, a well-known evolutionary psychologist who has worked in this area for decades has shown that although male college students in both America and China outperform their female counterparts on 3-D mental rotations (in a 2001 study with DeSoto they found between 81-82% of the top scorers were male and 63-64% of the bottom scorers were female), there was no consistent sex difference on 2-D mental rotations. They also found that different methods of assessing mental rotation led to different results. All of this means these tests are not equivalently good predictors of success in STEM fields. For example, Sorby and Bartmaans reported in 2000 that the mental rotation skills tapped by the *Differential Aptitude Test* are better predictors of freshmen engineering performance in a visual graphics course than are other spatial tests.

To recap, sex differences involving spatial skills, specifically mental rotation ability of three-dimensional objects, are among the largest reported cognitive differences between boys and girls, and they have been linked to sex differences in later mathematics grades, and occasionally to differences in aptitude scores like the SAT-M. As we will show, some researchers have parlayed this finding into an attempt to account for the underrepresentation of women in math-intensive fields, notwithstanding the large gains women have made in educational accomplishments over the past 30 years. They do this by arguing that, despite getting better grades than men in math and science classes, fewer women score in the very highest region on mental rotation ability and also in the very highest region on math aptitude tests. It comes down

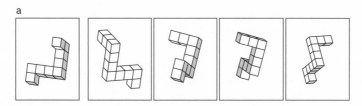

FIGURE **1.2.** Example of items on the 20-item Mental Rotation Test (MRT) where the item on the left must be matched with the two figures on the right that are identical to it after rotation in space, yielding a maximum score of 40.

FIGURE **1.3.** Child-adapted version of the Mental Rotation Test. Is the teddy bear raising the same arm in the 120-degree rotated form? Reprinted with permission of Claudia Quaiser-Pohl (2003).

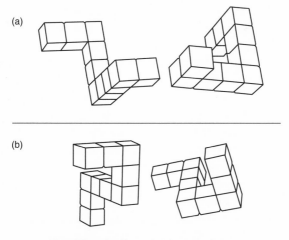

Mental Rotation Test—Are these two figures the same except for their orientation?

FIGURE **1.4.** Ten-cube shapes that are 2-D representations of 3-D shapes, with angles between shapes varying between 0 and 80 degrees. The task is to determine if the two figures labeled A and the two figures labeled B can be made identical by rotating them in space. Source: Adapted from Halpern, D., et al. (2007). The science of sex differences in science and mathematics. *Psychological Science in the Public Interest, 8*, 1–51. With permission of Wiley-Blackwell.

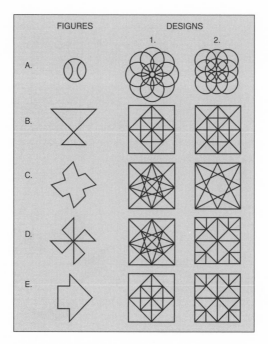

FIGURE **1.5.** *Disembedding Figures Task*: Select figure on right that contains the figure on left. © 2009 Allen D. Bragdon Publishers. Reprinted with permission.

A prism, consisting of three rectangles and two Equilateral triangles at the ends (as seen on the Figure below) is going to be cut by a plane. Which of the cut surfaces I, II, III can result?

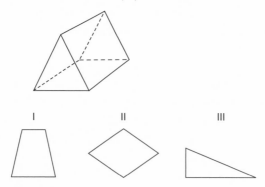

(A) only I and II
(B) only II and III
(C) only I and III
(D) I, II, and III
(E) none of those cut surfaces can emerge

FIGURE **1.6.** Only one of the five possible answers given is correct. In this example the correct answer would be C (only I and III). Reprinted with permission of Claudia Quaiser-Pohl (2003).

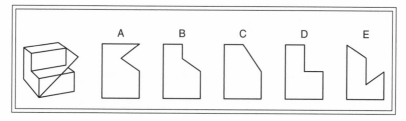

FIGURE **1.7.** On the Mental Cutting Test (MCT), students are shown a figure that must be cut with a specified plane and they must choose the correct resulting cross-section from five alternatives. Source: CEEB Special Aptitude Test in Spatial Relations (MCT). Copyright © 1939. The College Board, www.collegeboard.com. Reproduced with permission.

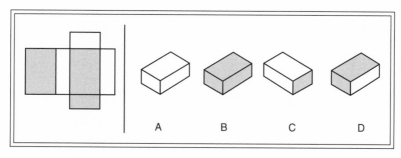

FIGURE **1.8.** From Differential Aptitude Tests. Copyright © Pearson Education, Inc. and/or its affiliates. Reproduced with permission. All rights reserved.

to a contrast between female superiority on virtually all school and college grades, including science and math grades, versus male superiority on tests of mathematical aptitude (SAT-M) and spatial skills (3-D mental rotation). Which set of advantages, if either, is related to STEM career success, and how malleable are they? Stay tuned. But first we must journey through arguments about the alleged causes of such advantages, both environmental and biological.

Opening arguments: Environment

"Where I am today has everything to do with the years I spent hanging on to my career by my fingernails."
— Barbara Aronstein Black, on appointment as dean of Columbia Law School after raising a family and returning to her studies

In this chapter we delve into the nonbiological and noncognitive factors that have been touted by some researchers as causes of the underrepresentation of women in math-intensive STEM fields. The discussion will focus on claims about the influences of early experiences, preferences, parental and teacher biases, societal stereotypes, and claims of discrimination.

OVERVIEW OF ENVIRONMENTAL FACTORS

We begin with some snapshots of research showing environmental influences (or failing to show biological influences) on sex differences in STEM careers. For example:

- Guiso et al.'s 2008 demonstration that cultures that value gender egalitarianism exhibit narrower sex differences in math achievement, a finding independent of genetic differences between cultures, thus reinforcing the power of cultural mechanisms as explanations of sex differences in math performance

- Spelke's[1] refutation of the argument about sex differences in the putative "people versus object" orientation
- Halari et al.'s[2] failure to find sex differences in brain activation during performance of tasks associated with the largest sex differences, and specifically the claim of greater lateralization for spatial tasks in the right hemisphere of men and greater bilateral representation of some verbal tasks in women
- Newcombe's 2007 critique of evolutionary accounts of sex differences in spatial cognition; the argument about evolutionary evidence more broadly—that much of its content is nonspecific, tied to undemonstrated areas of competence, or not focused on particular cognitive abilities that are directly related to math and science performance
- Eccles's 2007 model of early socialization differences that lead to adult outcome differences (as well as myriad other environmental arguments we report below)
- Findings by Hyde,[3] Jones et al.,[4] and others showing that sex differences in mathematics performance can be altered by changing the social environment
- The finding that if the ability to master new, challenging mathematical material over extended periods of time is the criterion, then college men and women show equal aptitude for mathematics[5]
- The revelation that females from some other nations outperform U.S. and Canadian males on mathematical aptitude tests,[6] often by greater margins than those that separate U.S. males and females
- Changes in the pattern of sex differences within the United States over time.

ENVIRONMENTAL CORRELATES OF LATER COMPETENCE

As has already been made clear, there are a great deal of data showing an underrepresentation of girls scoring at the outer right tail of the math and spatial ability distributions (those whose aptitudes rank in the top 1% and higher). Although they start school being equal to boys or even superior in math, as adolescents, girls begin to score less and less at the right tail on mathematics tests that are not directly tied to what is taught in school, tests such as the Scholastic Assessment Test-Mathematics (SAT-M).[7] In the most recent extensive reporting, Janet Hyde and Marcia Linn—two highly respected sex-differences researchers—and their colleagues show that eleventh-grade white boys in Minnesota outnumber white girls among the top 1% by a 2.06-to-1 ratio. Similar overrepresentation at the top 1% exists for other states.

In view of this, one might imagine that very few women would succeed in mathematically intensive high school, undergraduate, and graduate programs. But, as the so-called Nation's Report Card, the National Assessment of Educational Progress (NAEP), shows, this is far from the case. For example, there are no longer gender differences in the number of demanding mathematics courses taken in high school, and as we have shown, girls do better on average than boys in these courses.[8] Females get better grades in all math classes, even in college, and they comprise 48% of mathematics majors in college. This leads some to question the claim of biological superiority of men. We will return to this issue, but first we present evidence for various environmental influences.

Noncognitive Factors: Motivation and Personal Choice

Some have offered[9] a "high-powered job" hypothesis, according to which women and men differ in their motivation. These differences are seen as encompassing both their motivation to succeed in STEM fields and their choices about how they spent their time when they were younger and how they wish to spend it as adults. These differences could potentially partly explain women's underrepresentation in STEM professions. To the extent that they do, one need not invoke innate biological bases as a primary cause of women's underrepresentation. We say "partly explain" because women clearly have no motivational deficits for many fields of science that are not mathematically intensive; they obtain as many or more doctorates as men in a host of scientific fields—between 48% and 75% of doctorates in biology, veterinary medicine, psychology, dentistry, medicine, and others.

This female preponderance renders explanations based on how women spend their time and on the nature of their motivation curious, since to explain the data these explanations need to apply only to mathematically intensive fields where women are underrepresented (earning only between 17% and 32% of PhDs). So, unless one wishes to claim that math-intensive fields are avoided by women because they require longer hours, or greater effort, to master (claims for which there are no data to support), the motivational deficit argument is unsatisfactory. Certainly fields such as medicine, law, biology, and veterinary medicine require at least as much effort and years to master as math-intensive fields, yet women currently receive half or more of the doctorates in these fields.

To shed light on this seeming inconsistency, we begin with a developmental analysis of motivational issues. But first an observation of relevance: To some feminists, the substitution of deficits in motivation for alleged deficits in biologically based math and spatial ability hardly represents progress. Both positions portray the underrepresentation of women in STEM careers as a result of some deficit, either internal or external. As we will see later, some find it far more palatable to claim women's underrepresentation is due to discriminatory hiring, funding, and promotion practices, or results from sexist stereotypes and cultural beliefs that deter women from achieving all they are capable of achieving, rather than resulting from either differences in biology or motivation. This shifts the level of discourse—from women's culpability to society's shortcomings.

Baron-Cohen[10] has argued that girls come into the world with an orientation toward people, whereas boys come into the world with an orientation toward objects, and that these different orientations lead them down differing paths of interests. He cites as evidence for this position a study by Connellan et al. of newborn infants, which found that male babies looked longer at a screen image of an object while females looked longer at an image of a person. To some, this early preference is the genesis of a lifelong sex difference in preferences that leads men to become fascinated with systematizing objects and exploring their relationships and leads women to an interest in social relationships.

Spelke[11] has argued against this view, citing data and studies inconsistent with it. She states that an extensive literature review suggests that "male and female infants are equally interested in people and objects,"[12] and she views the Connellan et al. study as an aberration, criticizing it on methodological grounds, as well as pointing out that it has not been replicated. She concludes, "Thousands of studies of human infants, conducted over three decades, provide no evidence for a male advantage in perceiving, learning, or reasoning about objects, their motions, and their mechanical interactions. Instead, male and female infants perceive and learn about objects in highly convergent ways."[13]

Others have claimed that differences in how boys and girls spend their time (playing with Legos, blocks, and erector sets versus dolls and dress-ups) might result from early differences between them that lead to differences in spatial and mathematical abilities that in turn get amplified by the encouragement of gender bias in play styles[14] and toy selection.[15] Some of this work, especially claims that teachers shower attention on boys and neglect girls, is open to a criticism we describe below. Notwithstanding this criticism, Kersh et al. have provided persuasive arguments and data suggesting a causal link between early block playing and later mathematical ability. And there is some evidence that feelings of self-efficacy in math predict sex differences in math achievement, whereas girls' superior grades are predicted by their mastery orientation in schoolwork,[16] as well as their greater self-discipline—which is particularly important for getting good grades, but not, it is alleged, as important for getting high scores on aptitude tests such as the SAT-M which do not simply test for rehearsed learning.[17] However, some oft-cited studies purporting to show experiential reasons for boys' superior math skills lack convincing evidence. Entwisle et al. in a 1994 report suggested that boys' large-group, outdoor sports contribute to their superior math skill development because, for example, "choosing up sides to play a game is like ensuring equivalence of sets."[18] Without comparable analysis of girls' play or any analysis of the supposed link between team sports and set theory, it is difficult to know what to make of this hypothesis.

Entwisle et al. (1997) cite older work by Lever as support for the link between sex differences in early activities and later math competence. Work by Lever in 1976 and 1978 analyzed children's play patterns and attempted to classify activities by complexity. She suggested that boys develop superior social skills by playing team sports, while girls miss out on complex social skill development by playing simpler games and engaging in fantasy role-play. However, although it may be easier to see the complexity of sports because the rules are codified and known to researchers, this does not mean that less formal games lack comparable complexity, as demonstrated by observations of girls' pretense play and use of counterfactuals. Entwisle et al. interpret Lever's work as suggesting that boys' team-playing experiences would lead to the development of superior math and problem-solving skills. However, it is surprising to see team sports credited with fostering mathematical ability in contrast to activities Lever classifies as low complexity, such as chess and imaginary play, that are often seen to facilitate cognitive development.[19] In contrast, our image of the school jock does not include membership on the Math Olympiad team.

Lever[20] discussed her results in terms of social skill development rather than mathematical skill development, acknowledging that "we do not know what effect playing games might have on later life."[21] She hypothesized that "a girl engaged in pastimes with one of a series of 'best friends' may be gaining training appropriate for later dating experiences where sensitivity skills are called for, but she is less likely than her sports-oriented brother to learn organizationally relevant skills."[22] However, Lever noted that this claim was merely suggestive, writing that, "the above thoughts are speculative."[23]

Thus, the relationship, if any, between these activities and the dearth of women in STEM fields is in need of empirical support that is presently lacking. Finally, Levine et al.[24] also suggested that girls' lack of outdoor exploratory play may have led to their lower spatial cognition scores. However, it is unclear what to make of the fascinating race/social class interactions she and her colleagues reported; poor kids in their study didn't display this gender effect and white middle-class girls were superior to poor boys in spatial ability. Intuitively, it would seem that poor inner-city children engage in the most unsupervised outdoor play, roaming farthest from home, unless one makes an argument that because of safety issues they are restricted to closer quarters. Until someone is able to find an ethical way to randomly assign boys and girls to various exploratory play experiences, we simply will not know what, if any, causal role these experiences have on later mental rotation and math differences. This is true notwithstanding Kersh et al.'s compelling argument for a causal connection between early block playing and later mathematical ability and notwithstanding the data showing that male 4-month-old infants already exhibit a spatial advantage on mental rotation tasks.

Numerous other nonbiological factors have been mentioned as possible causes of women's underrepresentation in STEM fields. For example, some have argued that the images of female scientists in past science materials and radio and television programs have resulted in fewer women identifying with being a scientist. Terzian[25] described the depictions of women scientists in *Science World*, a popular magazine subscribed to by thousands of schools between 1957 and 1963. He argued that many of the women portrayed in the magazine were described as popular and attractive, creating a burden on females who may have gotten the message that science careers require attractiveness and femininity in addition to intellectual ability and devotion. As was true of the claims about sex differences in children's play, it is impossible to judge how causal such depictions of women scientists were in reducing the entry of women into STEM careers back in the 1950s and '60s. One could imagine that if the depictions of female scientists in magazines and on television had been of unattractive women, some would seize on this as a reason why fewer women of that epoch entered STEM fields, (i.e., they resisted identifying with unattractive adult role models). This same caveat applies to many of the alleged factors that have been offered to account for the underrepresentation of women in math-intensive fields.

The Role of Personal Choice and the "High-Powered" Job Hypothesis

There are also suggestions that differences in motivation and personal choice in adulthood have led to the underrepresentation of women at the top of STEM professions. One set of factors concerns former Harvard president Lawrence Summers' "high-powered job hypothesis." In his words:

> Twenty or twenty-five years ago, we started to see very substantial increases in the number of women who were in graduate school in this field. Now the people who went to graduate school when that started are forty, forty-five, fifty years old. If you look at the top cohort (for example, STEM scientists), it is not only nothing like 50–50, it is nothing like what we thought it was when we started having a third of the women, a third of the law school class being female, twenty or twenty-five years ago. And the relatively few women who are in the highest ranking places are disproportionately either unmarried or without children. . . . What does

one make of that? . . . I am speaking completely descriptively and non-normatively-to say that . . . the most prestigious activities in our society expect of people who are going to rise to leadership positions in their forties near total commitments to their work. They expect a large number of hours in the office, they expect a flexibility of schedules to respond to contingency, they expect a continuity of effort through the life cycle, and they expect—and this is harder to measure—but they expect that the mind is always working on the problems that are in the job, even when the job is not taking place. And it is a fact about our society that that is a level of commitment that a much higher fraction of married men have been historically prepared to make than of married women. That's not a judgment about how it should be, not a judgment about what they should expect. But it seems to me that it is very hard to look at the data and escape the conclusion that that expectation is meeting with the choices that people make and is contributing substantially to the outcomes that we observe. . . . Another way to put the point is to say, what fraction of young women in their mid-twenties make a decision that they don't want to have a job that they think about eighty hours a week. What fraction of young men make a decision that they're unwilling to have a job that they think about eighty hours a week, and to observe what the difference is. And that has got to be a large part of what is observed.[26]

To bolster his argument, Summers pointed out that he hears this same story in many prestigious venues—major law firms, teaching hospitals, and universities: Fewer women are willing to prioritize jobs over family, and those who do are disproportionately unmarried and/or childless. As odious as many found this claim, there are actually several sources of evidence consistent with it. First, consider the work of Vanderbilt's David Lubinski.[27] Lubinksi and his colleague and wife, Camilla Benbow, are two of the foremost researchers of mathematically gifted youth. In one of their many analyses, they reported data on the amount of time that nearly two thousand 33-year-olds, who were identified during adolescence as being at the extreme right tail of math ability by scoring above 700 on the SAT-M as 13-year-olds (placing them in the top 1 in 10,000), typically devote to their current jobs, and the amount of time they would devote to their ideal jobs.

As can be seen in Figure 2.1, in both cases, men report working more hours—for example, roughly twice as many high-aptitude men report typically working 60-plus hours per week as do high-aptitude females. Conversely, approximately three times more high-aptitude women report typically working less than 40 hours per week than do men. Lubinski and Benbow reported a similar sex difference in another study of nearly 10,000 high-aptitude math persons, leading to their suggestion that "one only needs to imagine the differences in research productivity likely to accrue over a 5- to 10-year interval between two faculty members working 45- versus 65-hour weeks (other things being equal) to understand the possible impact. The same pattern would emerge for advancing and achieving distinction in any other demanding pursuit."[28]

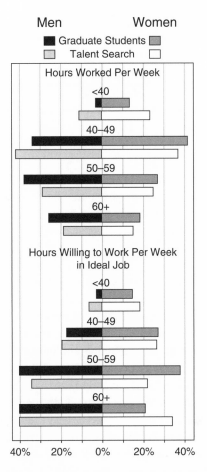

FIGURE **2.1.** Number of hours graduate student (GS) and talent-search (TS) participants worked per week and were willing to work per week in the ideal job. The data for hours worked are based on *n*'s of 276 and 264 for male and female GS participants, respectively, and 217 and 54 for male and female TS participants, respectively. The data for hours participants were willing to work are based on *n*'s of 269 and 268 for male and female GS participants, respectively, and 206 and 57 for male and female TS participants, respectively. Source: Lubinski, D., Benbow, C.P., Webb, R. M., & Bleske-Rechek, A. (2006). Tracking exceptional human talent over two decades. *Psychological Science, 17*, 194–199. Reprinted with permission of Wiley-Blackwell.

Further support of the high-powered job hypothesis comes from the faculty survey by Mason and Goulden conducted in 2004. Their analysis of a nationally representative sample of doctoral recipients, as well as their analysis of 4,459 tenure-track faculty at the nine University of California campuses, revealed that although 66% of faculty fathers report working over 60 hours per week at their careers, only 50% of faculty mothers do. (Mothers report working more hours per week than fathers when combined across their multiple demands of career, housework, and caregiving—101 hours for women with children versus 88 hours for men with children.) Childless men and women both work 78 hours across careers and homes. On average, female faculty with children report working 4 hours less per week at their careers than do childless women faculty.[29] (It is unlikely that men are exaggerating their estimates because childless men and women both report working 78 hours.)

Recently, David Leslie analyzed four large-scale surveys by the National Center for Education Statistics. He demonstrated that there is a linear trend between the number of children and the number of hours worked at an academic job, with more children reducing women's hours of working at their academic jobs but actually increasing men's hours on the job (Figure 2.2). Leslie concluded, "It is increasingly clear that having children has a particularly serious effect on women's careers."[30]

The fourth piece of evidence supporting the high-powered job hypothesis that more men than women are willing to devote themselves completely to their jobs comes from Catherine Hakim, a sociologist in the United Kingdom who has analyzed surveys of men's and women's lifestyles in Britain and the United States. As can be seen in Table 2.1, she presented data showing that 10%–30% of women in various surveys prefer home-centered lifestyles and prefer not to work outside the home, and another 60% prefer adapted work lifestyles in which work can be fitted in with family and personal goals, the latter being paramount. However, only approximately 20% of women in these surveys prefer work-centered lifestyles in which the main commitment is to career. In contrast, more men are work centered, and far fewer of them are home centered, according to a national survey in Britain.[31] Hakim notes that

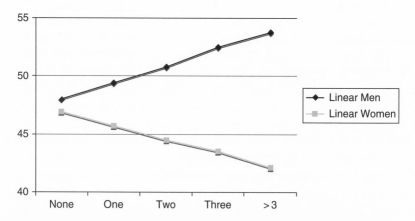

FIGURE 2.2. Number of dependent children and hours worked per week, linear trends. Source: Adapted from Leslie, 2007. *The reshaping of America's academic workforce.* TIAA-CREF Institute, #87. Retrieved 10/22/08, from www.tiaa-crefinstitute.org

TABLE **2.1.** Classification of Women's Work-Lifestyle Preferences in the Twenty-First Century.

HOME-CENTERED (BETWEEN 10%–30% OF WOMEN)	ADAPTIVE (60% OF WOMEN)	WORK-CENTERED 20% OF WOMEN
Children and family are main priorities throughout life.	Want to work but not committed to career.	Main priority is career (work, politics, sports, art, and so forth). Disproportionate number of childless women here.
Prefer not to work.	Qualifications obtained with intent to work. Very responsive to government policy, equal opportunities policy/propaganda, economy, school schedules, childcare provisions public attitudes toward working women availability of part-time work and flexible working schedules.	Committed to work.
	Compromise between family values and marketplace values.	
Qualifications obtained as cultural capital.		Large investment in gaining qualifications/training.
Family size affected by government policy, family wealth, etc. Not responsive to employment policy.		Responsive to economic opportunity, political opportunity, artistic opportunity, and so forth. Not responsive to social/family policies.

Source: Hakim, C. (2006) Women, Careers, and Work-life Preferences. *British Journal of Guidance and Counselling, 34*, 273–294.

these categories run into each other and are probably a continuum rather than discrete categories. This led her to conclude that:

> ... there is solid evidence that men and women continue to differ, on average, in their work orientations and labour market behaviour, and that these differences are linked to broader differences in life goals, the relative importance of competitiveness versus consensus-seeking values, and the relative importance of family life and careers.[32]

It is likely that real sex differences do exist in work preferences and hours worked per week and that this affects productivity; however, these are averages and obviously many women are work centered (and thriving at their jobs) and many men prefer adapted work lifestyles in which their careers are secondary to personal and family goals. Although some research[33] suggests that productivity differences among senior male and female scientists vanish when the type of institution and available resources are taken into account (for instance, large research universities versus small teaching colleges), such data are open to alternative explanations. For example, the type of institution and resources of current senior professors may be partly a consequence of the earlier productivity differences between men and women. If true, then statistically adjusting women's productivity for level of current resources will underestimate the role of past productivity in explaining current productivity differences. Something like this probably is at work, because other evidence we will describe points to sex differences in productivity starting very early in one's STEM career, in graduate school and postdocs (Sigma Xi Postdoc Survey Methods, 2006).

For example, in a large-scale 2006 Sigma Xi survey, Freeman and Goroff found significant sex differences in productivity, even after controlling for family structure and number of children, type of institution, and training. Freeman and Goroff found that male postdocs worked 2.6 hours per week more than female postdocs (mean 52 hours versus 49.4 hours). A similar male advantage shows up in National Science Foundation's Survey of Doctoral Recipients for women with children under age 18.[34] The male variability in the hours worked per week was greater than the female variability (standard deviations for men and women were 12.1 and 11.1, respectively). This suggests that more men probably worked the highest numbers of hours per week, which, if true, could help explain some of the productivity differences they found. Consider: sole-authored peer-reviewed articles (0.3 versus 0.2 for men and women, respectively); co-authored peer-reviewed articles as first author (1.7 versus 1.2); co-authored peer reviewed articles as non-first author (1.7 versus 1.3); and non–peer-reviewed papers (1.7 versus 1.3).

Two areas of comparability between male and female postdocs were number of chapters written (both 0.2) and number of patents and conference presentations. And male postdocs actually submitted fewer grant applications on which they were the principal investigator than did female postdocs (0.8 versus 1.1 for men and women, respectively), although males were co-principal investigators slightly more frequently (0.7 versus 0.6). There were no sex differences in teaching or service duties. Taken together, these findings suggest that men and women allocate their resources somewhat differently, with men tending to focus on publication more than women, and women focusing more on grants. Although these differences in productivity are not large, they could become important if they continued beyond a few years.

TABLE **2.2.** Percentages of Women in Select STEM Careers.

OCCUPATION	% OF PROFESSION COMPOSED OF WOMEN
Psychologist	67.3
Biologist	48.7
Physician	32.3
Architect	24.4
Industrial engineer	14.9
Chemical engineer	14.3
Aerospace engineer	13.3
Civil engineer	13.2
Computer hardware engineer	10.8
Electrical and electronics engineer	7.1
Mechanical engineer	5.8

Source: U.S. Department of Labor, Bureau of Labor Statistics. (2005). Current population survey. Retrieved, on September 2, 2007, from http://www.bls.gov/cps/wlf-table11-2006.pdf.

None of the above four pieces of evidence on women's lifestyle preferences needs necessarily to be valid for the high-powered job hypothesis to be possible. The fact that these four pieces of evidence came from established researchers, usually (but not always) published in peer-reviewed journals, makes it reasonable for someone to arrive at the conclusion that women differ from men in ways that may reduce their STEM participation. An irony in this contentious area of research is that one frequently encounters statements by partisans on each side of the debate that are based on far less supporting evidence, yet their proponents escape condemnation—at least by those who hold similar positions.

As intuitively plausible as the high-powered job hypothesis may seem— in which more women simply have a different and more home-centered life focus than men—there are some important unanswered questions with this hypothesis. If women are diminishing their careers in fields such as mathematics, physics, chemistry, operations research, computer science, and engineering because they devote fewer hours due to prioritizing family over career, then why aren't they foregoing careers in such fields as medicine, law, veterinary medicine, dentistry, biology, and psychology? Being a medical doctor or veterinarian makes inroads into family life every bit as great as do mathematically intensive careers. After all, doctors often must be on duty for 48-hour shifts, must be on call through the night, and are unable to stay home with sick children or attend their school functions. And yet, women have flocked to medicine, veterinary practice, law, psychology, dentistry, and biology in droves in the past few decades. Women comprise between one-third and two-thirds of the total profession in biology, psychology, and medicine (see Table 2.2), and because they are now either nearly at parity or in the majority among new doctorates in these careers (for instance, half of all new MDs are women), they can be expected to comprise increasingly larger proportions of the total professions in the coming years.

It is not obvious how the high-powered job hypothesis explains this, unless it manifests itself not in the raw numbers of newly minted doctorates but in their success in the years following completion of the doctorate. What remains unknown is whether the progress women have made in getting their doctorates in fields such as medicine, veterinary practice, law, psychology, dentistry, and biology will later be paralleled by comparable progress in getting full professorships, center directorships, deanships, and so on. It does not necessarily follow that this must occur. In fact, historically in fields in which women are a majority, such as nursing and restaurant cooking, men have still predominated in the top posts.[35]

Relatedly, if more women than men opt for part-time employment, this could impede promotion and appointments to leadership positions. Several colleagues, upon reading this section of the book, opined that the difference between mathematically intensive fields and the rest is that the latter provide more flexibility for women to take short-term detours and later become reintegrated into their profession, whereas in academia, including mathematically intensive fields, it is not easy to reintegrate after a prolonged leave. In other words, a female medical doctor can reduce her practice to part time during early childrearing years and return to full-time practice with seeming ease. The same is true in other fields (law, clinical psychology, dentistry, and veterinary medicine).

In contrast, until now it has been very difficult for women to take a detour from a tenure-track assistant professorship and return to the tenure track after working several years part time. The academy rarely allows this. And yet, there is the suspicion that even in those fields in which women can take detours, doing so may jeopardize their career in subtle ways. Perhaps the doctors and attorneys who reduce their practice to part time can reenter full time a few years later, but at the cost of making partner. If true, women in these non-math fields may still be affected by the high-powered job hypothesis, yielding fewer women who become full professors, partners of law firms and medical practices, chairs of departments, and deans of schools and colleges. The Gender Equity Committee of the University of Pennsylvania noted in its 2001 report that:

> Within the clinical departments of the Medical School, women were 18% of senior faculty (Full and Associate Professors) on the clinician educator track, and they were 9% of the senior faculty on the tenure track [p. II].... The resignation rate among female Assistant Professors-CE [clinician educator] (16%) is significantly higher than that of male Assistant Professors-CE (9%) [p. III].... Thus, this large group of junior faculty women is experiencing particular difficulty reconciling their professional responsibilities with the demands of family and home life, resulting in an unusually high resignation rate.[36]

It is possible that pipeline issues might account for some of the sex differences noted, as the greater dropout rate of young women versus men has been observed in many STEM fields.[37] So when explaining the dearth of women at the very top (as opposed to those who are newly hired), the situation in math-intensive STEM fields may also be the norm even in fields that are less mathematically intensive such as medicine.

We agree with these colleagues that it may indeed be that the underrepresentation of women in the top levels of math-intensive fields is now somewhat of a red herring. This may be true even if women reached the point where they were no longer underrepresented among new PhDs and junior-status professors. This is because, although women occupy well below 50% of the top positions in mathematical fields, they also occupy well below 50% of the top positions in most other high-prestige occupations, a fact not unnoticed by headlines in the popular press: "Top Wall Street jobs still elude women, minorities"[38]; "Why do so few women reach the top of big law firms?"[39]; and "10 Best-paid executives: They're all men."[40] This male domination at the top occurs despite large increases in numbers of women entering the pipeline in these fields. The print media are laden with these accounts.

Even in academia, there are still disproportionately few women at the top. At Harvard, for example, the portion of senior faculty who are women is only 13% across all disciplines—not just in mathematically intensive STEM fields.[41] And across the United States, in the field of philosophy, the portion of top women (full professors and department heads) is also small. Although women earn nearly half of the PhDs in biological sciences, only approximately 17% of the full professors at the top 100 universities in this field are women. However, Ginther and Kahn's 2006 analysis shows that women are hired and promoted, including promoted to full professor, at rates similar to men, once fertility decisions are taken into account. Their finding suggests that the underrepresentation of women in senior positions can be explained on the basis of earlier differences in research productivity and will probably persist into the foreseeable future, because women are more likely than men to slow down or discontinue tenure-track careers to have families in all fields. This trend is relatively more easily offset in fields with high concentrations of female PhDs, such as biology and psychology, so that women who leave the tenure track can be replaced, due to the full PhD pipeline. For example, approximately two-thirds of new PhDs in psychology are women which means a ready reserve to replace women who depart, though only 48.2% of assistant professors in the top 100 psychology departments are women—in part the result of many PhDs specialized in clinical/practice and never intending to be academics.) This point needs some explanation.

Consider newly hired assistant professors. The tenure system requires that they demonstrate excellence at a young age and work full time (or more).

This system is especially inhospitable for women; despite greater equality in domestic responsibilities between men and women today, women continue to carry the major burden in family matters, as we document below. Although some may find this fact distasteful, it also bears noting that historically, women were far more likely to abandon their own career aspirations in favor of their male partners'. For example, Schiebinger[42] noted that:

> High-achieving women have a tendency to marry high-achieving men and this holds consequences for their own geographic mobility and advancement. For example, 43 percent of married female physicists are married to other physicists, whereas only 6 percent of male physicists have physicist spouses. Where there are two professionals in a family, it's hard for each to pursue opportunities for advancement when they come by[43]

None of this makes universities congenial settings for female faculty, especially young female faculty with preschool-aged children (a point confirmed in a number of internal faculty surveys). Newly hired faculty typically have 5–6 years to demonstrate their research and teaching competence, at which time a decision is made about whether they will be given life-long tenure or not. Liberal family leave policies are not sufficient to buffer a young mother trying to care for infants and young children while carrying out the myriad demands of being a pretenure professor, preparing new courses, setting up labs, training and mentoring graduate students, and establishing a successful program of research. One response to this state of affairs has been to propose pretenure leaves of absence, in which women or men with young children can go off the pretenure clock for 1 or more years and then return to the tenure clock when their children are somewhat less needy. This policy might result in a young faculty parent being given 7–9 years to amass a record of publishing and teaching before being voted on for tenure. Variants of such modifications include allowing faculty to have a half-time tenure position in which they would be expected to accomplish half of what a full-time faculty member accomplishes, or, alternatively, giving them twice as long to demonstrate their accomplishments before being voted on for tenure.

However, a great deal more data are needed before such proposals can be implemented in a manner that is fair to faculty (men and women) who must strive to earn tenure under the regime of the regular tenure clock. Questions to be answered include: Can scientists ultimately be as successful when they reduce their scientific effort for a period of years early in their careers, or will this result in losing ground permanently in some fields? Are some fields of research fast moving, such that being away from the lab for a prolonged period will result in knowledge becoming obsolete? Perhaps this may not become a real issue until one has been out of the mainstream for 2 or more years, or until one has been working half time for several years.

But a number of PhD mothers we have talked to about this option have expressed a desire to be off tenure track for even longer—until their youngest child starts kindergarten, which can run up to 10 years if they have multiple children. One highly talented colleague opted not to apply for tenure-track positions until her youngest child was an adolescent. She is extremely smart, and in between driving her children to practices and engaging in myriad family activities, she has managed to keep up publishing research in excellent journals. A decade after finishing her doctorate, she is well published, but her chances of getting a tenure-track position commensurate with her talents is very low, despite her steady record of publishing while she raised her family. Currently, few universities and colleges will hire someone who has been raising children for a decade without an academic appointment, even if the individual has an impressive publication record like our colleague. We have worked with her on a number of projects during the past decade while she was rearing her children, and we have seen her technique of finding time to work on her part of our joint projects at times that don't overly interfere with her parenting. She is an outstanding scholar and we feel fortunate to be able to work with her. But there is no way she could do the research she does and take on even half-time teaching and service duties unless she abandoned what for her is the most important job—raising her children.

Evaluating Past Productivity and Predicting Future Contributions

The practice of voting on assistant professors for lifetime tenure after 5 or 6 years on the job assumes that research productivity during these early postdoctoral years predicts their research productivity throughout their lifetime as a scholar. This traditional assumption bears scrutiny. In fact, numerous instances exist of an early burst of activity (in those able to temporarily put aside other cares to focus on academic pursuits full time) that actually is unrepresentative of later productivity. Many of us who are academics know of colleagues who "pecked before reinforcement," that is, managed to publish just enough in the pretenure years to earn a positive tenure vote, then relaxed into a long period of reduced productivity and unenthusiastic teaching. Such examples are nowhere near as common as some academy bashers seem to think,[44] but they certainly exist at all levels and at all types of colleges and universities. The question lingers: Are there other ways to accurately evaluate past productivity and to predict future contributions?

No doubt fields of scientific inquiry differ in the consequences associated with delayed start-up or part-time work to raise children. Some research from the early 1980s indicates that fields vary in how fast their research becomes out of date. Once research becomes obsolete, researchers cease referring to it in their publications.[45] Because some fields abandon their past scientific literature more quickly than others, anyone who leaves active research in them for a long time might experience the feeling of being left behind upon their return. The studies, paradigms, and methodologies that one relied on before going on leave may have been replaced with newer ones that must be learned, and this can conceivably take a very long time. (And prospective graduate students may not gravitate to work with such persons in view of their lower productivity.)

In contrast, fields that change very little will not pose a problem for someone dividing time between work and family. This is because, regardless of when one returns from a family leave, the same studies that one built their research around before leaving the field will still be relevant. (We imagine medieval history scholars can safely reenter full-time scholarship without penalty, but the fields in which women are seriously underrepresented, such as physics, may be another matter.) McDowell[46] studied this issue by classifying the shelf life of research publications to determine how frequently old articles were still being cited. He took this citation-rate data as evidence that it was possible to take a childcare leave for several years and resume working without having fallen behind in the knowledge needed to conduct research. He found that scientific articles in the STEM fields became obsolete particularly fast, and concluded that there is a bigger child penalty in these fields for women.

Consequently, math-intensive STEM fields could be associated with greater penalties for someone who took a multiyear break from or reduced her time spent on research for several years, because she will need to retool upon returning to full-time work. Summers invoked this as a possible explanation for the dearth of women at the top of math-intensive careers:

> We would like to believe that you can take a year off, or two years off, or three years off, or be half-time for five years, and it affects your productivity during the time, but that it really doesn't have any fundamental effect on the career path. And a whole set of conclusions would follow from that in terms of flexible work arrangements and so forth. The question is, in what areas of academic life and in what ways is it actually true?[47]

To reprise Barbara Aronstein Black's opening quote in this chapter, she was able to delay her education to have children and then start a highly successful career. But if she had delayed having and raising children until after she launched her career, we wonder if her rise would have been as meteoric. The moral is that having children while in school is hard, but having them as an assistant professor and launching an academic career at the same time is even harder. Leslie's data in Figure 4.2 reveal an interesting gender asymmetry: Men actually appear to spend more time at work as their families get larger, whereas women spend less time at their academic jobs. A number of surveys accord with this finding. Men seem to enhance their chances of being promoted as their family size expands, while women's chances of promotion decline.

Since MacDowell studied the shelf life of STEM articles, there have been important changes in the academy that prompt us to wonder if the multiyear child leave penalty still applies. Wuchty et al. in 2007 reported an extensive analysis of the authorship of nearly 20 million scientific papers and patents, and how authorship has changed over the past 50 years. Their analyses reveal that a sea change has occurred in the way scientists do their work, with teams increasingly replacing individual investigators in nearly all fields of scientific research. In fact, teams produce the highest-impact work today, significantly higher than sole-authored investigators, so it may not be as difficult to reenter the tenure stream today as it was 25 years ago due to the role played by various team members in these joint-authored projects.

The relevant experiment that would need to be conducted to answer such questions is impossible, because those denied tenure are not given the opportunity to show what they could have done later in their careers had universities and colleges allowed them to leave for several years of childrearing, and return later to rejoin their teams. There may be some merit in studying countries with different employment systems that would permit an examination of the predictive power of early academic output, to determine whether it is possible to reduce effort early in one's career, resume it later, and experience high ultimate levels of productivity. But it would be difficult to persuade fields to experiment with the impact of early part-time employment on later productivity. All the same, these are the sort of data that are lacking at present, with the exception of only a few studies that we describe next, none of which spans multiple fields or types of institutions.

An investigation of the careers of people with biochemistry PhDs by Long[48] supports the view that the timing of the tenure system is structurally tilted against women, putting them in a position in which they have to make personal choices that may be damaging to their careers. This is because, as was just seen, the pretenure system punishes a temporary reduction in productivity with a permanent withdrawal of opportunities. This happens precisely at the time when many women are likely to have to make such a reduction in their productivity—early during child-bearing years. Whether this lock-step progression is justified by the particular nature of academic work is open to debate.

In Long's study, the number of articles published and citations to them was studied in a cohort of researchers who obtained their doctorates in biochemistry in the 1950s and 1960s. For those who obtained PhDs between 1956 and 1963, men's citations rose steeply in the first few years post-PhD, then leveled off. For women, however, the data curve looked different; their articles and citations fell significantly in the fourth year post-PhD when some began having children, but later their productivity and citations rose steeply and caught up with men.[49] Overall, men produced more articles, but women had higher-impact articles (their articles tended to be cited more often than men's articles, suggesting they were having greater impact on the thinking of peers). Long concluded: "By year seventeen the average paper by a female is cited 1.5 times *more often* than the average paper by a male."[50] So, even though women biochemistry professors went through an early period of lower productivity and never caught up with men in total productivity (number of publications), they surpassed men in the impact of their published work.

Similar findings have been reported for other fields. For example, Mauleon and Bordons[51] analyzed the bibliometric records of 333 Spanish scientists in the field of Materials Science between 1996 and 2001. Consistent with Long's 1992 study, these authors found that female scientists published in higher-impact journals than their male colleagues at the same rank, and this trend was especially evident at the senior rank. However, Mauleon and Bordons cautioned against assuming that the Spanish system of promoting scholars was biased against women. They argued instead that a lack of significant differences between male and female scientists within a given rank argued against sex-based promotion. Instead, they suggested that sex differences in promotion were due in part to women's lower overall productivity, particularly at the lower ranks. In their words:

> Productivity increases with professional category (rank) for both men and women. . . . Gender differences in productivity within each professional category (rank) were not found, an issue that might indicate that scientific requirements for promotion are independent of sex. However, a different 'life-cycle' of productivity for men and women is found in the area. The lower productivity of women as a group can be due to their lower presence in the upper and most productive categories, but also to their lower productivity at specific age classes, whose reasons would require further analysis.[52]

These two studies[53] are suggestive of a structural tilt in the way tenure and promotion are apportioned, especially in the timing of such decisions. The largest sex differences in productivity occurred exactly around the time tenure decisions are made. Predictions of future impact (how often peers cited one's research publications) that are based on productivity during the first 5 years after attaining the doctorate (the period on which tenure or permanent job security is based) were not good among these biochemists and material scientists. If the goal of the tenure process is to select those based on a snapshot of performance who are expected to exhibit future impact, these studies— particularly Long's—suggest that the process is flawed. (Although these data do not speak to the situation of family-focused male scientists, the same effective bias may also be acting against men who decide to temporarily divert a substantial portion of their energies to caring for the needs of their family early in their careers.)

However, given the cohort that Long studied (women who obtained their PhDs in the late 1950s to early 1960s), it could be argued that they are unrepresentative of both male and female academics today, in the sense that they were almost certainly more select than the typical biologist today— far fewer women entered and obtained PhDs at that time, and even fewer went on tenure track in biochemistry. Perhaps they are not a good group to gauge the predictiveness of publishing and citations inasmuch as they are superior to the average men and women who today enter STEM fields.

Having said this, in both of these studies, early productivity did predict later productivity (early number of publications was predictive of later number of publications) even though early number of publications did not predict later impact (the average number of citations to one's publications). One could argue that professional recognition may be influenced to a greater degree by total number of citations rather than by the average number of citations per article. For example, someone who published 80 articles that were cited on average 20 times each may have greater recognition than a colleague who published only 30 articles that were cited on average 30 times each. The former individual would have amassed 1,600 citations versus only 900 for the latter person, despite the average being higher.

We will return to this issue later when we consider claims of outright discrimination against female job seekers and job candidates,[54] authors,[55] and grant applicants.[56] But for now we suggest that gender may be a weak proxy for a host of variables that predict tenure and promotion but which themselves are not causally related to gender. That is, if the same curriculum vitae (CV, or an academic job resume) were blinded, the same promotional decisions might be made regardless of the gender attached to them, and female raters would not differ from male raters in preferring the portfolios of those given grants, tenure, or promotion. This will become clearer when we discuss the discrimination studies, particularly that of Steinpreiss et al.

The Larger Societal Context

No discussion of the dearth of women in science is complete without acknowledging the societal forces that impinge on women's success in the academy. There is more to success as a scientist than scoring in the right tail of the distribution of math and spatial test scores, no matter how important this may prove to be. In several large-scale surveys of academic men and women, a picture emerges that seems inescapable: Women's success in academia is on a collision course with their success as parent and partner.

According to Maryann Mason and Mark Goulden's 2004 analysis of a nationally representative sample of doctoral recipients, as well as their analysis of 4,459 tenure-track faculty working during fall–winter 2002–2003 at the nine University of California campuses, the factors that affect women's success and satisfaction spill over into the family. To reprise some statistics we reported earlier, although 66% of faculty fathers reported working over 60 hours per week at their careers, only 50% of faculty mothers reported doing so. As the reason for their lower number of hours devoted to their careers, mothers report working more hours per week than men when combined across their multiple demands of career, housework, and caregiving: The totals are 101 hours per week for women with children versus 88 hours per week for men with children. (Men and women without children report working, on average, 78 hours per week across all of these domains.)

Additionally, married faculty mothers work 4 hours less per week at their academic jobs than do single women without children.[57] (These data are consistent with Leslie's referred to earlier.) Women in academia also report lower rates of marriage and fewer children: 41% of female academics report being married with children versus 69% for male academics. Only 30% of women hired in tenure-track positions have children within the first 12 years of being hired, which for most women means they never will. In contrast, 50% of men hired on tenure track have children within the first 12 years. Of course, you might argue that many of the women are content with this state of affairs, but that does not appear to be the case. The women express dissatisfaction: Among 40- to 60-year-old academics, 40% of females report desiring more children versus only 29% of men. Finally, male academics are much more likely to be married than women, and women academics have higher rates of divorce (144% of the men's rate). Taken together, these findings prompted Mason and Goulden to remark:

> Thirty-odd years after the second-wave feminist revolution, equality in the workplace remains more of an aspiration than a reality.... In focusing solely on the professional outcomes as the measure of gender equality, scholars have failed to acknowledge that the gap between the family outcomes of men and women, as measured by marriage, children, and divorce, is as wide as the gap in employment.[58]

Recently, Hamel et al. took this argument a step further in an editorial in the *New England Journal of Medicine*, suggesting that the increasing numbers of women in the medical pipeline may eventually neccesitate a relaxation of the rigid schedule for tenure and promotion evaluation:

In 1960, only about 5 percent of medical students in the United States were women; today, the numbers of women and men in medical school are approximately equal. This apparent success story, however, is tempered by observations that women who enter academic medicine have been less likely than men to be promoted or to serve in leadership positions. As of 2005, only 15 percent of full professors and 11 percent of department chairs were women. . . . Jagsi et al. (2006) document similar trends for women as authors of articles in prominent medical journals. They report that nearly five times as many women authored original articles published in six major journals in 2004 than in 1970. Despite this progress, in 2004 small proportions of first and senior (last listed) authors were women (29.3 percent and 19.3 percent, respectively). . . . In many medical schools, promotion criteria and timelines require academic productivity that is unattainable without devotion of most waking hours to career activities, leaving little time for family and other priorities. This approach may prove untenable in the future, as women make up an increasing portion of the physician pool and as many male physicians take on more responsibility for child rearing and want more time for personal life.[59]

The economist Donna Ginther[60] analyzed data from the U.S. Survey of Doctoral Recipients, a nationally representative sample of those receiving doctorates in the sciences that tracks individuals over a 25-year period from 1975–2000. She discovered gender differences in promotion and tenure (although she found that promotion probability was not significant for the most recent cohort by itself), after controlling for productivity (quantity of papers published and presented) and demographics. She also found that women were paid less, though for the younger faculty most of the differences in pay were explainable in terms of such performance indicators as number of citations. For female full professors, however, their lower pay could not entirely be accounted for in terms of performance differences. In Ginther's statistical model the same level of performance brought less pay for a senior woman than a man.

But in an extension and update of this analysis, with more recent data, Ginther and Kahn[61] found that, although women doctoral recipients are less likely to take tenure-track positions in science, the gender gap is entirely explained by fertility decisions. For example, "Children create a marked divergence between men and women. The presence of a pre-kindergarten-aged child lowers women's likelihood of having a tenure-track job by 8.2 percent . . . [while having] no effect on men's likelihood at all."[62] An older child actually increases a man's likelihood of getting a tenure-track job but has no effect on a woman's. Ginther and Kahn hypothesize that the beneficial effect of children for men reflects other characteristics of the kinds of men who are married with children. They tend to be viewed as more reliable than men without children (e.g., perhaps not as likely to stay out all night clubbing, coming to work hung-over), and more reliable than women with children (less likely to miss work because of a sick child, for instance).

The good news is that in Ginther and Kahn's recent 2006 analysis, the gender difference in hiring and promotion to both associate and full professor (after controlling for demographics, family size, and productivity) was no longer present. Women academics were promoted at the same rate as men when they were comparable in terms of number of children, number of publications, and so on. However, the authors did find that in some fields, such as the physical sciences, having school-aged children reduces the likelihood of a woman being promoted to full professor by 9.6%, but does not affect men's likelihood of promotion because of their reduced childcare responsibilities even among two-career professional couples. Therefore, it seems in some cases that women may have to make a very sad choice between having a family and optimizing their academic career—a choice that men are not forced to make. In the authors' words:

> Marriage greatly increases the likelihood that men get tenure track jobs (by 22 percent), but has smaller and generally less significant effects on men's promotion at either level. Marriage tends *not* to hurt women's likelihood of getting tenure track jobs, being granted tenure or becoming full (professor). Often, it helps. It is striking that marriage does not hurt women in science. Dual career problems do not seem to deter women from getting a tenure track job, from getting tenure, or from becoming a full professor, despite the fact that more than 60 percent of women scientists are married to scientists (Rosser 2004). The presence of children, however, does disadvantage women during the early post-PhD years that coincide with the child-bearing window in life sciences and physical sciences. The single exception is a 6% lower chance of achieving full (professor) in life sciences. Children make it less likely for women to make it through the postdoc hurdle and get a tenure track job. In engineering, people tend to go directly from the doctorate receipt to jobs, bypassing the postdoc stage. Here, too, however, children make it less likely for women to be successful in academia during the early career years, lowering their likelihood of receiving tenure. Our results indicate that to some extent, women in science must make a choice between a family and an academic career. Opting out of academic career jobs because of children dovetails with some of Preston's (2004) results that show a major reason that women leave science is because of childcare responsibilities.[63]

It can be argued that women self-handicap in their early years by choosing to start families or follow their partners' careers in lieu of competing for tenure-track jobs that require a single-minded dedication that allows no more than a one- or two-semester leave following pregnancy. Women are less likely to go on tenure track, or remain on tenure track following pregnancy, and are more likely to be at small colleges and/or in adjunct/part-time positions.[64] Men appear less likely to sacrifice their career aspirations to facilitate their partners' careers[65]; men are also less likely to take time off to rear children and care for elderly parents. Unlike some female scientists who have opted to devote a major part of their energies to raising their young children, male scientists usually need not make such decisions.

As an illustration, it is interesting to observe the parents of the classmates of our two youngest daughters. A number of these mothers have doctorates (two have PhDs in chemistry, one in architecture, two in psychology) and worked as professionals prior to the birth of their children, but they resigned from their jobs to raise their children. All but one of them have been doing this for 8–10 years and plan to do it for the foreseeable future. Each morning these mothers drop their children off at school, many of them staying on to volunteer in their child's classroom, while others return after school to take their children to various activities. We know several who literally spend several hours per day chauffeuring children—a fifth-grader to ski club, even though she herself cannot ski because she must leave immediately after dropping her off to drive another child to soccer in a city an hour away, and a third child to another event before returning to collect her fifth-grade skier. Many of these mothers are eager to remain intellectually connected to the academy, but none wishes to work full time (or even part time) until their children are older. They can, and sometimes do, continue doing research as a sideline. But teaching is usually not an attractive option, and several have declined offers from our university to teach part time because it would cut into their childrearing, and they do not need the money. They all understand that part time teaching does not segue to a tenure track job.

This story will probably surprise some readers who assume that if only universities allowed new mothers to take off for a semester or a year following birth, everything would be fine. Granted, for some new mothers this is a desirable solution, but many mothers desire longer leaves or part-time options that allow them to remain on tenure track for several years before returning to work full time. As some survey data indicate, many mothers who return to full-time work following a one- or two-semester leave express dissatisfaction with their harried lives. They find it stressful to accomplish all of the demands of their academic jobs while attending to the needs of their young children in daycare with the predictable absences due to illness, school closings, class trips, and so forth, coupled with the race to exit faculty meetings in time to collect toddlers from preschool. This is the genesis of many new mothers' decisions to go off tenure track and opt for part-time nontenured posts.

When one first learns of such stories, one's impulse may be to criticize these new mothers. They made choices that were not working out for them and it was not society's responsibility to solve them. No one forced them into careers and motherhood, and bending long-established rules such as the tenure clock to facilitate their needs presents significant problems for the academy that we will discuss later. Upon reflection, however, we think that views about the plight of such mothers may change in the future. We will return to this point later. For now, it is important for readers to be aware of the tremendous resources we are now wasting as a society by subsidizing the training of women who spend many postbaccalaureate years gaining technical skills that are underutilized at a time when our influx of international graduate students has ceased growing and has even declined in some sectors. Many of these international students in the past remained in STEM careers in the U.S. following the completion of their training. We need to maximize our domestic talent pool to replace them.

Until now, mothers who opted for part-time employment in the academy were on a one-way downward slide as far as career success is concerned. As Ginther and Kahn's 2006 analysis reveals, and as Mason and Goulden's survey data show, once a woman decides to go off tenure track—or delays going on tenure track after completing her doctoral studies—the chances of getting on tenure track are greatly reduced. Those outside of academia may find this assertion surprising, but it is a fact of life in most academic fields, with a few exceptions. No matter how promising someone is in graduate school in a STEM discpline, the longer she (or he) delays competing for a tenure-track job, the duller her (or his) luster becomes, and the less likely the person is to be offered a prestigious tenure-track post. This is because some faculty on search committees view the candidate's willingness to prioritize personal needs as an indication that she or he is not devoted to career, and lacks "fire in the belly." Others view the lack of a prior tenure-track job as an indication that the individual has been trying to become hired on tenure track but unsuccessfully so "perhaps she is not good enough to get a tenure-track job".

Regardless of the specific excuse, this delay pattern is an important reason why women are less often in tenured positions and earn less than men. The situation with women who successfully landed tenure-track positions but later decided to segue to part time to rear children or care for an elderly parent also results in a downward slide. Few universities allow pretenure faculty to reduce their effort to anything less than 100%, save a semester or two of family leave. There are many reasons for this, but one that outsiders may not have realized has to do with the perceived fairness of permitting some faculty to have twice as long as others to amass a record compatible with the granting of tenure. The thinking goes like this: "If one faculty member is allowed to reduce her effort to half time and is given twice as long to obtain tenure, say 10 years rather than 5, then how can we be sure she is not 'gaming' the system? If she has the financial means to exist on partial salary (perhaps due to a partner's earnings or a private trust fund), she could, in theory, be doing less childcare, perhaps paying for help, while secretly writing and publishing, unencumbered by the normal teaching and service responsibilities of her childless untenured peers. When she eventually comes up for her tenure review, she could have amassed a record of publishing that is far superior to her peers who had to cope with full-time teaching, advising, and committee responsibilities while also doing research. Because it is research that accounts for most of the tenure decision in the top 100 universities, anyone who can afford to reduce their teaching and committee effort will have more time to do research.

There are many job characteristics that can reasonably be expected to affect pay, such as rank (senior scientists earn more than junior ones), years since earning a PhD, type of institution (large PhD-granting universities pay more than 4-year colleges; private select institutions usually pay more than state institutions), field (economists earn much more than psychologists; humanists earn far less than business/management professors), and so on. In Ginther and Kahn's analyses, when these characteristics are taken into consideration, the salary gap between the sexes is greatly reduced, even abolished in most cases. Although Ginther appears to regard her findings as demonstrating that some residual of the gender gap in pay cannot be explained by these observable job characteristics, we think the real message is that the unexplained portion of the salary gap is quite small—overall, it is only 2%, mostly the result of higher unexplained differences among full professors. Among assistant and associate professors, the unadjusted 2001 salary gender gaps of 5% and 4%, respectively, are virtually completely explained by observables (criteria such as the field one is in). Such small pay differences can not be the reason that fewer women enroll in math-intensive STEM graduate programs. Graduate students rarely know the salaries of academics, and it is not a driving force in their decision to earn a PhD in STEM fields. Furthermore, there could be other factors that were not included in Ginther's model of observables that could account for the unexplained difference in pay among full professors.

In sum, the survey data from several independent sources point to the deck being stacked against women, who assume greater responsibility for children and who are more likely to defer to their partners' career aspirations. The claim that women are burdened by extra-academic demands that only rarely affect men, such as child rearing and caring for an elderly parent or ill partner, is to some[66] evidence of an institutional barrier that has prevented women from rapid promotion and advancement, because it permanently penalizes them for an early interruption in their work. Consider:

> Academia is one of the few places where young talent has to prove itself at a young age in order to keep their job. If graduate school is followed by a post doc (as many in the sciences will do) and then six years at the assistant professor level, the young academic will be approximately 36 years old before applying for tenure. . . . For women, tenure clocks and biological clocks run on the same time zone, and although maternal and paternal leaves are available at most universities, there are also subtle and not-so-subtle pressures not to take advantage of these leaves. The conditions of academic life are particularly difficult for any woman who has caregiving responsibilities such as child care, which is a more likely reason for the underrepresentation of women in academic science, with its additional requirements for laboratory hours, than the fewer number of women at the highest tails of math and science standardized tests.[67]

To be completely fair, however, one could interpret this as an admission that when any sex differences in salary and rank occur, they are defensible, because male scientists invest longer hours in their careers, uninterrupted by family demands. Some suggest that women's fewer hours working at their careers may be limiting their success during the early years of their career, but the evidence for this assertion is not plentiful. When women and men have similar cognitive profiles and put in similar hours, so it is argued, there are no differences in rates of promotion.[68] Summers entertained this as a potential cause of the scarcity of women in math-intensive careers, as we noted in the introductory chapter. His argument bears repeating:

> ...what do we know, or what can we learn, about the costs of career interruptions.... We would like to believe that you can take a year off, or two years off, or three years off, or be half-time for five years, and it affects your productivity during the time, but that it really doesn't have any fundamental effect on the career path. And a whole set of conclusions would follow from that in terms of flexible work arrangements and so forth. The question is, in what areas of academic life and in what ways is it actually true?[69]

We end this section with an issue that seems to be gaining momentum in some policy and political circles, though it is a minority view among members of the scientific world. We are referring to the argument that the culture of STEM disciplines is male oriented and this conflicts with female values and results in an unfair male advantage when it comes to promotion and pay raises. According to its proponents, male values such as a competitive, assertive, autonomous (as opposed to collectivist), single-minded obsession with winning is valued for success in STEM fields rather than female values of democratic, interdisciplinary, cooperative, less obsessive, nurturant, expressive, concerned about others, and less stressful. Instead of arguing that women's underrepresentation is the result of cognitive or motivational factors, these proponents seem to favor changing the rules of the game, according to Christine Hoff Sommers,[70] who critically describes attempts to "Title 9" academic departments in which women are greatly underrepresented. Sommers notes that during her presidential campaign, Hillary Clinton said that "women comprise 43 percent of the workforce but only 23 percent of scientists and engineers" and insisted that government take "diversity into account when awarding education and research grants."[71] Sommers describes congressional testimony by some proponents of this view, claiming that it encourages men to develop "a strong commitment to earning and prestige, great dedication to the job, and an intense desire for achievement. That inevitably results in a permanently unfair advantage for men."[72] This is why we used the phrase "changing the rules of the game"—because it sidesteps sex differences in productivity that are due to uninterrupted hours worked, prioritizing of career over family, and so forth (all male values), and by fiat declares that institutions with more men in them should be penalized, or Title 9'ed. By a similar token, the NBA could be considered actionable. Having said this, there are biological differences between the sexes that tilt them in somewhat different directions in research and family matters. For example, in randomized, double blind trials of oxytocin nasal spray, Zak et al. (2007) demonstrated that men who sprayed oxytocin into their noses became more trusting and cooperative in an economic competition. Oxytocin is home-grown in women and associated with bonding, trust, and cooperation. Such findings bolster the argument that the rules of the game have been based on male values of competition, autonomy and obsessive work, and have not considered female values of cooperation, nurturance, and democratization. Later, we will discuss other sex hormones' alleged influence.

The Same Evidence Can Be Used by Both Sides

When we edited our 2007 volume, *Why Aren't More Women in Science?* we learned something interesting. The same evidence is often interpreted differently by opponents in the debate over sex differences in cognitive abilities as a cause of women's underrepresentation in math-intensive careers. We wrote in our synthesis of 15 chapters, each written by an expert in this debate:

> Now that we have read these top scholars' position papers, we realize it was probably naive to have assumed that anything as complex as this topic could be resolved by tallying the pros and cons on a point-by-point basis. Many of the arguments and counterarguments do not align perfectly, making it difficult to use one type of evidence to nullify another. But even more importantly, all sides in the debate often draw on the very same evidence. In other words, it is not the case that one side in this multi-sided debate is unaware of the evidence that the other sides rely on, but rather that the same or similar evidence is often invoked by proponents on all sides—but interpreted differently. . . . At this stage the most one can hope for is a critical appraisal of evidence in support of various views, and a qualitative assessment of where the preponderance of strong evidence lies.[73]

An example of similar evidence being interpreted differently can be found with the data demonstrating that women tend to pursue people-oriented or organic fields, whereas men with similar math and science abilities tend to pursue object-oriented fields. A number of researchers[74] have argued that we should explicitly factor students' interests into the predictive mix, noting that men and women often have different interests that propel them into different careers.[75] In some analyses, sex differences in job preferences account for more of the differences in the prediction of later careers than do sex differences in either the SATs or Graduate Record Exams (GREs).[76]

What this means is that what people want to do, and are interested in doing, may be even more important than their cognitive profile when it comes to choosing a career. But is it a bad thing if men and women differ in their pre- ferred field of study? Fields have their own life histories, with the gender mix in them changing over time. Our own field of psychology has become increasingly attractive to females to such an extent that most of its subfields have been producing a majority of female doctorates (overall, 68% of all new psychology PhDs are attained by women). It would be deeply unfortunate if talented individuals were impeded from entering a field in which they were interested and capable of doing well. However, it seems benign if women are, on average, more interested in different fields than men—say, interested in medicine as opposed to engineering, in biology instead of chemistry, or in veterinary science as opposed to physics.

Throughout history there have been male–female shifts in dominance within professions such as teaching, secretarial work, and medicine. These shifts are easily explained in terms of changes in prestige and income, rather than by changes in hormones or genes, as we explain in Chapter 3. In their longitudinal program of research, Jacquelyn Eccles and her colleagues at the University of Michigan have demonstrated that young women were more attracted to health-related careers primarily because they placed higher value on a people/society-oriented job than did their male peers. This was the case even when their mathematical ability was taken into consideration. Men and women with similar math ability tended to prefer different careers.

Whether different interests are to some degree the modern vestiges of patterns of intrasexual competition and mate choice, as evolutionary psy- chologists have suggested,[77] or the result of more proximal forces such as contemporary gender stereotypes that constrain girls' early choices[78] is an interesting theoretical issue that is addressed elsewhere.[79] We worry that implementing incentives to encourage greater female participation in nonpre- ferred fields could result in women finding such professions less satisfying, which in turn could lower their chance of success. For example, suppose we induce more women who currently prefer to be psychologists to become engi- neers. If these women are unhappy as engineers, we have achieved greater gender equity in engineering at the cost of these women's satisfaction. But some research[80] indicates that high school students often possess erroneous ideas about the career options available in fields such as engineering, and that should be rectified by presenting accurate information about careers. It is one thing to be disinterested in a career for valid reasons (if one does not prefer it for legitimate reasons); it is quite a different matter to be disinterested in it for the wrong reasons. Students need to be exposed to a range of career options in STEM fields so they appreciate the possibilities when they begin to ponder which careers are worth the effort and delayed gratification. But we should be prepared to discover that for many, the choices could end up being gender differentiated, with young women preferring different careers than young men at different points in history.

Missing from the aforementioned argument is the fact that sex differences in career choice can represent a very positive story: talented men and women have been deciding how they would like to develop, even if it results in them excelling in different areas. If this process eventuates in more women than men going into biology, law, and medicine, and more men going into physics, chemistry, and engineering, this outcome does not seem like an inherently bad thing. As our colleague Susan Barnett asked, is it more valuable to encourage women to shift from their dominance in fields of biology to mathematics, so they can end up working on a search algorithm for Google rather than on a cure for AIDS?

3

Opening arguments: Biology

"The emotional, sexual, and psychological stereotyping of females begins when the doctor says: 'It's a girl.' "

—Shirley Chisholm

"We will have equality when a female schlemiel moves ahead as fast as a male schlemiel."

—Estelle Ramey, past president of the
Association of Women in Science

In this chapter, we review evidence for the alleged role of *biology* in producing sex differences in math-intensive fields, to parallel what we did in Chapter 2 for the alleged role of the *environment*. Here we will describe findings on brain organization, hormones, and putative evolutionary influences. We will also delve into differences in early spatial skills that show up prior to the onset of schooling, which suggest biological rather than environmental origin—at least to many researchers.

There are ample grounds for positing some causal role for biology in explaining the dearth of successful women in math-intensive STEM fields. We withhold our opinion about the persuasiveness of this evidence until after we have presented it, as well as the counterevidence, so that for the time being readers can form their own opinion without being unduly influenced by ours. So for now we make the following point: None of the claims about the biological bases of sex differences that have been made in the media by high-profile policy makers needs to be correct for them to be regarded as reasonable hypotheses, given the frequency with which scholars have raised the same points in journal articles. All of the studies we will review in evaluating the validity of biological claims were published in peer-reviewed scientific journals. This alone justifies their use in a debate—unless they have been definitively refuted in subsequent peer-reviewed journals before one knowingly invoked them. It is the job of those who oppose such biological interpretations to provide cogent peer-reviewed counterarguments, rather than *ad hominem* assertions and personal testimonials as sometimes occurs following suggestions of biological causes of the gender gap in the media.

This is not meant to claim that no cogent criticism has been offered in response to biological assertions. But sadly, too much of the reaction in response to claims of biological causation of sex differences is directed at what critics view as character flaws and misogyny of the people who believe in biological differences rather than a refutation of the scientific basis for their claims. We will describe the pro and con evidence related to biological claims, but at the outset of this enterprise it merits noting that commentators often speculate about policy topics with far less support than the proponents of biological differences have. As will be seen, there is support for some of the biological claims, though we later will provide criticisms of some of the supporting evidence.

This brings us to an important disclosure about our personal scientific values because they influence the evidence gathering that went into this book. We favor free speech in science, even on hot-button issues such as race, gender, abortion, and immigration. Generally, in scientific investigations, premises resulting from informed inquisitiveness are tested and retained, refined, or refuted on the basis of empiricism and logic. We have written elsewhere that "when scholars are silenced by colleagues, employers, editors, and funders who believe that simply *asking certain questions* is inappropriate, the process begins to resemble religion rather than science. Under such a regime, we risk losing a generation of desperately needed research."[1] Granted, there are real costs associated with this view; entire groups—women, minorities, and religious communities—may feel abused by the publication or broadcast of claims that disparage their abilities. "However, racial and gender hatred did not emanate from allowing scientists to publish or broadcast their views, and indeed pernicious folk-theories of racial and gender inferiority predated by centuries the onset of scientific studies claiming to support a biological basis of gender and racial inferiority. Just as research did not cause such hatred, censuring it will not make the problem go away." And it could lead to missed opportunities to enlighten others and make unanticipated research gains that come about in the process of refuting one's critics.

In our own field of science, worthwhile and important scientific progress on racial and gender equality would never have occurred without the added incentive of disproving critics who were permitted to express their data and hypotheses without fear of censure or even dismissal, as happens on occasion. None of the foregoing argument for free speech in scientific discourse is meant to imply our wholehearted endorsement of biological views because, as readers will see, we have serious criticisms. But it is meant to argue that once we cast opprobrium on opponents for arguing their case, we slide into one-party science. Under one-party science, the current consensus regarding gender and racial cognitive equality might never have occurred, and this would have represented a loss to the entire scientific and world community. The key evidence for equality emanated from informed debate, and would not have been generated had rivals been muzzled.

OVERVIEW OF BIOLOGICAL FACTORS

Substantial journal space has been filled with reports of male superiority in math and spatial reasoning, some of it alleging a biological basis. For example, consider the following snapshots of the biological evidence, which we elaborate upon below:

- Geary's 1998 suggestion that evolutionarily important behaviors such as male–male competition involve greater reliance on the ability to represent three-dimensional space geometrically. This is a skill at which men excel, and one which (as we noted) some have suggested underpins sex differences in advanced mathematics. Male superiority has been documented across both developed and less developed nations.
- Numerous studies report that men's greater cerebral lateralization is associated with sex differences in spatial cognition as well as with women's superiority at verbal processing, because such processing is more bilaterally represented in their brains[2]; also see Haier et al.'s 2005 review of sex differences in neural organization and cortical activation while solving cognitive tasks.
- Kimura's 2000 and 2002 arguments about the role of prenatal and postnatal hormones on spatial cognition; Resnick et al.'s 1986 work showing that men with low early androgen levels (due to idiopathic hypogonadotropic hypogonadism) have lower spatial ability than men with normal androgen levels; Slabbekoorn et al.'s 1999 demonstration that androgen therapy for

genetic female transsexuals results in higher three-dimensional rotation ability compared to their preandrogen therapy ability.

- Studies demonstrating that male rats outperform female rats on a water maze problem, but that their advantage disappears following castration or following injection of testosterone into newborn female rats.[3]
- Baron-Cohen's 2007 argument that female babies come into the world with an orientation toward people whereas males come into the world with an orientation toward objects, which leads them down differing paths of inter-ests and divergent styles of systematizing; research showing that women gravitate toward "people" and men gravitate toward mechanical things[4]; Lippa (in press) analysis of responses to the BBC's survey of approximately 200,000 adults, revealing the "people–things" dimension was stable across 53 countries ($d = 1.40$) and unrelated to countries' level of gender equality.
- Studies by Quinn and Liben (2008) and Moore and Johnson (2008) showing that very young male babies are better at mental rotation tasks than female babies.
- Gur and Gur's 2007 suggestion that male brains are optimized for enhanced connectivity *within* hemispheres, whereas female brains are optimized for communication *between* hemispheres, especially in language processing and posterior brain regions, as indicated by the larger callosal splenia (Dubb et al., 2003).
- Kucian et al.'s 2005 finding that for spatial tasks, better performance of men when solving the harder problems is associated with more focal activation of right visual association areas of the brain. In contrast, for the more challenging spatial and arithmetical tests, women's performance entails bilateral activation of additional brain regions.
- Haier et al.'s 2005 finding that the amount of gray and white matter in the frontal areas of the brain is more important in women, whereas it is the gray matter in the parietal areas of the brain that is more important in men.

BIOLOGICAL CORRELATES OF LATER COMPETENCE

The above snapshots are the tip of a huge mountain of evidence that behavioral endocrinologists, neuroscientists, developmental psychologists, and evolu-tionary scholars have amassed on the role of sex differences in hormones and brain architecture in spatial and mathematical ability. We describe some exemplars of this work next and, although intrigued and respectful of it, we point to some problems of inconsistency and methodology.

Recent biological work on cognitive sex differences investigates brain size, brain organization, and hormonal differences. Elsewhere we have reviewed this evidence in detail; here we provide an abbreviated review. The interested reader can consult more technical reviews for details.[5] At the core of biological accounts of sex differences in cognition is evolutionary theory. Simply put, it holds that to succeed in a Darwinian sense, one must be more reproductively successful, and do a better job of surviving and of having one's offspring survive, than do one's peers. Genes associated with enhanced spatial skills needed for expert hunting, way finding, waging war, and navigating were preferred across generations. Evolutionists posit that because the offspring of homo sapiens have a long period of parental dependency, hunters/gatherers who did not have the spatial skills to defend their young and successfully hunt for their food may themselves have survived to procreate again, but their offspring were less likely to survive to procreate. The result was a human brain that has powerful information-processing ability, due to the preferential procreation by those with strong spatial skills who produced offspring who were better fed and protected, and hence lived to procreate themselves. There are numerous implied assumptions in this argument, and some scholars have argued oppositely, as we describe in a later chapter.

Brain Size

Prior to the availability of data from modern neuroimaging studies, a number of investigations of head volume and perimeter differences in favor of men were reported. In fact, Francis Galton, a second cousin of Charles Darwin, made this claim in the late 1880s when he measured the head sizes of Londoners, as did the Italian criminologist, Cesare Lombroso, around the same time.

Over the years, some theorists have suggested that women are biologically less adept at mathematics as a direct consequence of their smaller brain size: For example, there were "attempts by nineteenth-century craniologists to prove that the female brain was too small for scientific reasoning."[6] More recently, J. Phillipe Rushton[7] calculated the measurements of several thousand U.S. Army personnel's head sizes. He reported that even after taking into account their smaller body size and stature, women had smaller brains than men by 110 cm^3. Human brains reach their maximum size around age 25, a time at which Ankney found men's outweigh women's by 175 g—about 17%. He also found men's brains outweighed women's by approximately 142 g even after adjusting for body size differences. Such reports have led to the suggestion that male superiority in math and spatial ability is a result of the brain mass superiority of males: "Surely, no one would claim that the sex difference in brain size is due to, for example, girls having poorer nutrition than boys in North America or Western Europe. Therefore, I propose that the difference is genetically based . . . and that it is related to men's, on average, greater spatial and mathematical reasoning ability."[8]

Lest one dismiss the brain size argument on the grounds that it is highly imprecise, numerous studies using neuroimaging techniques have essentially replicated these findings. For example, recent estimates of intracranial volume using magnetic resonance imaging data reveal quite high correlations with more primitive estimation methods of brain sizes based on external skull length and width, usually well over 0.5, and as high as 0.66.[9] What makes this research germane to the topic of women's underrepresentation in math-intensive fields is that brain size appears to correlate modestly with general intelligence. As Deary et al. point out:

> There is a correlation of about .33 between intelligence and brain volume in healthy adults assessed using magnetic resonance imaging (McDaniel, 2005). Rushton and Ankney's (2007) more recent estimate is .37. In a sample of healthy older men residing in Scotland, we found a correlation of .42 between g (the general factor in intelligence) and brain volume.[10]

Although a gross difference in brain size could well have cognitive consequences, this does not explain why such a difference would result in a particular deficit in mathematical or spatial ability as opposed to some other cognitive abilities, many of which favor women, or in general intelligence, which displays little in the way of sex differences. For example, although men excel at three-dimensional mental rotation, women excel at spatial memory, perceptual speed, and many verbal tasks. As we show later, research does not support the notion that men are on average more intelligent than women. And as is the case with most of the research on biological correlates of sex differences, the focus is on means, whereas the focus on sex differences in the STEM fields is on the extreme right tail (the top 1% or even the top 0.1% or the top 0.01%) of the distribution—a population that has not been the focus of brain studies. As interesting as we find studies of brain size, none of the above studies was conducted to compare right-tail samples. Finally, an analogy to computers seems unavoidably alluring: The laptop computers of today are capable of doing what it took room-size computers to do as recently as 30 years ago, suggesting that the sheer size of the hardware may not be the determining factor in cognitive processing.

Neuroscience Findings

Studies by neuroscientists have identified many subtle male–female brain differences. For example, Haier et al.[11] used Magnetic Resonance Imaging (MRI) and asked whether sex differences in the amount of gray and white matter in different brain regions was associated with differences in IQ test performance in 48 normal volunteers.

These researchers concluded that in various regions throughout the brain the amount of gray matter or white matter predicts IQ scores.[12] Regions associated with language in the frontal and parietal lobes appear to be particularly important. Other researchers have shown that the volume of these same brain areas appears to be under genetic control.[13] In Haier's words:

> Since there does not appear to be reliable sex differences in general intelligence (and this is true irrespective of efforts by test manufacturers to sanitize IQ tests of gender differences), we had no reason to expect sex differences in the brain structures related to IQ. However, we were wrong. When we reanalyzed our MRI data separately for men and women, we found completely different brain areas correlated to IQ (the men and women in these samples were matched on IQ). The amount of gray and white matter in the frontal areas seems more important in the women; the gray matter in the parietal areas seems more important in the men.[14]

This apparent sex difference is the finding that received a great deal of public attention following former Harvard president Summers's remarks in 2005. If this difference holds up in independent replications with representative samples, it can be concluded that men and women achieve the same general cognitive capability using somewhat different brain architectures. However, it is not yet clear what, if anything, these possible differences in typical male–female brain architecture imply for the causes of sex differences at the extremes of mathematical and spatial ability. These investigators did not examine that population, as it was not part of their research question. Much additional research using functional Magnetic Resonance Imaging (fMRI), including some undertaken while men and women performed mental rotation tasks,[15] has reported sex differences in brain optimization, although it too has not been conducted with participants from the extreme right tail of the mental rotation or mathematics distributions. Again, we do not presuppose how extreme the right tail must be for one to have a successful career in a math-intensive STEM field, because this will remain unknown until researchers gather prospective, longitudinal data. Perhaps it will be found that successful STEM scientists do not need to be in the top 1% or top 0.1% of ability. Later, we review the available but limited evidence related to this issue, and readers will see that it is mixed. This is important because sex differences become much more pronounced as one moves toward the extremes (top 10%, top 1%, top 0.1%), whereas they are far less pronounced at less extreme values, such as at the top 25% of the ability distribution. For example, Geary and DeSoto (2001) found in their sample that males comprised 84% of the individuals who scored in the top 10% on the Mental Rotation Test (MRT) in the U.S. and China, but only 70% of those scoring in the top 25%. (It is noteworthy that these investigators also reported inconsistency across other rotation tests, with Chinese women outscoring Chinese men on one of them that requires both 2-D and 3-D rotations, and U.S. women outperforming Chinese men and women on a 2-D rotation task.)

Hormonal Influences on Sex Differences in Cognition

In addressing sex differences in STEM fields, one long-standing candidate for a causal role has been pre- and postnatal hormones. Hormonal explanations for sex differences in spatial cognition have invoked both the organizing effects of prenatal sex hormones on the brain and the activating effects of hormones produced postnatally (onset of puberty, menstrual cycle, menopause, time-of-day fluctuations) on mental rotation and mathematical ability.[16] Many readers are familiar with the striking findings showing that male rats are superior at figuring their way around a maze compared with female rats, but that if they are castrated, their superiority disappears. Equally striking findings from individuals seeking sex-change operations show that when biological women are given estrogen-suppressing drugs coupled with large doses of male hormones, their spatial ability is enhanced. Because of their well-known role in sex differences, we spend considerable time below reviewing hormone research and assessing the likelihood that hormones are a major source of women's underrepresentation in math-intensive STEM careers.

It is beyond our scope here to delve into the mechanisms by which prenatal hormonal exposure is thought to influence brain organization, the ways postnatal exposure to hormones affects brain functioning, and how their possible interaction influences behavior. Here we restrict the discussion to what this very large and complex literature can tell us about the influence of hormones on sex differences in spatial ability, particularly mental rotation ability, and mathematical aptitude. In our recent analysis of this literature we[17] concluded that the research on hormones is internally inconsistent and, despite the many intriguing findings in individual studies, the literature as a whole is filled with contradictions, small effects, and occasional results that are only significant after questionable statistical manipulations are carried out.

Consequently, we believe that hormones, while possibly accounting for some of the sex differences observed among average men and women, are unlikely to be a major cause of sex differences in STEM careers. This is mainly because very few hormone studies have examined hormonal influences in individuals who score at the extreme right tail of spatial and mathematical ability. The majority of hormone trials have been carried out with special populations (women with Turner syndrome or congenital adrenal hyperplasia, transsexuals seeking sex changes, men with hypogonadotrophic hypogonadism), and few studies have been population studies of free-circulating testosterone levels that could examine individuals at each level of math and spatial ability.

As mentioned earlier, the evidence for a linkage between hormones and spatial ability includes Doreen Kimura's[18] influential arguments about the role of prenatal and postnatal hormones on spatial cognition; Resnick et al.'s 1986 study showing that men with low early androgen levels have lower spatial ability than men with normal levels; Slabbekoorn et al.'s 1999 demonstration that androgen therapy given to genetic female transsexuals results in higher three-dimensional mental rotation ability compared with their preandrogen therapy scores; and Fink et al.'s 2006 demonstration of a relationship between the ratio of the lengths of the second to fourth fingers (2:4 digit ratio) and arithmetic competence. This finger ratio is an indicator of the relative levels of prenatal testosterone, or T, as well as estrogen.[19] T is the best known androgen, and it stimulates and controls many masculine characteristics. It is closer to parity in heterosexual women (their second and fourth fingers are more nearly the same length), whereas for men and lesbians the second finger is usually considerably shorter than the fourth finger, resulting in a lower 2:4 digit ratio. Prenatal T is thought to influence many limb markers such as finger ridge counts. The Homeobox genes *Hoxa* and *Hoxd* control the differentiation of both digit growth and the urinogenital system (HOXA13), and are thought to affect the production of testicular androgen in utero.[20] We reviewed this evidence in detail[21]:

> The evidence that such characteristics are markers for prenatal T levels includes demonstrations that gonadal and limb development are genetically linked. The Homeobox genes (*Hoxa* and *Hoxd*) are critical for the development of the urogenital system, limbs, and digits of mammals (see Sanders et al., 2000 for citations). Hence, prenatal gonadal growth is genetically tied to the development of the hands and feet, supporting the view that distal limb characteristics reflect prenatal T levels. Therefore, the fact that performance on sex-dimorphic tasks is associated with limb markers is consistent with a prenatal organizational effect of T on brain development and certain cognitive abilities.[22]

Many researchers such as Fink et al.[23] have reported a correlation between finger-length digit ratios and sex differences in arithmetical ability, whereby women's higher digit ratios (the second and fourth finger or 2D:4D ratio being more similar in length for them) correlate with lower numerical ability. Cambridge University professor Simon Baron-Cohen and his colleagues[24] reviewed evidence for the link between male hormones present in fetal and amniotic fluid and later spatial and mathematical ability. Despite the evidence that the 2D:4D ratio is a marker for prenatal T levels for the fourth finger and estrogen for the second finger,[25] some researchers have not found an effect of prenatal hormone levels on cognitive ability,[26] and Puts et al.[27] found only very small correlations between the 2:4 digit ratio and spatial ability in their large meta-analyses. Studying normal variations in postnatal activating hormones, Moffat and Hampson (1996)[28] found a strong effect of T on visual-spatial tests, but Davison and Susman,[29] while reporting a relationship between T and spatial performance for boys in six out of six comparisons they ran, found for girls a relationship between T and performance in only one of six comparisons. Thilers et al.[30] failed to find any association between spatial cognition and T.

This is a very small survey of the hormone literature, but it serves to illustrate the inconsistencies we found when reviewing the entire corpus. The more important obstacle, however, to concluding that levels of prenatal hormones limit women in STEM fields is that little research has examined STEM women. Falter et al.[31] found the 2:4 digit ratio and current T levels were significantly correlated ($r = -0.295$) in a sample of 69 Cambridge University students, and sex accounted for 19% of the variance in mental rotation speed, with males 361 milliseconds (about one-third second) faster and also 5% more accurate. However, importantly, these researchers reported that T (manifested in the 2:4 digit ratio) did not predict mental rotation ability. Others have reported associations between the 2:4 digit ratio and some types of cognitive performance but not others, or for one hand but not the other, or for one sex but not the other. For example, Brosnan[32] studied a group of seventy-five 7-year-olds and found that boys demonstrated a significant correlation between their 2:4 digit ratio and numeracy scores (-0.35) but girls did not (0.16); and boys did not demonstrate a correlation between their 2:4 digit ratio and literacy scores (0.03) whereas girls did (0.26), but the difference between the two correlations with the 2:4 digit ratio (literacy and numeracy) was significant for boys (-0.37) but not for girls (0.09). The relationship was stronger for the left hand than the right hand with numeracy and for girls the relationship with literacy was stronger for the left hand than the right hand (0.23). In sum, we return to the core observation that we set out attempting to explain—namely, that there are large sex differences in mental rotation and they occur with regularity all over the world. But we are no closer to understanding their genesis in terms of hormone differences between men and women.

Recently, Hampson and Moffat[33] reviewed some of the literature on the activational effects of postnatal hormones (that is, not prenatal hormone levels reflected in the finger digit ratio but postnatal hormones due to puberty, menopause, circadian changes, hormone supplements, and so forth), arguing that the data were mostly consistent with a spatial enhancement by steroid hormones. The role of prenatal organizational effects is less clear.[34]

Kimura[35] has described various bodies of evidence for the role of male hormones in cognitive functioning. For example, a U-shaped relationship has been found between levels of free-circulating testosterone and measures of spatial ability in right-handers but not in left-handers.[36] (Later, we explain why handedness is theoretically relevant.) According to Kimura, "Women with higher testosterone achieve better scores than women with lower levels of it, but in men, the reverse is true.... This has given rise to the suggestion that there is an optimal level of testosterone for certain kinds of spatial ability, and that this optimal level is in the low male range."[37] In other words, neither men with high levels of testosterone nor women with very low levels of it do well on mental rotation tasks; the ideal level is around the low-average male level.

It has been known for a long time that boys afflicted with extreme androgen deficiency (idiopathic hypogonadotrophic hypogonadism) exhibit low spatial ability early in life compared both to normal boys and to boys who develop androgen deficiency later in life.[38] Furthermore, prenatally androgenized girls (those with congenital adrenal hyperplasia, or CAH) exhibit higher spatial ability than their non-CAH peers.[39] However, one problem with most early studies of CAH girls is that the control groups employed were not ideal matches; that is, they were not sisters or cousins of the CAH girls. It turned out to be very difficult to match CAH girls otherwise, so that original claims for superior ability, including above-average IQs, disappeared in later studies when sisters were used as controls.

It has been suggested by Lacreuse et al.[40] that declining T levels seen in adult male monkeys might be the reason their spatial-memory declines, because reductions in spatial ability are associated with a gradual reduction in T—perhaps a consequence of its influence on the hippocampus, a brain structure involved in spatial ability. Research studying the androgen levels of successful professors in STEM fields at various stages of their lives might be useful in exploring this hypothesis further. One study indicates that physical scientists' second-to-fourth digit ratios (again, an index of their prenatal T level) are closer to the second-to-fourth digit ratios of women than to male social scientists' ratios, lending some support to the notion that T levels are related to digit ratios in a curvilinear, U-shaped manner.[41] However, this study combined myriad disciplines under the rubric of "Social Science-Humanities-Management Faculty," including some that would seem to be highly math intensive (management), while also finding that engineering faculty—a quintessentially math-intensive field—had digit ratios no different from both social science-humanities-management on the one hand and science faculty on the other. This clearly calls for more research before concluding that there is a U-shaped relationship between the finger ratio and math and spatial ability. And the role of T in cognitive performance may be mediated by its influence on social and emotional behaviors rather than its direct influence on cognition. In a recent study,

Coates, Gurnell, and Rustichini (2009) compared profit and losses (P&L) of 49 London stock traders. (On the trading floor in the City of London there are only three females out of 200 traders.) P&L was used as the measure for how well the traders did compared to each other. Higher P&L profits were associated with lower digit ratios, suggesting that prenatal T levels influence risk-taking and fast reactions, whereas success in financial positions that require more analytic decision making have been associated with female digit ratios.

For Kimura,[42] the issue of the underrepresentation of women in STEM fields is, in her words, a "misrepresentation." This is because her analysis of the hormone literature leads her to the expectation that there *should* be gender asymmetries in STEM fields. She summarized what she regarded as six convergent lines of evidence that, taken together, led her to argue for a biological basis of sex differences in cognitive ability. In her words:

> Research into cognitive sex differences over the past half-century has shown that many human cognitive sex differences are: 1) significantly influenced by both pre-natal and current levels of sex hormones (see Kimura, 2000 for this and following points). Prenatal androgen levels are almost certainly a major factor in the level of adult spatial ability. However, even in adulthood, variations in hormone levels (across the menstrual cycle in women and across seasons and time of day in men) are associated with variations in specific cognitive abilities; 2) (cognitive sex differences are) present very early in life, before major differences in life experience (e.g., Levine et al., 1999). Thus not all cognitive sex differences develop gradually through post-elementary school years. Of course, even those that do not appear until after puberty are not necessarily determined solely by experience, but may be influenced by the pubertal alterations in sex hormone levels; 3) (cognitive sex differences) are present across cultures that vary in social pressures to conform to a gender norm. This has been documented for both mathematical reasoning and spatial ability (e.g., Geary & DeSoto, 2001); 4) (such differences are) apparently uninfluenced by systematic training in adulthood. While both sexes benefit from short-term intensive training on spatial tasks, men's and women's scores do not converge (Baenninger & Newcombe, 1995); 5) (cognitive sex differences are) mostly unchanged in magnitude over the past three or four decades, a period in which women's roles and access to higher education have changed substantially (Feingold, 1996; Kimura, 2002); 6) (such differences are) parallel to certain sex differences found in nonhumans where social influences are, either naturally or by virtue of a laboratory environment, absent or minimal. For example, male rats are superior to female rats in learning spatial mazes, and these sex differences can be reversed by hormonal manipulation in early postnatal life (Williams & Meck, 1991).[43]

Kimura is correct; there are many supportive studies of the causal link between hormones and cognitive performance. However, as we argued above, a number of attempts to relate spatial ability to prenatal androgens have not succeeded in demonstrating a causal link, and other efforts have resulted in findings that are inconsistent. In addition to the handful of failed attempts we mentioned above, Collaer et al.[44] studied the performance of females with Turner syndrome, who have lower levels of female sex hormones from early in life. The authors found that although those with Turner syndrome were impaired on many cognitive measures compared to matched controls, there was no difference in the degree of their impairment for abilities in which males usually excel, such as spatial tasks, versus those in which females usually excel, such as memory span tests. This does not support the claim that sex hormone levels are the cause of male cognitive superiority on STEM-relevant tasks. In addition, females with Turner syndrome are missing gonads altogether, so they are lacking testosterone, which the ovaries manufacture in addition to estrogens. They are missing an entire chromosome as well. And as a group they are unhealthy and have below-average IQs, so any results could be due to missing genes or low IQ instead of hormone levels.

Although the strongest evidence for a causal link between spatial ability and hormones comes from animal studies in which hormonal levels can be precisely controlled and dosed very high, there is a danger of overestimating the causal influence of hormones on humans based on those found with animals. The evidence for hormonal mechanisms in humans is more limited, and less impressive than what is found in animal studies.

As one example of the danger of generalizing from animal studies to humans, the correlation between exposure to male sex hormones and playing roughly has been demonstrated with animals but has not been found with human children. In fact, Hines and Kaufman[45] expected to find increased rough-and-tumble play in 3- to 8-year-old children with elevated prenatal exposure to androgens in CAH, but they reported that CAH girls were similar to normal girls. Additionally, CAH boys actually exhibited *less* rough-and-tumble play than unaffected boys, despite having higher male hormones. Possibly the best human data showing that prenatal sex hormones are important to children's social behavior is from the studies of children's toy preferences, where CAH girls score nearly twice as high as unaffected girls on a preschool inventory of play behaviors.[46] So, there is a need to be cautious in extrapolating the animal neuroendocrine findings to human behavior.

Lest readers imagine that the weakness of the hormonal evidence is confined to studies of social behaviors such as rough-and-tumble playing and toy preferences, the scientific literature relating spatial ability to hormones is also mired in inconsistencies, although it is stronger than the social literature alluded to previously.[47] And even this endorsement may be an overstatement, because, in fact, we could find only a couple studies in the literature in which spatial abilities have been unambiguously related to prenatal androgen exposure.[48] Other attempts to study spatial ability and relate it to prenatal androgens have not succeeded in demonstrating a substantial association,[49] showing at best a modest relationship.

Hines, Fane, et al.[50] studied a group of 30 women and girls and 29 men and boys with CAH (aged between 12 and 45) and a nearly equally sized control group. Among the measures administered were two mental rotation tasks. They found that although control men and boys outperformed control women and girls ($d = 0.92$ indicates the difference among these normal male and female subjects was quite large), the relative performance among women and girls did not correlate with their degree of androgen exposure, and CAH men and boys who had the highest androgen levels actually performed worse than control men and boys, a result that follows from Kimura's[51] U-shaped expectation. Figure 3.1 illustrates this curvilinear function by showing that, for females, high T is associated with superior mental rotation ability, whereas for males, it is associated with low spatial ability. So, if you combine male and female data, the result is a U-shaped function in which spatial ability rises as T approaches the average male level, then declines as T rises above this level. In fact, based on our analysis of many such studies, the optimal level of T as far as spatial ability is concerned is around the low-average male level. Contrary to popular portrayals such as the manly Marlboro man hunting bison in the outback, so-called macho men with high T levels are *not* notably better at spatial ability than men who are slightly below average in T, and may even be worse than them.

On another spatial task, CAH women and girls were superior in their ability to aim darts or balls accurately at a point in space (which has a sex effect size even larger than that for mental rotation ability, $d \sim 1.3 - 1.9$)—but this was not true of CAH men and boys. Further complicating matters, the difference between females with CAH and those without CAH was large on the dart targeting task ($d = 0.76$, $p < 0.001$), but only approached significance on a

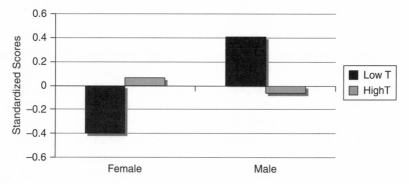

FIGURE **3.1.** The relationship between testosterone (T) and spatial ability in males and females.

similar ball target task ($d = 0.47$, $p = 0.057$). It is unclear what to make of such results. The authors suggest that androgen, if it affects mental rotation ability at all, may have a time course starting sometime after the prenatal period, possibly 6 months postnatally. Primates, including humans, have markedly elevated testosterone levels during the first postnatal month, but little is known about the cognitive consequences of this elevation, although it cannot be ignored in thinking about hypotheses relating hormones to sex differences in spatial ability. Hines et al. also point out that because targeting performance involves muscle systems as well as neural systems, there is a possibility that the action of androgen is on the developing musculature rather than on the developing brain. Studies using measures of targeting ability that are void of muscle strength (such as computerized target tasks) could help evaluate this hypothesis.

The link between hormones and spatial ability found among CAH girls and androgen-deficient boys has not been supported by a linear correlation between masculinizing hormones and spatial ability among normally developing children.[52] Van Goozen et al.[53] have provided intriguing findings regarding the influence of hormones postnatally—they can have rapid and enduring effects of large magnitude. Van Goozen and her Dutch colleagues demonstrated a significant relationship between androgen dosage and two-dimensional mental rotation. They assessed spatial cognition (as well as noncognitive behaviors such as aggression) both before and after the administration of hormones in a group of female-to-male transsexuals ($n = 35$) and a group of male-to-female transsexuals ($n = 15$). They found a moderate magnitude androgen enhancement effect ($d = 0.56$). As we summarized recently:

> Biological females given androgen along with estrogen-suppressing hormones improved on spatial ability, while genetic males given estrogen therapy and androgen-suppressing drugs became less accurate in rotating two-dimensional objects. Interestingly, the latter group also improved on verbal measures following the administration of female hormones, conforming to what is commonly regarded as a female hormone profile.[54]

What makes Van Goozen et al.'s spatial cognition findings somewhat challenging to interpret is that in follow-up work, she and her colleagues reported a very large effect size for androgen therapy on a task requiring three-dimensional rotation used in the above study.[55] In this latter study, the enhancing effect of testosterone on spatial ability performance was not quickly reversible over a 1-year period. In contrast with their earlier study, antiandrogen treatment in combination with estrogen therapy did not result in diminished spatial ability, nor did it have an enhancing effect on verbal fluency in adult men who were given female hormones, as had been found in their earlier study.

What all of this data shows is that no clear hormonal pattern of effects is apparent: Among biological women attempting transsexual conversion, testosterone administration enhanced three-dimensional spatial ability, whereas in biological men seeking sex conversion to women, deprivation of testosterone did not alter this particular spatial ability. Of course, one can posit that it is living a lifetime with high T levels that fosters spatial ability rather than a recent surge in T, or that it is particularly prenatal T levels that affect the organization of the newly emerging brain rather than contemporaneous activational effects in adults given T. But such hypothesizing is in need of rigorous testing before we can confidently conclude that hormones play an important causal role in the dearth of women in STEM careers.

In women, some positive relationships between free-circulating testosterone and different spatial ability tests have been found on three-dimensional spatial ability.[56] However, the magnitude of this effect did not increase as a linear function of hormone levels over a period of 7 months, and their improved spatial abilities did not decline 5 weeks after stopping the hormone treatment. Androgen suppression did not result in a decline in three-dimensional spatial performance for male-to-female transsexuals, suggesting either some prenatal or later (perhaps pubertal) organizational effects on these abilities. However, it could be reasonably argued that exposure to testosterone as an adult results in irreversible cognitive changes, much the same way that testosterone given to adult women masculinizes their voice pitch/larynx, and this change persists permanently.

To study the activational effects of sex hormones on cognitive functioning in humans somewhat more directly, two types of studies have commonly been conducted. First, in women, the cognitive effects of fluctuating hormone levels during the menstrual cycle have been investigated. Women do better on a speeded motor coordination test during the midluteal phase, when levels of estrogen and progesterone are high,[57] and they show an enhanced verbal articulation during the preovulatory phase, when only levels of estrogens are ascended.[58] These two studies showed that the spatial scores of women were lower during the midluteal and preovulatory phases than during menses, when hormonal levels are relatively lower. Similar findings were found in the case of both two-dimensional mental rotations[59] as well as three-dimensional rotations.[60] Performances on these tests were better during the menstrual phase. Menstrual studies are correlational, of course, and they leave open alternate possibilities: In addition to hormonal changes with the menstrual cycle, other aspects of physiology also vary (for example, PMS, once viewed as the direct result of hormones, is now understood as emanating from other causes).

Secondly, hormone levels have been manipulated directly in nonclinical samples of humans through hormone administration. Our colleague at

Cornell, Elizabeth Adkins-Regan, a behavioral endocrinologist, regards these as the best studies, with clean experimental designs and excellent control of the independent variables. For example, Gordon et al.[61] tested healthy young men before and 1 week after an injection of luteinizing hormone–releasing hormone (LHRH) and compared these findings with placebo-injected men. The LHRH-injected group improved more on verbal ability tasks, while the placebo-injected group improved more on some spatial ability tasks. Therefore, LHRH administration, which is associated with increased gonadotropins (luteinizing hormone [LH] and follicle-stimulation hormone [FSH]), fostered verbal performance and prevented learning effects on some spatial ability tasks.

The same experiment was repeated with testosterone injections by Gordon et al.[62] in a different group of healthy young men. However, this time no relation was found between testosterone fluctuations and cognitive functioning. Two possible explanations were offered for this result. First, it was suggested that T levels measured at the time of testing were not related to the amount of exposure to androgens prenatally. Second, the increase of the T level in blood might have been faster than its effect on cognitive functioning,[63] particularly if the cognitive changes require neural remodeling. Finally, Bhasin et al. have conducted a number of studies of nonclinical samples of men who were administered testosterone, and these researchers failed to find any systematic effect of visual cognition, regardless of dose level.[64] In these authors' words:

> Although men, on average, perform better on tests of spatial cognition than women, testosterone replacement has not been consistently shown to improve spatial cognition in hypogonadal men (1, 29, 48). We did not find changes in spatial cognition at any dose. The effect size of gender differences in spatial cognition is small.[65]

In sum, the literature based on animal studies shows pronounced hormone effects on spatial cognition, and it seems most robust, but also less applicable to human cognition. As was seen, the human hormone literature, usually based on small unrepresentative samples and clinical groups, is often contradictory. In a large population-based sample, attempts were made to address shortcomings that have potentially contributed to discrepancies in the clinical and small sample literatures. Thilers et al.[66] analyzed the serum free-circulating testosterone of 2,383 German men and women, ranging in age from 35 to 90 years. Their spatial measure was the Block Design subtest from the Wechsler Adult Intelligence Scales, a task that requires adults to work from a two-dimensional perspective drawing of a two-color figure to construct a three-dimensional structure out of red and white colored blocks, so it involves some degree of mental rotation.

The authors found that elevated T levels were associated with better spatial abilities for men, and this improvement increased with age, similar to what has been found with rhesus monkeys.[67] For women, however, T levels were unrelated to spatial abilities. So in the population at large there appears to be sex-specific correlation of hormones with cognitive ability and, even more troubling, there was inconsistent evidence for the expected male and female cognitive–hormonal links: For women, as expected, lower levels of T were associated with higher levels of verbal ability. For men, however, there was also an association between T levels and verbal fluency, albeit marginal, indicating that higher male hormone levels enhanced what is ordinarily viewed as a female profile. Such reversals in expected outcomes present a challenge to the alluringly simple assumption of causal influence of hormones on cognition.

We conclude that the pattern across studies of hormones and cognitive ability differences between women and men is not strong and consistent enough to justify claiming that hormones are the *primary* cause of sex differences in STEM careers. Hormones appear to play a secondary role, and as we will show, other factors are more likely to play a larger role in explaining the dearth of women in math-intensive fields. Pockets of like-minded researchers endorse various positions across the nature–nurture spectrum, and although most researchers would agree that no single factor fully explains the dearth of women in these fields, their positions can be classified on the continuum from "primarily environmental" to "primarily biological."[68] What is lacking is a single large-scale, representative study that unequivocally demonstrates the predicted pattern: spatial ability of talented men and women enhanced as a function of higher levels of androgen (up to the low male level), along with a simultaneous reduction in verbal fluency. Small-scale therapeutic studies of such persons are valuable bases for creating and testing hypotheses, but we must ultimately await testing with randomized experiments and large-scale population studies that include ample numbers of extreme right-tail individuals to determine whether their very high spatial ability is associated with hormone levels.

Until such time as more representative studies are available, some of the best methodological treatments have failed to yield the expected pattern. Consider Bhasin et al.'s work: They employed a double-blind randomized experiment over a 40-week period to assess a group of 61 adult males who were assigned to one of five conditions. These men were administered monthly injections of a long-acting gonadotropin-releasing hormone (GnRH) agonist to suppress their endogenous T levels. They were then given weekly injections of 25, 50, 125, 300, or 600 mg of testosterone enanthate for 20 consecutive weeks, and their energy and protein intakes were standardized. The agonist, in combination with supplementation of T, resulted in circulating testosterone concentrations during treatment that were proportional to the administered dose of testosterone enanthate: The administration of the GnRH agonist plus graded doses of testosterone resulted in mean nadir testosterone concentrations of 253, 306, 542, 1,345, and 2,370 ng/dl at the 25, 50, 125, 300, and 600 mg doses. Bhasin et al. created the ideal conditions under which to observe any relationship that might exist between T and visual-spatial memory. Despite these ideal conditions, they failed to find any dose-dependent relationship for visual-spatial memory, which did not change at any dose. This led Bhasin et al. to conclude that only very low levels of T are needed to promote spatial ability, probably levels that are below those possessed by nearly all women. One could counter that spatial memory is not the same as mental rotation ability, and it is the latter where we should be looking for hormone effects. However, spatial memory is usually associated with superior female performance, yet in Bhasin's work there was no relationship—women did not get better on this measure at higher dose levels.

The Bottom Line on Hormonal Influences

This is why we have come to the conclusion that hormones have not been satisfactorily established as a *primary* cause of sex differences in spatial or mathematical ability among men and women at the right tail. Despite finding mean effects at the midpoint in the distribution, there are important inconsistencies[69] and the differences at the midpoint cannot be generalized to the extreme right tail. It is important to remember an earlier caveat, namely, that the optimal level of testosterone is thought by researchers to hover around the low end of the normal male range,[70] or hover near the moderately high end of the combined male–female range. Therefore, very high levels of T are often associated with reduced spatial ability rather than enhanced ability. Combining male and female levels of T results in an inverted U-shaped function, with both very low and very high levels associated with lower scores on mental rotation and mathematics tests.

Despite a number of studies showing a clear nonlinear relationship between activational or postnatal[71] effects of T on mental rotation and mathematics performance,[72] there are a number of studies that failed to find such relationships.[73] As one example, a 3-month cross-over random trial showed that 200 mg of Enanthate had no effect on elderly men's mental rotation.[74] To further call into question the murkiness of this presumed relationship, some of the studies that do report a significant relationship for an organizational effect of prenatal T do so only after dropping subjects who are outliers in the statistical sense that their scores are so far from the nearest ones that they engender skepticism[75] or the size of the effect is quite marginal.[76] Bhasin et al.'s conclusion[77] seems prudent, so we return to it: "Although men, on average, perform better on tests of spatial cognition than women, T replacement has not been consistently shown to improve spatial cognition in hypogonadal men. We did not find changes in spatial cognition at any dose."[78]

To summarize, most studies dealing with the organizational effects of hormones are small, not confined to the right tail of mathematical ability distribution, and sometimes unreplicated, and many important inconsistencies are in need of resolution before one can regard these findings as more than suggestive, such as why the finger digit ratio is thought to be a result of a linear hormone dose relationship whereas activational studies typically find U-shaped (nonlinear) dose relationships, when they find relationships at all. (That is, the 2:4 digit ratio is not due to the HOX genes controlling prenatal T levels extending finger length to a point and then ceasing to do so, but rather that the ratio gets progressively smaller—relatively longer fourth digit—with linearly increasing hormone levels.) This conclusion about the small role of hormones in accounting for the dearth of women in math-intensive careers came as a surprise to us because we had begun reading this literature with a belief that the hormone–cognition connection in women was far stronger and more consistent than we now believe it to be. In other words, both of us began writing this book with a strong pro-hormone belief, so our conclusion was definitely not preordained. Nor is it simply the manifestation of a bias by antibiological advocates, because both of us believe that biology is very important in virtually all types of cognition (and have written books with subtitles such as "The Bioecology of Intellectual Development"). Gradually we shifted away from our pro-hormone belief as the evidence became more problematic and less scientifically satisfying. We found ourselves backing off our original beliefs. And although we are open to the possibility that future research may establish a clearer role for hormones, we will show later that nonhormonal factors emerge as far more likely primary explanations for the shortage of women in math-intensive fields.

RECAP OF BIOLOGICAL EVIDENCE

There is support from several different biological approaches for the view that there are biologically related sex differences in many behaviors that *might* be related to performance in STEM fields. However, researchers differ regarding the conclusions that can be reliably drawn from this evidence, and important inconsistencies and outright contradictions are in need of resolution, especially about the role of prenatal hormones. Importantly for the theme of this book, more direct data are needed on men and women from the extreme right tail of the ability distribution. The most prudent position is that *if* hormones play a role in the underrepresentation of women at the extreme right tail of the math-ability distribution, it is likely that they play a secondary role vis-à-vis other factors that we will cover later in this book—factors such as personal choices and preferences, societal stereotypes, and work–family conflicts.

Challenges to the environmental position

"Can we today measure devotion to husband and children by our indifference to everything else?"

—Golda Meir

Lest the reader assume that our critique of the role of hormones and brain volume lead us to endorse the role of social influences, we do not believe that many of the environmental claims hold up to scrutiny any better than the hormonal claims. Before delving into these environmental claims, we will complete our excursion through the remaining biological claims, then segue to the social and environmental claims. So in this chapter, we start by reprising other biological arguments against the strong environmental position. These consist of claims that fewer women are succeeding in math-intensive careers because of inherent sex differences in both general and specific cognitive abilities, and the neurological substrates that support them. We follow this with a consideration of nonbiological claims.

LOGICAL ARGUMENTS AND CONUNDRUMS

Sex differences are not always found, and even when they are found they are not observed across the board, but rather sometimes only in the cognitive domain and at other times in the biological or social domains. Even when they are found in a given domain, they are usually unevenly distributed in that domain, occurring more on some measures than on others or for some age groups than for others, or at some ability levels but not others. Four broad categories of sex differences have been studied. The first are measures of early cognitive performance that many consider precursors to later mathematical competence (such as the ability of infants to mentally rotate three-dimensional shapes). The second are biological correlates of some of these measures (such as organizing and activating hormones we described in Chapter 3). The third are social and emotional factors that could plausibly underpin both the cognitive and biological measures (motivation, stereotypes, and personal choices). The fourth are environmental factors that might lead to performance differences (such as differences in children's exploratory play, or inconsistent teacher attention). We discuss each of these four categories of sex differences in turn.

Cognitive Precursors of Later Competence

To explain the underrepresentation of women in math-intensive STEM fields, we need information about the prevalence of boys and girls and women and men who have the capabilities to succeed in the STEM sciences regardless of whether they enter these scientific fields later. Are there more men with the capabilities to succeed than women, and/or do more men with these capabilities actually go on to succeed? Answering these questions is complicated greatly by the fact that we do not know what the necessary capabilities are to succeed in these professions. To put it bluntly, we are looking for sex differences in precursor characteristics (the abilities one needs under one's belt before heading down the road to success) without being sure what the relevant *criterion* characteristics are—and by criterion, we mean demonstrated abilities essential to success. We need answers to questions such as, Exactly how much mathematics and spatial ability is needed to be a successful physicist, chemist, computer scientist, engineer, operations researcher, or mathematician? And at what age must this ability be manifest?

Researchers have studied sex differences in a wide variety of possible precursor measures. These include global characteristics such as intelligence as well as scores on specific cognitive tasks, spatial tasks, and aptitude tests such as the Scholastic Assessment Test-Mathematics (SAT-M) and the Graduate Record Exam-Quantitative (GRE-Q). Researchers have also studied various biological measures and the relation between these biological measures and the alleged precursors. Unfortunately, the research usually catalogs male–female differences on these precursors without relating them to success in math-intensive careers, because much of this research was not designed to answer the women-in-STEM question (with the exception of some of the work discussed later). This leaves us with much data but few definitive conclusions. More prospective longitudinal research focused directly on determining the antecedents of success in these fields is clearly needed. Here we describe what is known so far.

GENERAL INTELLIGENCE: ARE WOMEN GENERALLY SMART ENOUGH?

Some theorists have attempted to use very general characteristics, such as intelligence, to account for the dearth of women in STEM fields. For example, Lynn[1] argued for an evolutionary account of what he maintained was lower general intelligence of women. He pointed out that throughout most of the animal kingdom, males compete with each other to secure mates, but females do not. Consequently, during the evolution of hominids, intelligence became an important determinant of success. According to this account, evolution selected men more rigorously for intelligence than women. Relatedly, Lynn and others[2] have suggested that male specializations in hunting and the making of artifacts may have been more cognitively demanding than female specializations in gathering plant foods, weaving, and childrearing. Lynn[3] suggests that although a subhuman female is intelligent enough to rear her offspring as satisfactorily as a human female, no subhuman male is capable of performing the roles of a human male. We confess to some confusion here. Male lions, tigers, wolves, and so forth are highly proficient hunters and protectors, but no other species raises such complex-language-using young as do humans. We are not talking about basic language acquisition, but rather the fact that men hunt, but tigers hunt just as well; dogs rear their pups and women rear their children—but a human child reared by a dog would not be a successful member of even a stone-age society; he or she certainly would not score in the right tail on the SAT-M.

The claim that the sexes differ in general intelligence is complicated. Consider two meta-analyses (these are large-scale integrative analyses of many individual studies). Lynn and Irwing reported that the adult male average IQ on general intelligence tests (*Ravens Progressive Matrices*) is approximately 5 IQ points higher than the female average IQ.[4] However, other evidence suggests that when sampling is representative, women perform as well as men on tests of general intelligence, including the *Ravens Progressive Matrices*.[5] Recently, Brouwers et al.[6] did a meta-analysis of cross-national *Ravens* scores between 1944 and 2003. When the scores were transformed by him from their raw mean to a 0–100 scale and then averaged across the Advanced, Colored, and Standard Versions of the test, the authors found no significant sex differences. Overall average IQ for the 175 men in this study was 61.71, and for the 113 women it was 62.76, a difference that is not statistically significant.[7] Including various statistical controls in the analysis did not make a difference.

At the outset of the mass intelligence testing movement, sex differences in general intelligence were small to negligible, though sex differences on later measures were eliminated by design.[8] For example, a population study of 87,400 children born in Scotland in 1921 found that when the children were 11 years old, their average intelligence test score was 43.1 for boys and 43.5 for girls.[9] And the scores of 97 of these surviving individuals tested in 1998 on the *Ravens Matrices* revealed differences favoring men that were not statistically significant.[10] These results urge caution against differential intelligence as an explanation for sex differences in STEM fields. Having stated this, it is incumbent to mention that although Deary et al.'s age 11 test results showed no sex difference in the center of the distribution (that is, in average male and female intelligence scores were 43.1 and 43.5 respectively), there was a larger male standard deviation (male IQ scores were more variable and spread out from the mean than were females'), leading to an excess of males at both the low and high extremes of IQ: The ratio of girls to boys was 1:1.4 at the right tail (IQs > 130). This means that many more boys had very high IQs than girls (just as more boys had very low IQs than girls), even though the average IQs did not differ for the two sexes. If STEM scientists need very high IQs to succeed, then one could argue that more men are available with very high levels of ability to succeed. We return to this point later. Finally, Spinath et al.[11] examined a large group of British twins (9-year-olds) using quantitative genetic methods. They found that the best predictor of sex differences in math, on which boys were superior, was general intelligence. (It was also the best predictor of English scores, on which girls were superior.) General intelligence also predicted boys' and girls' beliefs about their ability in each of these domains. So, the evidence that links general intelligence to math differences is mixed, and notwithstanding positive findings, the effect sizes are not large enough to render it a primary cause of the lack of women in math-intensive fields. Next, we examine the possibility that even if sex differences in general intelligence may not be a primary cause of the underrepresentation of women in science, perhaps less general cognitive measures such as spatial reasoning, mathematical ability, or specific scientific aptitude could be the culprits.

SPECIFIC COGNITIVE ABILITIES

Rather than focusing on sex differences in general intelligence, other researchers have examined sex differences in specific cognitive functions. One thing that becomes apparent in wading through hundreds of published studies on sex differences in cognitive functioning is that the pattern of sex differences is much more nuanced than that depicted in undergraduate textbooks (for example, male = superiority on tasks that depend on the right hemisphere such as visualization; female = superiority on tasks that depend on the left hemisphere such as reading comprehension). Most psychologists and educators, if they have read anything at all about sex differences in cognitive ability, have probably heard that men excel on skills subserved by the right side of their cortex, such as quantitative and spatial skills, and women excel on skills subserved by their left cerebral cortex, such as verbal measures. However, the actual differences between the sexes are far more complex than this. For example, men excel on some verbal tasks, and women excel on some quantitative tasks.

The following is generally agreed upon[12]: Women tend to be somewhat superior on tests of verbal fluency, arithmetic calculation, associative memory, perceptual speed, and memory for spatial locations. On the other hand, men tend to be somewhat superior on tests of verbal analogies, mathematical word problems, and memory for the geometric configuration of landscapes. Far from the monolithic stereotype of female superiority in verbal domains and male dominance in quantitative/spatial domains, women excel at some forms of calculation and are better at spatial location memory, and men tend to excel at spatial reasoning, as well as at social studies and some forms of verbal analogical reasoning. The magnitudes of the differences at the midpoint (average scores) on most, but not all, of these measures are fairly small (d's < 0.2).[13] Later, we will present evidence that even tiny effect sizes can at times be important—for example, a $d = 0.06$ can translate into several thousand additional women starting college with advanced placement (AP) calculus credit. But for the most part, effect sizes this small are unimpressive and do not suggest important policy implications.

Sex differences also change with development: Girls are initially better than boys at mathematical computation, but their superiority fades by adolescence, and although there is no initial difference in complex mathematical problem solving, boys pull ahead of girls in high school.[14] What we lack is a framework that links these cognitive tasks to talents required to perform the jobs of successful math-intensive scientists. Is spatial reasoning more important than memory span for a chemistry professor, for example? Is analogical reasoning as relevant as calculation skills for a computer scientist? Is spatial ability more important for a physicist or engineer than it is for an archeologist, radiologist, neurosurgeon, architect, or artist? Unfortunately, we do not know the answers to these and myriad related questions. We do not know what it takes to be a successful math, engineering, or physics professor, or a chemist or computer scientist. And even within a given field there are probably differences in reliance on spatial, mathematical, and reasoning ability, with some subfields requiring more or less. For example, in some areas of theoretical chemistry, the goal has been to infer eight-dimensional structures that project three-dimensional surfaces,[15] whereas other questions in chemistry seem far less spatial in nature. So, when we ask what it takes to be successful in a field, we need to further specify which subfield we are referring to.

So existing data do not offer a clear explanation for why more men make it to the top in these STEM fields. As already noted, women's college math grades are as good as men's and roughly as many of them major in math as men. Some have tried to reconcile the vagaries of this topic by making a distinction between *achievement* and *aptitude.* They argue that tests such as the SAT-M and GRE-Q are more reflective of mathematical aptitude because they do not contain content that has been explicitly taught and rehearsed in classrooms, but rather require somewhat novel applications of thinking, which is what is most important for math-intensive fields. In contrast to aptitude, achievement is measured by testing precisely what has been taught, and it often reflects effort and memorization more than novel thinking. We will revisit this argument in greater detail later. For now we can state that the distinction between aptitude and achievement is fuzzy—and many scholars do not accept it—and the two constructs correlate with each other very highly, indicating that those recognized for their high achievement also have high aptitude test scores.[16]

Spatial Transformation Tasks

In one of her earlier meta-analyses of gender differences, Hyde[17] concluded that "Gender differences in spatial ability are heterogeneous and declining. Differences that remain are responsive to training."[18] However, one spatial skill that is often proposed as a possible cause of sex differences in mathematical performance, and that stands out as a large magnitude effect, involves the spatial transformation we have been calling mental rotation. This occurs on tasks in which two-dimensional and three-dimensional perspective drawings are shown at different orientations and the test taker must determine whether they are the same object, or on tasks in which one is asked to judge whether a two-dimensional piece of paper can be folded into a three-dimensional shape. For example, on one popular task a subject must decide whether two shapes are identical or if one is a mirror image of the other. Response times increase as the angle of disparity between the two shapes increases. This is taken as evidence that an image must be mentally rotated and superimposed on the reference shape to determine whether the shapes are identical.[19]

On these kinds of tasks requiring mental rotation, the size of sex differences is large, often falling in the $d \sim 0.7-0.8$ range.[20] However, even here explanations can be tricky, because men are likelier to form an image of one object and rotate it mentally to see if it aligns with the other object. In contrast, women are likelier to engage in a feature-by-feature comparison of the objects.[21] Sometimes one strategy is more effective than the other, and both men and women can use both strategies. Furthermore, when they are constrained to use only one strategy, men and women tend to perform somewhat more similarly. For spatial targeting tasks (like dart throwing in three-dimensional space), the effect size is larger ($d = 1.3-1.9$) than for mental rotation tasks.[22] However, for these kinds of tasks the conceptual connection with high-level math skills is less obvious and the involvement of motor skills confounds matters, so most of the work on the link between spatial skills and high-level math skills focuses on mental rotation-type tasks rather than on the even larger-magnitude spatial targeting tasks.

Studies of sex differences in mental rotation beg the question of whether observed differences in spatial cognition are the cause or consequence of sex differences, because there is some research implicating experiential factors in brain changes. A lifetime of different experiences could bring about substantial changes in spatial behavior and/or the brain regions that support it,[23] which are not necessarily genetic in origin. As just one of many examples, adults learning to juggle balls undergo brain changes, as do taxi drivers learning to navigate large cities. Maguire et al. in 2000 demonstrated that the posterior hippocampi of 16 London taxi drivers expanded regionally in conjunction with their driving experience around London. If boys spent their childhoods building with Legos and erector sets and girls spent theirs playing with dolls,[24] it would not be surprising to find that this resulted in brain changes that in turn led to later spatial and social skill differences, but their existence would not prove their origin was innate. What is needed are data on performance differences that exist before substantial experiential differences of boys and girls have occurred. That is, one needs to study very young children longitudinally. Researchers have begun to do this and later we shall describe several promising beginnings.

David Lubinski, Camilla Benbow, and their colleagues have provided some intriguing "look-back" analyses that are the next best thing to prospectively studying children longitudinally. In their work, mathematically precocious seventh-grade girls and boys were assessed and followed for several decades.[25] The assumption is that because the girls were all in the top 1% of the math distribution when they were first examined in seventh grade, then it can be assumed that there were few motivational differences between boys and girls because, after all, they all achieved so highly in math and took similar math courses. We will return to these studies later.

Researchers have examined whether there are sex differences in the etiology of specific scientific aptitude during childhood that could help account for the lack of women in scientific careers.[26] Based on analyses of 3,000 pairs of English and Welsh twin 9- to 12-year-olds, these researchers found no evidence for quantitative or qualitative sex differences in the etiology of science excellence. Of those students who displayed high talent for science (top 15%), boys and girls did not differ genetically in their extreme scientific ability. These researchers concluded: "At 10 and 12 years we were able to equate the thresholds for males and females without worsening the fit of the model to the data, indicating roughly equal proportions of males and females in the high ability groups. . . . Finally, with respect to quantitative differences, we were able to equate the genetic and environmental parameters for males and females, indicating that these influence science performance to the same extent in males and females at all three ages. The prediction for molecular genetic research would be that specific genes associated with science will have similar effect sizes in males and females."[27]

Finally, there is an emerging consensus today about the gender equality in the genetic determinants of intelligence; most researchers, including ourselves, agree that genes do not explain gender differences, even if they account for some of the differences between individuals within the same gender group. The mechanisms that bring biological potential in individuals to fruition, however, remain unknown. No alleles for high intelligence have been identified, nor have causal pathways from sets of alleles to neural changes associated with intelligence. (In contrast, many more boys have various forms of mental retardation than girls; this occurs because of the existence of detrimental alleles that occur more often in boys.[28])

Standardized Aptitude Tests

In addition to research on sex differences in general intelligence and in specific cognitive abilities, another line of inquiry has attempted to pin the cause of the observed sex differences on so-called "aptitude" tests. These are standardized paper-and-pencil tests of various forms of reasoning ability that, as mentioned above, are not supposed to be directly taught in school. In this sense they resemble intelligence tests. Unsurprisingly, they correlate very highly with IQ tests (for example, SAT scores correlate very highly with IQ scores; individuals who score highly on the SATs or GREs usually score highly on IQ tests—so much so that researchers sometimes use them interchangeably when doing analyses in which they need to controll for general cognitive ability[29]).

We have added quotation marks around the word "aptitude" because the concept of aptitude is a source of contention among psychometric researchers, with some arguing that these tests are not as impervious to schooling and cultural factors (such as number of math and science courses taken) as was once thought.[30] This was the reason Educational Testing Service changed the original name of the SAT—"Scholastic Aptitude Test"—to its current name, "Scholastic Assessment Test," so as not to presuppose it was a measure of aptitude independent of achievement. Many regard these exams as achievement tests, rather than an index of innate ability that is genetically programmed to flourish, almost regardless of one's academic or home environment.

Although girls score as well as or better than boys in elementary school on science and mathematics tests, there is some slippage that becomes evident by high school, when fewer girls take AP chemistry and AP physics. Girls begin to score lower on some science and mathematics "aptitude" tests such as the SAT-M around this time. In Figure 4.1, it can be seen that any given percentile is associated with a higher SAT-M score for boys than girls. For instance, a score of 645 is needed to place a boy in the top 20% of the male distribution, whereas a score of only 600 on the same test is needed to place a girl in the top 20% of the female distribution. And as noted in the *Preface*, boys outnumbered girls 2 to 1 at scores of ≥750. Table 4.1 shows the male advantage in mathematics score percentiles for college-bound high school seniors in 2007, and a similar male advantage has been true prior to 2007.

Strand et al.[31] analyzed a large national database of over 320,000 British boys' scores on the *Cognitive Ability Test.* They reported a similar overrepresentation of boys at the right tail, starting at age 11. Although they found only small differences at the mean or midpoint of the ability distribution in mathematics, 11-year-old boys were overrepresented at both the upper and lower tails of the quantitative distribution. Recently, Lohman and Lakin[32] analyzed

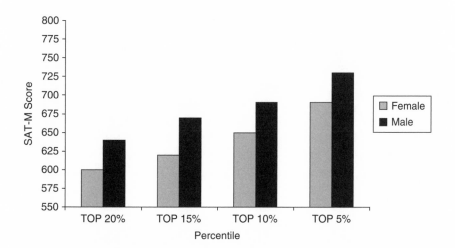

FIGURE **4.1.** College-bound seniors' SAT-M scores as a function of gender. At every percentile, boys outscore girls. Source: Percentile ranks for males, females and total group mathematics. 2006–2007 College Board data.

TABLE **4.1.** SAT® Percentile Ranks for Males, Females, and Total Group. 2007 College-Bound Seniors—Mathematics.

SCORE	Total		Male		Female	
	NUMBER	PERCENTILE	NUMBER	PERCENTILE	NUMBER	PERCENTILE
800	9,857	99	6,759	99	3,098	99+
790	4,447	99	3,113	99	1,334	99
780	2,928	99	1,890	98	1,037	99
770	5,936	98	3,841	98	2,095	99
760	5,703	98	3,728	97	1,973	99
750	6,265	98	3,950	97	2,315	99
740	6,953	97	4,411	96	2,538	98
730	7,191	97	4,507	95	2,681	98
720	8,825	96	5,486	95	3,331	97
710	15,072	95	9,296	93	5,774	97
700	16,067	94	9,806	92	6,256	96
690	19,601	93	11,786	90	7,808	95
680	20,916	91	12,405	88	8,504	94
670	21,962	90	12,885	86	9,070	93
660	25,740	88	14,713	84	11,006	91
650	32,714	86	17,955	82	14,740	90
640	32,113	84	17,957	79	14,130	88
630	28,289	82	15,346	77	12,928	86
620	30,548	80	16,415	74	14,112	84
610	30,731	78	16,202	72	14,507	83
600	34,376	75	17,781	70	16,555	80
590	47,328	72	23,748	66	23,536	78
580	40,074	70	19,950	63	20,060	75
570	38,404	67	19,004	60	19,341	73
560	46,860	64	22,938	57	23,866	70
550	41,214	61	19,503	54	21,649	67
540	52,880	58	24,159	51	28,639	63
530	47,341	54	22,091	48	25,136	60
520	50,140	51	23,069	44	26,929	57
510	45,141	48	20,337	41	24,681	54
500	51,933	45	23,021	38	28,764	50
490	55,039	41	23,196	35	31,691	46
480	52,895	37	22,694	31	30,031	42
470	42,081	35	17,573	29	24,373	39
460	49,938	31	20,872	26	28,814	36
450	43,616	28	17,561	23	25,849	32
440	41,937	26	16,642	21	25,087	29
430	42,253	23	16,812	18	25,191	26
420	45,858	20	17,338	16	28,263	23
410	43,492	17	16,687	13	26,509	19
400	29,343	15	10,825	12	18,301	17
390	31,664	13	11,935	10	19,473	15
380	26,376	11	9,728	9	16,395	12

370	27,562	9	10,125	7	17,171	10
360	18,635	8	7,120	6	11,285	9
350	20,379	6	7,542	5	12,610	7
340	15,308	5	5,683	4	9,447	6
330	14,188	4	5,124	4	8,896	5
320	8,751	4	3,219	3	5,419	4
310	12,449	3	4,693	2	7,562	3
300	8,976	2	3,225	2	5,600	3
290	7,199	2	2,712	2	4,358	2
280	6,255	2	2,349	1	3,786	2
270	4,390	1	1,655	1	2,658	1
260	3,514	1	1,344	1	2,115	1
250	1,725	1	648	1	1,044	1
240	3,571	1	1,327	1	2,167	1
230	1,424	1	556	1–	838	1
220	2,494	1–	996	1–	1,449	1–
210	1,067	1–	426	1–	616	1–
200	4,603	–	1,841	–	2,639	–
Number	1,494,531		690,500		798,030	
Mean	515		533		499	
Standard Deviation	114		116		110	

changes in the proportions of boys and girls at each level of the same *Cognitive Ability Test* in both the United Kingdom and the United States, but they did so for grades 3–11, and also for three different cohorts (1984, 1992, and 2000). They too found male overrepresentation across all dimensions of quantitative aptitude, despite large growth over time for both sexes. For example, at the highest and lowest levels of mathematical aptitude, boys outnumbered girls by roughly 2 to 1—approximately 65% of the highest aptitude students were boys and about 35% were girls (see solid versus dashed blue lines in Figure 4.2). Boys were also twice as likely to be the lowest scorers. (This is why we have been reporting so-called "standard deviations"—they index how much more variable male scores usually are than female scores, and by implication, how asymmetric the sexes will be at the right and left tails of the distribution.) So large-scale national studies of mathematical aptitude favor boys, and this holds for the most part across cohorts and test formats. Later, we shall see there is significant variation across countries in the ratios of boys to girls with the highest aptitude, although in Lohman and Lakin's data, the male advantage held firmly across both Britain and the United States and the 2-to-1 ratio at the top 1% or 2% of the math distribution is one that crops up in a number of these large data sets.

In juxtaposition to this "aptitude" gap among the top male and female mathematics scorers, girls actually achieve higher grades than boys in most science and math courses. As a result, many researchers have turned to aptitude

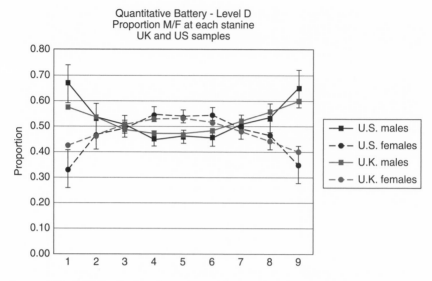

FIGURE **4.2.** CAT distributions for males and females from Lohman, D. F. & Lakin, J. M. (2009), Consistencies in sex differences on the Cognitive Abilities Test across countries, grades, test forms, and cohorts. *British Journal of Educational Psychology, 79*, 389–407.

as a possible explanation for the dominance of men at the top of STEM professions.[33] Their reasoning is that whereas aptitude test scores reflect raw mathematical reasoning ability, grades reflect such things as being obedient, being effortful, doing homework, and coming to school prepared—on all of which girls usually exceed boys. To some, it is aptitude, not teacher-pleasing behavior, that is most important for success in the most math-intensive STEM fields.

As Halpern[34] notes, however, this discrepancy between "aptitude" scores and grades in math and science classes has led to claims of bias from all sides in the debate over the causes of sex differences in STEM. One side has argued that teachers and schools are biased against boys, because they give them lower grades than their "aptitude" (as shown by measures like SAT-M scores) would appear to warrant. The argument is that schools penalize boys for their impulsiveness, lack of motivation, and challenges to teachers' authority, and they reward girls for their docility, compliance, and willingness to do homework and follow rules. One piece of evidence for this claim is a study of 67,000 college students taking calculus. Men who received grades of Ds and Fs had SAT advanced calculus scores that were equal to women who received grades of Bs.[35] Table 4.2 shows the sex breakdown for each grade in college as a function of the SAT scores in advanced mathematics. As can be seen, men with calculus scores of 579–580 got Ds and Fs, while women with these scores obtained Bs.

TABLE **4.2**. Sex Breakdown for Each Grade in College as a Function of the SAT Scores in Advanced Mathematics.

GRADE	SAT-M ADVANCED MATH MALES	SAT-M ADVANCED MATH FEMALES	SAT-M CALCULUS MALES	SAT-M CALCULUS FEMALES
A	713	677	635	604
B	686	665	615	580
C	666	631	597	559
D	642	611	580	540
F	651	600	579	537

Source: Modified from Wainer, H., & Steinberg, L. S. (1992). Sex differences in performance on the mathematics section of the Scholastic Aptitude Test: A bidirectional validity study. *Harvard Educational Review, 62*, 323–336.

As compelling as some may find these data, the other side could argue that standardized "aptitude" tests such as the SAT-M are biased against females because they underpredict their grades in high school and college math classes. When mathematical "aptitude" is equated by matching students on SAT-M scores, women outperform men in college mathematics courses, just as the above calculus example shows.[36] In other words, if one tries to predict college math performance from SAT-M scores, the result will be that one expects women not to do as well as they actually do.

The correct interpretation of this debate depends on which of these measures is closer to a true measure of the relevant math skills required to succeed at the highest levels in STEM fields. Note that this is not the same thing as determining which measure is the best at predicting success, because many predictors are unrelated to math ability. For instance, there need not be any cause–effect relationship between two variables, even if one predicts the other. Race and income, for instance, are good predictors of grades and aptitude scores, but few claim they achieve prediction because they are causally related. Arguments can get dangerously circular here.

Consider an example developed by our colleague, Susan Barnett, in our research synthesis[37]: *Most professors in math-intensive fields are men, and men do better on tests like the SAT-M; therefore, such tests must measure mathematical "aptitude" better than college grades (on which women do as well or better), so men have greater "aptitude" for math, and that's why a disproportionate number of professors are men.*

Barnett's tautology reveals the potential for circularity. It also drives home the need for a theory-driven explanation and measure that is known to relate a given variable to math aptitude and STEM success, not merely to another variable that predicts it or is correlated with it. The measure that comes closest to this is 3-D mental rotation. But this measure is not theoretically grounded, although it does make sense on its face (some engineering, cosmology, and chemistry coursework and research are heavily spatial, and some researchers such as Sheryl Sorby have shown that this is an area of particular difficulty for some women engineering majors).

Sorby et al. found that female undergraduates score lower than males on visual cognition tests both before and after participation in an engineering graphics course.[38] Even though men and women made gains in spatial ability over the semester, women's end-of-semester scores were usually lower than men's start-of-semester scores. Because of this, Sorby et al. implemented a spatial cognition course that entailed both teaching and practice at solving complex spatial rotations. She first selected male and female engineering majors who failed a visual cognition pretest that included mental rotation along one or more axes. These individuals were given a visual cognition course in their freshman year. Women who took the course not only earned higher spatial posttest scores, but also earned higher grade point averages several years later by approximately 0.3 of a letter grade point (2.7–3.0), and were more likely to remain engineering majors (63.6% versus 53.1% of control group women who had not taken the course). Comparable figures were 69.2% for men who had taken the course versus 62.5% for those who had not (see Figure 4.3). Spatial ability has also been singled out as a significant predictor of sex differences in other fields, such as medicine,[39] chemistry,[40] and mathematics,[41] though not with the same empirical basis as Sorby. Thus, the limited work available indicates that the gap separating men and women majoring in math-intensive STEM fields can be narrowed with intensive semester-long training.

Despite its promise as an explanatory variable, so far there has not been a showing that superiority in mental rotation is any more important in fields in which women are underrepresented than it is in fields that are not as math intensive, such as architecture, art, radiology, and archeology. In fact, it has

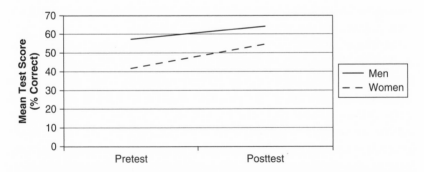

FIGURE **4.3.** Freshmen male and female engineering students' scores on the Purdue Spatial Visualization Test-Revised. Source: Data adapted from Sorby, S. A. (2001). A course in spatial visualization and its impact on the retention of female engineering students. *Journal of Women and Minorities in Science and Engineering, 7*, 153–172.

not yet been shown to be a predictor of success in mathematically intensive fields, either, except in the case of the limited work by Sorby alluded to previously.

In her cogent analysis of this issue, Harvard's Elizabeth Spelke[42] put more emphasis on the relevance of college grades than on math and spatial aptitude scores, and concluded that the weight of evidence suggests the SAT-M underpredicts female aptitude in mathematics. In her words:

> Men and women get equal grades in math classes that are matched for difficulty (Bridgeman & Lewis, 1996), and they major in math in nearly equal numbers. . . . By the most meaningful measure—the ability to master new, challenging mathematical material over extended periods of time—college men and women show equal aptitude for mathematics. The contrast between the performance of high school students on the SAT-M and the performance of college students in mathematics classes suggests that the SAT-M systematically underpredicts the performance of high school girls, relative to boys. Further analyses support that suggestion. When the SAT-M scores of boys and girls are matched, girls go on to earn higher grades in college mathematics classes. The SAT-M's underprediction of girls' mathematics performance is widely known (e.g., Gallagher & Kaufman, 2005; Nature Neuroscience Board of Editors, 2005; Willingham & Cole, 1997).[43]

As a thought experiment, one can ask the following: What if the SAT-M led to the prediction that African American students would get *better* grades in college than they actually do get? Would some claim the SATs were unfair since they overpredicted African American students' classroom performance? We suspect many might argue the opposite, that African American students' lower grades were unfair because they were a reflection of societal biases, and that these students' mathematical potential (indexed by their SAT-M score) is greater than their grades convey. Certainly, few would claim that the grades are proof that Caucasians have better mathematical aptitude than African Americans merely because of their higher grades. Yet this seems analogous to arguing that girls' better grades trump their lower SAT-M scores as indicators of their math aptitude.

This is not merely a hypothetical issue: African Americans' grades in college *are* overpredicted by their SAT scores: On the basis of their SAT scores, they are expected to obtain higher grades than they actually get. The usual interpretation is that this grade outcome shows the SAT is not racially biased against African Americans, and if anything is actually biased in favor of them because it leads college admissions officers to expect them to achieve higher grades. So one could argue that college math grades are biased against African American students because on the basis of their SAT scores, one would expect them to be capable of achieving higher grades than they actually get. By a similar logic, some parents may feel that college grades are biased against their sons, because they believe the SAT is a fairer measure of their sons' aptitude in mathematics than are the grades given to them. The point of this thought experiment is to note that, until we know what tests truly measure the relevant skills required for success in STEM careers, we are stuck guessing about what leads to success in them.

How Select Are STEM Scientists?

Although the SAT-M is the most widely used index of math ability in the debate over sex differences, it was never designed to answer this question of causality. We know little about whether the questions on the SAT-M are the ones that tap mathematical abilities needed for success in STEM careers. This is not to say that we know nothing about its predictiveness of college students' grades in math and science courses, though. Many studies show that the SAT-M does modestly predict math and science grades in college, and it does so for both sexes, and all ethnic groups, with some overprediction of African American students as already noted. And when the SAT is added to other information, such as high school grade point average, student values, and occupational preference measures, it improves the prediction even more.

As noted above, however, race, birthweight, income, and even height predict school grades, and yet they may have little to do with aptitude in math and science. To make this argument concrete, there is a 0.4 correlation between a student's SAT score and her parents' socioeconomic status (SES, based on education and occupational prestige), with students of higher SES parents getting higher SAT scores, on average.[44] But we would not rush to the conclusion that the correlation is the result of a genetic meritocracy whereby those with better genes for higher SAT scores get higher-income jobs and pass on their genes to their children who in turn get higher SAT scores. Or to take an even less compelling correlation, we suspect that if anyone ever bothered to test the correlation between SAT scores and having a tropical fish tank at home, they would discover that the sign of the correlation is negative: Fish tanks are more likely to be found in lower SES homes today, and on average children from lower SES homes do poorly on the SAT. However, no serious scholar would imagine that having a goldfish tank in the home lowers cognitive potential. It simply proxies for income and education. Such arguments quickly devolve into circularity, because the sole touchstone is the SAT score, which cannot be used to validate itself. Parental social class variables may be proxies for a stream of unmeasured variables and conditions that are related to achievement, but for reasons that are independent of mathematical aptitude.

What this means is that the SAT-M alone cannot tell us whether scoring in the top 1% (where there are pronounced sex differences)—as opposed to, say, scoring in the top 25% (where the sex differences are not as pronounced)—taps the skills that are needed to be a successful scientist in a mathematically intensive field. Are there specific SAT-M problems that must be answered correctly by people who become successful in STEM careers? What abilities do these problems reflect—are they spatial (for example, geometry)? And how strongly predictive are they when considered within a larger tapestry of skills, along with creativity, "stick-with-it-ness," intellectual risk taking, other forms of mathematical skill, communicative ability, leadership skills, and preferences? We do not know.

As alluded to earlier, some of the most intriguing analyses that bear on this question have been conducted by Lubinski et al.[45] These longitudinal analyses contrasted two groups of extremely talented adolescents from a sample of talent search participants nominated at age 13 who were administered the SAT-M and scored in the top 1%. The researchers followed those who scored in the *top* quartile of the *top* 1% versus those who scored in the *bottom* quartile of the *top* 1%. Even though all of these adolescents had scored in the top 1%, those who scored in the *top* quarter of 1% on the SAT-M when assessed 20 to 30 years later had received significantly greater numbers of PhDs in STEM fields, were more likely to be tenured STEM professors at top universities, and were credited with more inventions/patents. This would seem to indicate that those who are successful in STEM fields are disproportionately likely to come from the very top of the SAT-M distribution, assuming that the top and bottom quarters of the top 1% were both highly motivated to reach the top of STEM professions, took equal numbers of math classes later in their education, came from similar SES backgrounds, and were subject to similar cultural beliefs and pressures. But because of the limited sample size and greater variability among male scores, the findings cannot readily be applied to sex differences, as these authors note. Also, we do not know what other potentially causal factors may have correlated with aptitude test scores, although the ones that the authors examined did not interact.

Still, many individuals with scores in the bottom quarter of the top 1% did in fact become successful STEM scientists, so the question of whether there is a threshold below which one cannot succeed as a STEM scientist is unanswerable from this and other studies. For instance, can individuals with SAT-M scores in the top 10% (but not the top 1%) be successful STEM scientists? If so, what is it about them that allows them to overcome their relatively low scores (low relative to other STEM scientists, that is)? Again, we sadly note that there is nothing in the literature that addresses this question, save anecdotal reports such as the Putnam fellowships we described in the Preface, which suggest that future mathematicians come from the very top of the distribution, too.

In response to the evidence that boys are overrepresented among the top scorers of the SAT-M and tests of cognitive aptitude, critics have taken two different tacks. On the one hand, they have argued that so-called "aptitude" tests such as the SAT-M and cognitive abilities test (CAT) are biased against girls. We already have seen that they underpredict female math grades in high school and college. Therefore, if males excel on them, this is seen as irrelevant, because boys and men do not excel on high school or college math grades, including calculus.

On the other hand, some influential critics have argued that the individuals who fill the ranks of professional STEM scientists did not score highly on tests like the SAT-M. This is the tack taken in the prestigious National Academy of Sciences report spearheaded by former U.S. Department of Health and Human Services secretary Donna Shalala and 17 members of her blue-ribbon panel.[46] In this report an allusion was made that most STEM men score below 650 on the SAT-M, but later these authors backed off of this claim, noting some problems with it. Here is how these eminent scholars argued that sex differences in mathematics aptitude cannot explain the dearth of women in STEM careers:

> Measures of aptitude for high school and college science have not proved to be predictive of success in later science and engineering careers. Notably, it is not just the top SAT scorers who continue on to successful careers; of the college-educated professional workforce in mathematics, science, and engineering, fewer than one-third of the men had SAT-M scores above 650, the lower end of the threshold typically presumed to be required for success in these fields. The differing social pressures and influences on boys and girls appear to have more influence than their underlying abilities on their motivations and preferences.[47]

Although the analysis that this assertion is based on does indeed support this point,[48] it is important to add a qualifier that Shalala and her coauthors mentioned later and which greatly moderates the claim. The careers analyzed by Weinberger were *not* exclusively or even primarily professorial math-intensive STEM ones; they include the legions of master's degree–level technical workers in laboratories, research assistants, and associates in fields that are not always math intensive. There is no evidence in Weinberger's analysis that the SAT-M scores of two-thirds of the individuals holding *professorial* positions in math-intensive STEM fields are below 650—and yet this is the professorial-level group that forms the core of intrinsic sex differences in ability argument, the ones who are the object of many commissions, policies, and interventions.

Unfortunately, in the aftermath of Shalala et al.'s assertion, numerous commentators repeated this claim.[49] It is true that Weinberger reported that among men and women with the same SAT scores, women were only half as likely to enter these careers, but this could be the result of women's unwillingness to work at tech jobs, rather than representing a barrier preventing them from doing so. Indeed, if policies and interventions were designed to increase women's presence in scientific careers merely by adding more of these women to the ranks of lab technicians and research assistants/associates, such policies and interventions would be met with outcries that there was an academic caste system, with men hired as STEM professors and women funneled into lower status and lower-paying lab posts. Note that we are not alleging that the SAT-M scores of those who occupy the most prestigious positions (STEM professorships) are 3, 4, or 5 standard deviations above the mean, as Lawrence Summers opined in his 2005 speech; we are simply remarking that it is misleading to imply that over two-thirds of the men in STEM professorial posts have SAT-M scores below 650.

There are three good reasons for suspecting this is not the case. First, in our effort to find out the scores of graduate students in math-intensive fields, it became clear to us that the men have extremely high scores. At our own university, PhD candidates in math-intensive STEM fields *rarely* have SAT-M scores below 650, and the typical candidate's score is above 700, often well above it. The mean GRE quantitative score for the 480 Cornell graduate students matriculated in math-intensive STEM fields is 760 (see Figure 4.4). Based on unsystematic sampling of several peer campuses, their students do not differ much from those at our institution. Bear in mind that the top 50 research universities train over 95% of the individuals who go on to occupy STEM professorships. The evidence at these top institutions points to GRE-Q scores well above 650. There are two other reasons for skepticism that we detail below.

In reading through Weinberger's analyses, a number of questions occur, several of which we discussed in our recent research synthesis:

> Weinberger's models are richly detailed but she is unable to shed light on a number of interesting hypotheses related to alleged barriers preventing women's participation in STEM fields. For example, approximately 30% of the cohort of 1972 high school seniors who were surveyed in 1979 (or 1986) in her analysis had not taken the SATs, a requisite for many top universities that produced STEM scientists at that time. She employed statistical imputation to translate their Cognitive Test of Mathematics scores to SAT-M scores, but while this allows her to estimate the proportions of high- and low-scoring men in mathematically-intensive STEM fields, it needs to be kept in mind that those who take the SAT are probably a more select group. Possibly, a significant proportion of the men she included in her analysis, even among the subset who entered graduate school, did so at programs tailored to training technicians rather than producing scholars. It would be of interest to know what proportion of STEM scientists at places such as Carnegie-Mellon, Harvard, Stanford, Duke, Purdue, Michigan, Rice, etc. had SAT-M scores below 650, and what proportion of them had scores that were comparable to or below those of the average humanities graduate ($\leq$ 550), which Weinberger found to be the case for a third of the males in her sample.[50]

Another reason for skepticism about Shalala et al.'s claim that over two-thirds of men in STEM fields have scores that are unexceptional comes from the work of Wise et al. They analyzed Project Talent participants who were

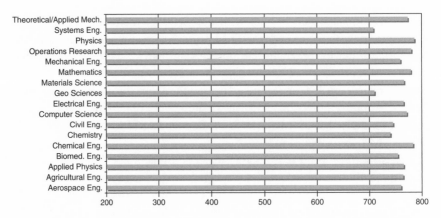

FIGURE **4.4.** Average GRE-Quantitative scores for Cornell University graduate students in math-intensive fields ($n = 480$). Special thanks to William Barnett, data specialist of the Cornell University Graduate School.

part of a large-scale national study begun over 40 years ago. These individuals were tested extensively in high school and followed from ninth grade through adulthood. Wise and et al. found that at age 30, disproportionately more of the individuals who gravitated toward careers in science had been in at least the top 10% of math aptitude in high school, and probably even higher if the most math-intensive careers could be examined separately.[51]

Finally, Lubinski et al. have demonstrated the increased likelihood of success in STEM careers as a function of very high math aptitude scores— the number of students who become STEM scientists increases with higher SAT-M scores. As we saw already, even among the top 1% of math talent, the top quartile does better in scientific careers. Moreover, these researchers provide other evidence that indicates the top 0.01%, or 1 in 10,000, does best of all. We will describe some of their findings later.

As noted, although there is no evidence in Weinberger's analysis that the SAT-M or GRE-Q scores of over two-thirds of individuals holding professorial positions in math-intensive fields are below 650, others picked up on this point and repeated the assertion. Soon, columnists and national speakers were claiming that because most male STEM professionals score below 650 on the SAT-M, it did not matter if women were underrepresented in the top 1% of scores on the SAT-M:

> [The] second over-hyped story, in my view, [is that] males are over-represented at the upper tail of distribution in math aptitude scores, and, therefore, are more highly represented in leadership positions in math and science. However, studies show only a weak relationship between scoring and the upper tail ability and eventual success in math and science careers. In fact, of the college educated professional workforce in math, science, and engineering, fewer than one-third of the men had SAT-M scores

above 650, which is the lower end of the threshold typically presumed to be required for success in these fields.[52]

None of the aforementioned four pieces of evidence proves that a top 1% score on the SAT-M is a requisite to becoming a successful STEM scientist in a math-intensive field, and there are undoubtedly highly regarded scientists whose scores are below 650. In the future we will have a better sense of how aberrant they are, when STEM professors at public and private universities are surveyed to determine their SAT-M and GRE-Q scores. We anticipate that although the occasional scholar will report having a score below 650, nowhere near two-thirds of professors of chemistry, computer science, engineering, operations research, mathematics, and physics will have SAT-M scores that low. In fact, we predict that most will report SAT-M and GRE-Q scores above 700 or even above 750, as the Cornell STEM data indicate.

Until such time as these data become available, the reader might try applying to a PhD program in computer science or engineering at Carnegie Mellon, MIT, Rice, Duke, Purdue, or any of the top 50 programs that produce the lion's share of STEM professors and see how far a score below 650 on the quantitative portion of the GRE gets her or him. Granted, some will get accepted if there are extenuating circumstances. But the vast majority probably will not. This is because graduate admission committees at these institutions do not trade off between high grades in mathematics and high quantitative aptitude scores; they demand both—and at selective institutions, they get both. From the point of view of an admissions committee, why use limited resources to support an applicant with low aptitude and high grades when you can easily admit other applicants who have high aptitude *and* high grades?

Microanalyses of the SAT-M

An impressive body of work has been conducted in recent years examining the possible causes of the differing patterns of results in school grades and aptitude tests. This work has looked at the specific SAT-M items on which boys and girls differ, and has examined the ways girls and boys answer them. Due to space constraints, we cannot detail all of these studies here, so we will provide a snapshot of the most important findings. To adumbrate our conclusion, the two sexes often achieve their SAT scores by answering different types of questions correctly. And even when answering the same question correctly, they often do so using different strategies. Because the SAT and GRE are not theory-driven measures (that is, they were not developed from theoretical constructs in a top-down manner), there is considerable confusion regarding what their scores mean.

Some have addressed this issue by examining mental rotation ability and its relationship to the SAT-M. For example, Casey et al.[53] found that, while mental rotation scores were predictive of overall SAT-M scores for college-bound youth and highly math-talented younger girls (controlling for SAT-Verbal [SAT-V]), mental rotation scores were not predictive for highly math-talented young boys—the group presumably producing a disproportionate share of the future STEM professors. However, consider follow-up work[54] with a less elite group, the top one-third of the college-bound sample (based on SAT-V scores). Here the authors found that the gender–SAT-M relationship was explained roughly two-thirds by mental rotation ability and one-third by math self-confidence, suggesting both are highly important for these students. These authors also explored the relationship of this to geometry grades in school, and found that most of the mediational effects of mental rotation and self-confidence were not explained by school geometry grades: So mental rotation measures appear to be indexing different abilities than geometry. This tells us that mental rotation may be important, but not as a predictor of grades in geometry and perhaps not within the top STEM subset in which we are most interested.

Another approach has been to look at the use of prior mathematical knowledge and strategies. For example, Byrnes and Takahira[55] showed that, for a sample of high school students, prior knowledge and strategies explained a great deal of the variance in SAT-M scores. No gender differences were found in amount of prior knowledge students had, but a gender difference was found for the conditional probability of getting an item right if one had the requisite prior knowledge and constructed an effective strategy. For boys the probability was 0.91, whereas for girls the probability was only 0.72, a highly significant difference. The authors suggest that perhaps "female students spend too much time on individual items or are more likely to fall prey to misleading choices."[56] But why would girls do this? It is possible that their greater time reflects slower processing speed or less crystallized and automated knowledge, but perhaps it simply reflects greater cautiousness. Exploring these possibilities will require further study, but there are older studies that do accord with the conclusion that female test takers are more cautious and weigh options more intensely than male test takers and check their answers more often before moving to the next question.

Several researchers[57] have investigated hypotheses that girls fall behind boys on ill-defined problems or those requiring unconventional solution methods, which might be considered examples of a phenomenon known as "far transfer."[58] Far transfer refers to the application of existing knowledge to problems that are different from those that one has applied the knowledge to before. Gallagher[59] found that boys did better than girls on SAT-M questions when solutions were not clearly defined, and girls did equal or better on problems requiring familiar solution strategies ("near transfer"). Fennema et al.[60] investigated possible forerunners of this effect in younger children, and found that girls used more standard algorithms and concrete solution strategies, whereas boys used more abstract, invented algorithms. Those using invented algorithms were more able to solve transfer problems requiring flexible use of their understanding.

It has been suggested that this apparent difference in abstract thinking ability may be caused partly by differences in the way teachers behave towards girls and boys in their class.[61] Later, we discuss evidence that teachers may engage in disproportionately more thought-provoking abstract interactions with boys,[62] although this is a hotly contested topic generating no consensus.[63] If these observations are used to claim that there are sex differences in abstract reasoning, the question is *why* do boys engage in more abstract reasoning? Is the cause innate or something environmental, such as classroom experience or parentally encouraged experiences? Later, we shall describe recent evidence from the current SAT-M showing that girls actually excel at abstract math items and boys excel at applied items. All of this harkens back to our concern that the SAT-M is not a theoretically driven instrument. Thus, the fact that such logical inconsistencies are rife in the measurement literature is unsurprising.

Gallagher and DeLisi,[64] following up on their earlier work showing that girls do better on well-defined problems and boys do better on ill-defined problems, interviewed high school students who had scored highly on the SAT-M. They found that the use of conventional strategies, which are good for solving well-defined problems, was correlated with more negative attitudes toward math. They hypothesized that girls used more conventional strategies. Perhaps this was because girls' lack of enthusiasm for or confidence in mathematics discouraged them from experimenting. Another interpretation, though, might be that girls' lack of confidence and enthusiasm stemmed from a lack of deeper understanding of the kind that permitted boys to experiment by extending algorithmic knowledge, given that the two sexes achieved their high scores by answering different types of questions correctly.

Gallagher et al.[65] applied a similar approach in their analysis of the quantitative section of the U.S. GRE. They found that it was possible to manipulate the relative performance of males and females on this test by changing the mix of question types. They concluded: "Qualitatively different approaches to mathematics problems that may be used by male and female test takers can lead to performance differences that may or may not be relevant to the test construct. Factors affecting performance should be evaluated with regard to their importance to mathematical reasoning. If deemed important, they should form part of the test specifications. If not, efforts should be made to minimize such factors."[66] In other words, because we lack a theory of what the SAT measures and how each of its items add incremental validity to it, it is unclear if changes in items that result in widening or narrowing sex differences do so validly.

Similarly, Harris and Carleton in 2006 reported their analysis of the item difficulty levels on the current SAT. They compared male and female students with equal overall SAT scores to determine which items presented gender-specific difficulties. Consistent with past research, they found that boys performed relatively better on geometry and trigonometry items compared to matched girls, who performed relatively better on miscellaneous and arithmetic/algebra items. But these sex differences were quite small. In contrast, girls did relatively better than matched boys on items that were abstract or that included variables such as X or *a(b),* whereas boys did better on items that were embedded in real-life applied contexts. The magnitude of these differences was fairly large, and led these researchers to suggest that "male students may use mathematics more than female students in everyday life and [this] could lend support to the argument that male students perform better in mathematics because they view it as more valuable or more applicable in their lives.[67] They also suggest that female students may benefit from greater curricular emphasis on various applications of mathematics."[68]

Spelke[69] has made a similar point, suggesting that the SAT is theoretically arbitrary. Changes are sometimes made to its content, some of which favor boys and others of which favor girls. Drawing on Gallagher et al.'s findings, she describes a case in which changes made to items on the SAT-M could have resulted in bias against women, depending on information that we do not know. Using her example, girls consistently outperform boys on data sufficiency problems. These are items for which the student must determine if the data provided are sufficient to answer the problem. These items have now been removed from the SAT-M because they are known to benefit from coaching. As Spelke argued, removal of items without a theory of the underlying test construct can result in biases:

> Removing a class of items on which girls score better nevertheless has the effect of lowering the scores of girls, relative to boys, and it raises a question: Did this change increase or decrease the fairness of the SAT-M as a measure of mathematical ability in men and women? If boys are more talented than girls, then this change may have increased the fairness of the test. If boys and girls are equally talented, then this change increased the test's bias against girls. Evaluation of the SAT-M therefore requires an independently motivated account of the nature of mathematical talent, its component processes, and its distribution across boys and girls.[70]

This approach suggests that what is needed is to ask what *each item* on the SAT-M measures, and how that item relates to both the underlying theoretical construct and later success. Once again, we find it appropriate to remark that we do not know the extent to which tests such as the SAT-M assess the skills that are critical for later STEM success in math-intensive careers, notwithstanding their modest correlations with college grades. Such tests may "proxy" for unmeasured variables that, even if they contribute to the prediction of college mathematics grades, are not of necessity key aspects of the mathematical skills needed to be a successful STEM scientist.

Gierl and McEwen[71] made this point more generally. They noted that the mere existence of items that favor one sex over the other is not evidence of bias, unless the performance differences that result from inclusion of the items create irrelevant test difficulty, which unfairly affects the test performance for members of one sex. In their words:

> If, on the other hand, the performance difference can be attributed to actual knowledge and experience differences the test is designed to measure, then the outcome can be interpreted as (unbiased) item impact. ... Typically, explanations for DIF (differential item functioning) are sought from panels of content specialists who study the items and try to identify why some items are more difficult for one group of examinees compared to another (Berk, 1982; Ramsey, 1993). However, experience and research has shown that it is unusually difficult to account for DIF using judgmental analyses (e.g., Angoff, 1993; Camilli & Shepard, 1994; Englehard, Hansche, & Rutledge, 1990; Gierl & McEwen, 1998; O'Neill & McPeek, 1993). Thus, more research is needed to substantively interpret DIF statistical outcomes when males and females are compared.[72]

So where does this all leave us? To sum up, boys and men score higher on a variety of cognitive and psychometric measures, both as children (as with mental rotation tasks) and as adults (as with the SAT-M). However, the findings are not always consistent, and their relation to career success in STEM fields remains unspecified. Furthermore, their theoretical rationale remains to be determined, as does their relation to differences, a topic we turn to next. Until these questions are answered, we do not know if the current test content is arbitrary and biased, on the one hand, or valid, on the other.

Recap: General Intelligence in Sex Differences

There is evidence of sex differences on many measures. These include measures of earlier cognitive performance (such as mental rotation ability during infancy) that might be considered necessary precursors to later mathematical competence at the highest levels. They also include biological correlates (such as hormone levels) of some of these measures. In addition, noncognitive factors (such as career and family choices and their consequences) and environmental factors (such as differential treatment by teachers and parents, and gendered beliefs about the maleness of math) have been invoked to explain performance differences. Any or all of these factors could be contributing to the observed underrepresentation of women at the top of math-intensive STEM professions, although the evidence is not strong enough for us to be certain that any of them plays an important primary role. Experimental evidence regarding sex differences in mental rotation ability is inconsistently related to sex differences in later mathematical ability, as are the associated hormonal findings. Evidence is stronger for differential career preferences and the detrimental effects of having children on women's careers.

However, the observation that women pick different careers does not explain why they do so (save the argument that early beliefs in gendered roles direct them away from later mathematical fields[73]). The magnitude of the effect of having children is not enough to fully explain the observed underrepresentation of women at the top of math-intensive professions, because women with children thrive in many professional careers that are less math intensive. In other words, it is not clear why this problem should be so much worse for math-intensive STEM fields than other high-powered professions, as it indeed appears to be:

- 48% of college teachers in nonscience fields are men;
- 57% of college psychology teachers are men;
- 74% of college biological science teachers are men;
- 71% of college social science teachers (summed across economists, sociologists, anthropologists, and political scientists) are men;
- 83% of college math teachers are men;
- 84% of college physical science teachers (summed across chemistry, astronomy, physics, and earth sciences) are men;
- 86% of college computer science teachers are men; and
- 93% of college engineering teachers are men.[74]

Finally, the evidence regarding differential treatment by teachers and parents is, in many cases, quite old and methodologically questionable. So we are left where we began, with many hypotheses but few robust conclusions.

THE ROLE OF THE SAMPLE IN SEX-DIFFERENCES FINDINGS

In addition to the lack of clarity and consensus concerning the nature and context of sex differences, a third source of disagreement concerns the sample used to assess sex differences. That is, for a given measure and within any particular cultural or ethnic group, the existence of sex differences depends on the specific sample being studied. To foreshadow our conclusion on this point, sex differences are unquestionably a function of where one looks, that is, the specific groups being compared. In particular, the magnitude of sex differences differs depending on where in the score distribution one looks (at the tails or at the center), the ages of the groups, and other sampling considerations we address next.

One of the most important distinctions to be made in the debate surrounding the dearth of women in math-intensive STEM fields is the contrast between the average performance of women versus the performance of women at the extreme right tail of the distribution. A large number of studies of and articles about sex differences, including many of those discussed earlier, focus on differences in average performance (see the 1985 meta-analyses by Linn and Petersen, all of the studies linking mathematical and mental rotation ability to sex hormones, and most of the teacher attention studies, as well as most studies of precursor capabilities and stereotype threat studies).

However, if we are interested in determinants of success at the highest levels in STEM fields, what matters are differences among men and women at the extreme right tail of the distribution, the highest-scoring individuals. A small difference at the mean can translate into a large difference at the extremes of the distribution, or none at all, depending on the variance and the shape of the distribution. Assuming a small average or mean difference and roughly equivalent degrees of variability (indexed by standard deviations) among male and female samples, bivariate normality (the distribution of one variable is normal for each and every value of the other variable), and equal sample sizes, then randomly selecting male and female scores from a combined sample of boys and girls may result in one sex slightly exceeding the other. But the biggest impact of such a small mean difference may be observed when the selection criterion is shifted rightward—when we attempt to select only elites (or, conversely, only the lowest performers). Here, the tails of the distribution may exhibit far greater gender asymmetry than is true at its midpoint or average.

The situation is further complicated by the fact that the variability or distribution functions may also differ. Based on our analysis of well over 100 published studies of score distributions, we estimate that men have somewhat larger variability for performance on most mathematical and spatial tests, usually 10%–20% larger than female variance.[75] So it is theoretically possible for the average woman to score equivalently to the average man on some measure. However, the top 1% of women's scores are significantly lower than the top 1% of men. As was seen, this is often the case for mathematical aptitude measures.

But we need to do more than simply state that differences in variance can magnify effects at the extremes of the distribution. For example, the usual normal curve deviates lead to the expectation that if only the top 5% of students in a class that is 50%–50% male–female is eligible for gifted/talented programs, such programs will have several times more men than women if there is a 0.5 standard deviation gap separating the sexes at the midpoint of their distributions. Or if we look at the top 1% of the distribution, men will outnumber women by approximately 7 to 1. These predictions follow from the logic of a normal distribution of scores with greater variability for male scores (e.g., Feingold, 1992).

This means that fewer women score at the right tail than do men, the part of the ability distribution where most scientists presumably reside, *if* such measures are relevant to becoming a scientist. This point is also made by Hedges and Nowell in their influential 1995 *Science* article: "Differences in the representation of the sexes at the tails of the ability distribution are likely to figure increasingly in policy about salary equity."[76]

For reading comprehension, perceptual speed, and associative memory, women outnumber men in the top 5% and 10% of performance, and men are 1.5–2.2 times as likely as women to score in the bottom 5% and 10% of the score distributions. For both spatial reasoning and mathematics, men are between 1.5 and 2.3 times more likely to be at the high end of the score distribution (including up to seven times more likely to be at the top 1% in some of the older studies). Where men are hugely overrepresented at the high end are in areas of mechanical/electronic reasoning (by a factor of nearly 10–1). Interestingly, there are also overrepresentations of men in social studies by factors of 1.7–3.5, which is rather odd given social studies' similarity to other types of verbal processing on which women excel.

In addition to the myriad other complexities that inhere in trying to analyze sex differences at the extreme right tail, there is one that we have not yet mentioned: Not all tests are the same, even when they purport to measure the same construct, such as mathematical achievement or "aptitude." One strategy that researchers have employed is to use linear equating techniques to map the score differences of one group on one test onto those from a different test. Although linear methods work very well in the interior of the distributions, they typically perform poorly at the tails.[77] This complicates the discussion of sex differences at the right tail enormously, because it is not possible to equate across the many different measures that have been reported in the literature—not if we are interested in the top 1% or the top 0.1%.

The sex difference in mathematical performance has been found to vary significantly depending on the selectiveness of the sample studied. For example, a meta-analysis by Hyde et al.[78] of over 100 studies of mathematical performance on standardized tests, covering a total of almost 4 million students, found virtually no sex difference ($d = 0.05$ in favor of girls) for nonselective samples but significant male superiority ($d > 0.3$) for selective samples. Selective samples included groups such as college-bound youth and groups of hand-picked highly precocious individuals. Of course, for the purpose of understanding sex differences in STEM fields, these select groups are the most relevant. The sociologist Andrew Penner[79] also has shown that the effect size for sex differences in math scores increases as the samples become higher functioning. He examined the TIMSS (Third International Mathematics and Science Survey) to evaluate whether "gender by item difficulty" interactions like those found in American mathematics distributions exist in mathematics and science in 10 other countries. For both mathematics and science, he found male advantages that were minimal on easy questions, but which increased significantly as questions became more difficult.

The Study of Mathematically Precocious Youth (SMPY) program, mentioned earlier, was one of the first major modern research efforts to focus specifically on the extreme right tail of the distribution. In the SMPY program, after screening large numbers of boys and girls, those scoring above the cutoff for admission were invited to participate. The necessary score was at least 700 on the SAT-M, which at age 13 or younger translates into a feat achieved by only 1 in 10,000. This is well above the 1% threshold on the SAT-M, and it is a level at which the sex disparity is very large. (Those admitted to the SMPY program were given accelerated exposure to mathematics.) But prior to this exposure to mathematics, there was a higher proportion of boys than girls who made the cutoff for admission into the program. At the end of high school, the students who had been admitted to the SMPY sample took the SAT-M again, and again there was a preponderance of boys at the upper tail of test scores.[80] The investigators concluded that there were more boys than girls in the pool from which future scientists and mathematicians are drawn.

This initial sex difference was obtained at age 13 or younger. This age is before students began to select their courses, so the male advantage wasn't explicable in terms of different coursework. In addition, because the students showed few sex differences in their reported attitudes toward mathematics, the investigators suggested that the sources of the later sex difference were probably, in part, genetic.[81] This assumes that the only sex-differentiated environmental variable that could explain such differences is course choices, which may not be the case. There are other potential nongenetically driven experiential differences between boys and girls that could lead to more boys desiring to participate in SMPY. And, of course, the sample itself was not scientifically assembled, but was rather a result of teacher nominations, opening it to systematic and unsystematic potential sources of bias, as the authors note. Since SMPY began assessing sex differences in math performance, the gap separating boys and girls at the extreme right tail has narrowed dramatically (see Figure 6.1 in Chapter 6).

Let us return to the Hedges and Nowell[82] study briefly mentioned earlier and which we return to in Chapter 6. In this study, the magnitude of the typically observed sex differences on tasks that require rotation in mental space of three-dimensional objects, or visualization of spatial relationships,

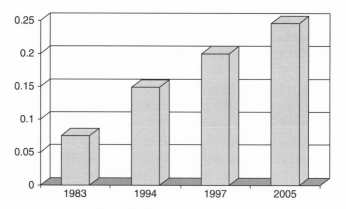

FIGURE **4.5.** Change in female representation at right tail (top 1%) of math score distribution at age 13.

could be large enough to have practical significance. This was because of greater variance for men's scores—*if* being in the top 1% of those possessing these skills is critically important for success in a STEM field. A moderately large gap of this size between men and women at the center of a spatial ability distribution will usually translate into very large gender asymmetries at the tails. We keep underscoring the word "if" because it truly becomes central to the issue of gender asymmetries in STEM careers. As we noted earlier, there is some evidence that spatial ability sex differences exist as early as 4 or 5 months of age.[83] There is evidence that such ability around 3 years of age predicts later math grades among elementary school children. There is also evidence that SAT-M scores between the sexes are comparable once they are controlled statistically for the sexes' differential mental rotation scores, suggesting that the latter is key to understanding male advantage on the SAT-M.

Some other studies have also looked at the right tail of the distribution. For example, there is Robinson et al.'s 1996 study of mathematically precocious young children, and LaChance and Mazzocco's 2006 analysis of the top quartile showing no consistent sex differences through third grade, with girls actually outperforming boys more often than not on math tests. As mentioned earlier, these authors did not find evidence of male superiority on most spatial measures, whereas other studies of similarly aged children often have found spatial skill differences in favor of boys. However, inasmuch as the measures used differ across these studies, it is difficult to make meaningful comparisons between groups in view of the low correlations between some measures of mental rotation.[84] Finally, a further complication in evaluating studies of the highest performers is that when differences in samples get amplified at the extreme tails of the score distribution, this can render conclusions about such small subsets statistically less reliable because the small number of individuals who achieve extreme scores on one test often do not achieve extreme scores on another. This is not a problem when matching individuals who score at less extreme parts of the distribution.

Unfortunately for our current purposes, most available studies of spatial and mathematical abilities and associated environmental factors do not focus on extreme right-tail samples. This makes much of the evidence somewhat irrelevant to our discussion, because sex differences at the mean or average are often small or nonexistent, and this is not where most STEM scientists score. In fact, the majority of the evidence published under the topic of sex differences in STEM fields may not pertain to the most relevant groups, the top scorers. For example, the biological work discussed earlier (such as brain organization and hormone studies) was generally performed on small samples of individuals who were not selected for their expertise in math. Extrapolating from these samples to extreme groups who comprise future scientists is logically hazardous.

A final complicating issue concerns how sex differences are assessed. This group of concerns includes variations in test content and context, differences in performance evaluation, and debates concerning the legitimacy of static versus dynamic testing. We will deal with each of these concerns in order.

Test Content and Context

If superior performance in STEM fields is an intrinsic function of maleness, as implied by one part (but not other parts) of Summers's remarks in 2005, then one might expect male superiority to be a highly robust finding. However, research has often shown the opposite. For one thing, male–female performance differences can be affected significantly by minor changes in the testing situation, such as the phrasing of test instructions in order to make gender salient. Any assessment of skills is, in some sense, a test of transfer of learning from one situation to another. Research has shown that transfer success varies with the content and context of the transfer situation.[85] So it is not surprising that, in research on sex differences in cognitive performance, varying the context of the testing procedure affects the results.

For example, in some cases the gender difference has been shown to be smaller when testing is in a group format rather than in an individual setting.[86] And if individual testing is used, gender differences are smaller when the tester is female rather than male.[87] These are just a couple of examples of the effects of social context on sex differences. The magnitude of these effects is usually not great, but they are statistically significant. Findings of social context sensitivity of sex differences are widespread in other areas, too[88]: Sex differences in video game aggression can be made to go away when the experimental context is made more anonymous,[89] and it has been shown that men demonstrate more helping behavior than women when they are being observed, but the sex difference disappears when they are not being observed.[90] Aspects of temporal context may also affect gender differences. For example, some have noted that tests in which there is time pressure (like mental rotation and the SAT) tend to result in a bigger male advantage than measures for which speed is not as important, such as spatial visualization and school grades.[91] Aspects of modality also matter: Stumpf and Stanley[92] found that in some subjects boys did better than girls on multiple-choice measures but not on free-response measures.

The specific content of the transfer measures can also affect the findings. Sex differences often depend on what skill is being assessed. For example, Vasta et al.[93] found training eradicated the sex difference in a water-line test (students were asked to draw the water line if the glass was tilted) when the outcome measure was getting the correct answer, but not when the outcome measure was verbalization of the correct physical principle. In other words, men did better than women at first, and then training eliminated this difference—as long as what one is measuring is getting the correct answer, as opposed to being able to explain why. Some variables can be even more sensitive to the particular outcome measure used. For example, Voyer at al[94] showed in a meta-analysis that the effect size of the sex difference on the mental rotation test was dependent on the particular scoring method used. When the test was scored out of 20 (the original scoring method used), the gender difference was bigger than when it was scored out of 40 (effect sizes 0.75–1.00 and 0.50–0.74, respectively). Other scoring methods reduced the effect size dramatically (to 0.10–0.19). Probably the best known difference is that the d for mental rotation of two-dimensional shapes is less than half the magnitude of d's for mental rotation of three-dimensional shapes. And finally, going back to the earliest meta-analysis of mental rotation, Linn and Petersen[95] showed that the effect size for gender depended significantly on the test used, and (as noted above) that several of the main rotation tasks do not correlate with each other as highly as one would expect if one wishes to speak of mental rotation ability as if it represents a unitary skill.

Such content and context sensitivity calls into question the presumed intrinsic nature of the male superiority on tests of mathematical ability and spatial ability, though reasonable justifications can be raised about some of these context-dependent effects (for example, that three-dimensional rotations are more complex than two-dimensional ones, and therefore yield higher d's because their greater difficulty taxes females' limited capacity quicker than it taxes males' greater capacity).

Static Versus Dynamic Testing

Most studies of sex differences in cognitive ability have used static measures. However, there is a long-standing literature showing that virtually all cognitive abilities are affected by experience.[96] A debate is raging more generally in the field of psychometric testing between those who argue that cognitive ability can be assessed using static tests and those who argue that dynamic testing yields a more powerful prediction of future performance.[97] Dynamic testing refers to a testing situation in which the test taker is given feedback on her or his answers while proceeding through the test questions. This can be used to determine how much the test taker is learning from the feedback and, some suggest, get closer to actual ability.

A few studies of cognitive sex differences have adopted more dynamic methods, with mixed results. For example, the spatial training of college students on the water-level task designed by Vasta et al.[98] totally eliminated one form of sex differences in spatial reasoning and reduced the magnitude of another, although in neither case did this training transfer to related types of tasks that were not directly trained. In their study, spatial training, using a self-discovery training procedure with progressively more difficult tasks, improved female students' knowledge of the spatial (invariance) principle, but it did not reach the level of males' knowledge. Newcombe[99] recently argued that the magnitude of the spatial gains due to training is often larger than the magnitude of the initial sex differences (see also Baenninger & Newcombe, 1989). Recall, for example, the Levine et al. study, mentioned earlier, in which a single 15-minute training session on a different day had an effect roughly equal to the entire male–female performance difference. Note again, however, that a sex difference in performance remained following training, because boys' gains were comparable to girls' gains.

As far as the malleability of cognitive skills is concerned, there are fascinating data showing that girls and boys often attempt to solve speeded test problems differently—but that when they are instructed to use the same strategies, they can do so. In other words, girls, while preferring certain strategies that are nonoptimal on speeded tests such as the SAT-M, can utilize optimal strategies. This suggests that they have more cognitive ability than displayed but choose, for whatever reason, to employ different strategies.[100] Training on appropriate strategy use can have large effects, again bringing into question the intrinsic nature of the male–female performance difference. However, results are mixed. Kimura[101] claims that "(such differences are) apparently uninfluenced by systematic training in adulthood. While both sexes benefit from short-term intensive training on spatial tasks, men's and women's scores do not converge (Baenninger & Newcombe, 1995)."

A Cautionary Note on Remediation of Sex Differences Through Training

Ceci and Papierno[102] reviewed some of the training literature aimed at gap closing. Gaps between the sexes are one important type of gap studied by researchers; others include ethnic/racial gaps and socioeconomic gaps. A key question facing our society today concerns how to reduce gaps that result from poverty, poor schooling, and other types of inequitable access to resources. Ceci and Papierno reported that sometimes training interventions actually *widen* preexisting gaps—if the interventions are made available to all students, not just to those in greatest need. This is because it is sometimes the case that the biggest gains in training studies are made by those who were the highest scoring before the intervention started. A dramatic example of this principle can be found in the experiments to create small classes for children. All children gain from being in small classes, including the bottom 10% of achievers. The problem is that the top 10% gain over twice as much from being in small classes, thus widening the preexisting gap between the top and bottom students even though all gain above the level seen in regular sized classes (Ceci & Konstantopolous, 2009).

The idea of targeting training interventions to one sex or ability level and excluding the others from its potential benefits raises many interesting political, economic, and moral questions that are beyond the scope of this book.[103] But in the context of the present debate, it bears noting that some interventions designed to elevate the numbers of women in STEM careers (such as informing high school students about the possibilities that each field offers to counter their erroneous impressions, or training adolescents on spatial reasoning skills) could result in increasing the interest of girls—but possibly increasing the interest of boys even more so. These are empirical questions worthy of study.

RECAP: CHALLENGES TO THE ENVIRONMENTAL POSITION

To sum up this chapter, research has shown that the manner in which sex differences are assessed can significantly affect the outcome of such assessments. In the next chapter we review the findings on stereotype threat, which has been proposed as a possible mechanism responsible for the gender gap in math and science, and we conclude that, notwithstanding the many fascinating findings in this literature, it is not likely to be a primary determinant of the sex gap. In the next chapter we also examine what may be the toughest evidence for proponents of a biological view of sex differences to refute:

The existence of sex differences will be shown to vary as a function of one's country, epoch, age group, and sociodemographic characteristics (race, ethnicity, and income). This research is important as we continue on our way to a synthesis of the entire data corpus, and what it tells us about the causes of women's underrepresentation in math-intensive fields.

5

Challenges to the biological position

"Women share with men the need for personal success, even the taste for power, and no longer are we willing to satisfy those needs through the achievements of surrogates, whether husbands, children, or merely role models."

—Elizabeth Dole

In this chapter we examine claims and counterclaims about the role of parents and teachers in causing sex differences in mathematics achievement in grades K–12 and college. We also assess research claiming that bias and stereotypes are important causes of sex differences in graduate school and beyond.

In addition to studying measures of what individuals can and cannot do and what they prefer to do, several researchers have studied how the environment shapes women and the differences women versus men elicit from their environment. Potential environmental influences include differential treatment by parents and teachers, as well as differences in the way children spend their time and, when it comes to older females, differences in the way colleagues, search committees, and grant review panels treat them. Some of the evidence we will describe may be surprising—even alarming—and some of it begs for replication and further exploration.

FAVORING BOYS AND IGNORING GIRLS

To begin with, there is evidence of discriminatory treatment of girls and boys in high school mathematics classrooms, using many measures. Becker[1] gathered frequency counts to compare teacher interactions with the children in their classes and added in-depth qualitative observational data. She studied 10 high school geometry teachers in the late 1970s, an era corresponding to the generation now reaching the top of many STEM fields. As seen in Figure 5.1, Becker found that girls were asked fewer direct and open questions by their teachers, and girls were offered fewer comments of praise and call-outs to sustain them in their high school math classes. Becker summarized these results as follows:

> The teachers in the sample treated females and males differently in (a) afforded response opportunities, (b) open questioning, (c) cognitive level of questions, (d) sustenance and persistence, (e) praise and criticism, (f) encouragement, (g) individual help, and (h) conversation and joking. The differences found generally work in a positive way for males—they received more teacher attention, reinforcement, and affect. Females, traditionally the "lesser sex," received less of all three . . . . In summary, the students were learning mathematics in an environment that sex-types the subject as male, that provided males more formal and informal reward and support in mathematics, and that provided males more outlets for classroom academic achievement and recognition. Whereas males were provided a good cognitive and affective environment in which to learn mathematics, females, relatively speaking, were treated with benign neglect.[2]

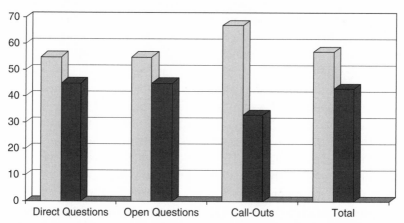

FIGURE **5.1.** The percentage of teacher-afforded response opportunities for males and females. Light bars refer to males; dark bars to females. Direct question refers to a time when a teacher directly calls on a student by name. Open question refers to a question addressed to the entire class, and the teacher calls on one who has his or her hand raised. Call-outs refers to when a student calls out an answer and the teacher directs the class's attention to the particular student. Source adapted from: Becker, J. R. (1981). Differential treatment of females and males in mathematics classes. *Journal for Research in Mathematics Education, 12*(1), 40–53.

It is not difficult to imagine how such differential treatment might have led to eventual differences in performance, such as boys excelling on far-transfer math problems and girls on near-transfer problems.[3] Elsewhere, research on the development of transferable skills has suggested that the style of interaction Becker identified as being used with boys may be more conducive to the development of far transfer skills,[4] such as applying math learning to novel situations. It would be interesting to know how classrooms have changed since Becker's study was undertaken nearly three decades ago. Today, national awareness seems to have sharpened, and many organizations offer programs for teachers and girls to increase their participation in STEM fields.

Notwithstanding such disturbing evidence of unequal treatment of male and female math students in the past, it is worth remembering that girls have continued to achieve higher grades than boys in high school mathematics classes, including in the geometry classes that Becker studied. So it is problematic to claim that teacher inattention leads the sexes to different careers—that is, unless aptitude tests such as the SAT-M, on which girls score lower than boys, are considered a more relevant outcome measure than is doing well in high school and college math classes. If school grades are considered the gold standard of the mathematical skills needed for high-level performance in STEM fields,[5] girls ought to be getting the message that counts most: They are better than boys. After all, girls persistently get better scores on school math tests and receive superior grades in math classes.

A colleague who read an early draft of this chapter argued that because school grades are a poorer predictor of success in graduate programs in math-intensive fields than are SAT-M scores (neither being very strong predictors, it might be noted), the differential treatment of girls and boys could play a role in their differing SAT-M patterns, and might partly explain the sex differences in success in STEM fields. It is not obvious to us, however, how teacher attention can lead both to lower grades for boys but superior SAT-M scores for them. Although logically possible, this argument begins to resemble grasping at straws. To advocates of the psychometric tradition, however, there is no contradiction here. This is because they regard the SAT-M as a better measure of underlying math aptitude than school grades, which they assume reflect various biases (like boys being penalized for their obstreperous behavior and more frequent absences; girls being rewarded for doing homework, raising their hands, and being compliant[6]). However, the direct evidence for this assertion is weak, and many classroom teachers bristle at being portrayed so simplistically, pointing out that they assign grades based on how well students grasp the content being taught, not on compliance or homework, which can be noted separately from the math grade. Teachers' testimonials are anecdotal, of course, and in need of systematic study.

A contemporaneous study by Parsons et al.[7] found fewer overall sex differences than Becker[8] in teachers' treatment of girls versus boys in a sample of fifth- to ninth-grade math classrooms. However, one notable exception to this pattern of null findings was that girls whom the teachers expected to do well in math received significantly less praise than other groups of students. This is presumably the group of girls from which future STEM professionals would come. It is possible that this lack of praise is a contributing factor to some of the behaviors of girls on the SAT-M, such as their low-risk-taking approach to solving math problems by unconventional means.[9] However, this, too, is little more than a hypothesis in need of rigorous testing. Far too much of this kind of speculation can be found in the literature, and far too often, no one gets around to testing such speculative assertions.

Finally, Kenney-Benson et al. have provided one possible explanation for the disjunction between girls' higher math grades and boys' higher SAT-M scores. Based on their analysis, they suggested that performance in formal testing contexts such as the SAT draw on different motivational resources than does day-to-day performance in the classroom. These authors see the former as drawing on self-efficacy and competitiveness and the latter as drawing on mastery-based strategies (asking for help, preparing, doing homework): "As a consequence, the testing situation may underestimate girls' abilities, but the classroom may underestimate boys' abilities."[10]

In addition to overt behavioral differences in the way teachers react to students, differences have also been found in the attitudes and perceptions of parents and teachers. For example, sixth-grade girls' mathematical abilities are underestimated by their mothers, while boys' abilities are overestimated.[11] In addition, abilities of high school girls are viewed less favorably than boys' abilities by both parents and teachers.[12] And these attitudes have an impact: Jacobs and Eccles[13] found that children are more influenced by their mothers' perceptions of their ability than by their actual grades, when developing opinions of their own abilities.

On the other hand, there are some data suggesting that parental encouragement and endorsement of math achievement will not close the sex gap in performance at the right tail on so-called aptitude tests such as the SAT-M. In his analysis of math achievement data from 21 countries, sociologist Andrew Penner[14] found that the students who report that their math achievement is important to their parents exhibit smaller sex differences—but only at the left tail of the math distribution (the lowest-scoring part). At the right tail, girls score 3% worse than boys among those who say that math achievement is unimportant to their parents, *but* they score 6% worse when they say math achievement is important to their parents. Parental encouragement of math achievement does not appear to be the answer, at least not in the absence of other interventions.

Over the last few decades, considerable attention has been devoted to the question of gender differences in teacher interactions. A 1992 American Association of University Women (AAUW) report concluded:

> A large body of research indicates that teachers give more classroom attention and more esteem-building encouragement to boys. In a study conducted by Myra and David Sadker, boys in elementary and middle school called out answers eight times more often than girls. When boys called out, teachers listened. But when girls called out, they were told to 'raise your hand if you want to speak.' Even when boys do not volunteer, teachers are more likely to encourage them to give an answer or an opinion than they are to encourage girls. Research reveals a tendency, beginning at the preschool level, for educators to choose classroom activities that appeal to boys' interests and select presentation formats in which boys excel. The teacher-student interaction patterns in science classes are often particularly biased. Even in math classes, where less-biased patterns are found, psychologist Jacquelynne Eccles reports that select boys in each math class she studied received particular attention to the exclusion of all other students, female or male.[15]

As further evidence, the authors of the AAUW report describe the results of a study showing that "79 percent of all student-assisted science demonstrations were carried out by boys."[16] A more recent summary of the state of knowledge on this topic by Sadker and Zittleman[17] reached similar conclusions:

> Although most teachers want to teach all children equitably, boys and girls often receive different treatment. Teachers call on boys more often than girls, wait longer for boys' answers, and provide more precise feedback to boys... Teachers often encourage boys to persist with and solve difficult problems, while assisting girls who ask for help.[18]

Counterarguments

In response to these concerns, attention has been paid in teacher training to eradicating gender biases in the distribution of teacher attention.[19] However, others disagree that attention *is* unfairly distributed. A 2006 review of relevant educational research by Beaman et al. focused specifically on evidence regarding "differential teacher attention to boys and girls in the classroom." The review covered work from the last 30 years, and found remarkable consistency over time in findings. This is despite changes in the popular conception from worries about boys' performance, to worries about girls', and recently back to worries about boys'. Although the review was not limited to studies in STEM subjects, some math and science classes were included. These authors refer to a substantial body of research and meta-analyses/reviews of research showing differential distribution of attention, but suggest that the supposed bias is more likely a response to student behavioral differences, with boys misbehaving more and therefore receiving more negative attention. They also note that boys expect to get more attention: "boys considered having two-thirds of the teacher's time as 'a fair deal,' " and felt discriminated against if they received less than this.

Beaman et al. criticize much of the research used to support claims of discrimination against girls in that the studies often do not distinguish between good and bad attention—that is, attention that fosters intellectual development versus attention doled out merely to maintain discipline. These authors concede that some studies did distinguish between types of interaction, referring to a meta-analysis by Kelly[20] showing that boys got "more instructional contacts, more high-level questions, more academic criticism and slightly more praise than girls,"[21] but they caution that the differences may be caused by a few individual boys rather than boys and girls in general.

However, before assuming the validity of the claim that teachers give preferential attention to boys, and that this contributes to girls' poor performance in math-related fields, a number of other paradoxes (in addition to the big one—that girls get better grades) need to be addressed. For example, in 1998, Diane Ravitch, former assistant secretary for educational research and improvement and counselor to the U.S. Department of Education, published an editorial in the *Wall Street Journal* in which she blasted the media for accepting claims that sex differences in scientific careers were the result of such factors as teachers showering more attention and praise on boys, or higher self-esteem among boys. Such ideas find little support in empirical studies, she argued:

> The schools, we were told, were heedlessly crushing girls' self-esteem while teachers (70% of them female) were showering attention on boys. Worst among their faults, according to the report (1992 American Association of University Women's document, entitled "How schools shortchange girls") was that the schools discouraged girls from taking the math and science courses that they would need to compete in the future. The report unleashed a plethora of gender-equity programs in the schools and a flood of books and articles about the maltreatment of girls in classrooms and textbooks.

Ravitch went on to criticize such claims, referring to published data from the U.S. Department of Education showing that, far from failing girls, schools were doing a good job in closing gender gaps in mathematics and science. With the sole exception of high school physics, in which 27% of boys compared to only 22% of girls were enrolled, girls were taking as many courses in mathematics and science as boys, and this state of affairs has been true at least since the late 1980s. For example, Ravitch pointed out:

> Female high school graduates in 1990 had higher enrollments than boys in first- and second-year algebra and in geometry; and among the graduates of 1994, there were

few sex differences in precalculus, AP calculus, trigonometry, statistics, and a host of science courses; in fact, females were more likely to enroll in chemistry and biology than males.... Overall, 43% of female graduates took a rigorous college-preparatory program in 1994, compared with only 35% of boys. This suggests that the notion that teacher treatment of girls has led to a lack of motivation to take STEM-relevant courses is mistaken.

In Figure 5.2 we see that girls are not only outperforming boys in grades, but also they are doing so in courses that are every bit as demanding as those boys are taking.

Given our goal of understanding the development of mathematical ability at the extreme right tail of performance, differential treatment of the subset of boys or girls who have the most math aptitude may be relevant, even if, on average, boys and girls are not treated differently. Unfortunately, we do not know of data regarding the differential treatment of the subset of boys and girls who are most likely to be potential STEM professionals.

As an illustration of the conflicting interpretations of these sorts of data, consider the implications of evidence showing that teacher eye gaze is mostly directed at boys. Beaman et al. suggest that this could mean either that girls are being shortchanged or that teachers are wisely keeping an eye on potentially disruptive boys to maintain classroom control. If the latter, then increased attention by the teacher could have adverse consequences, inasmuch as boys might view it as regulatory and punitive. And more generally, the impression

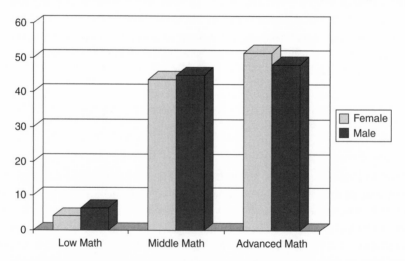

FIGURE **5.2.** Percentage of high school graduates who completed low-level math courses (either no math or nonacademic math), middle-level math courses (Algebra I, Geometry, Algebra II), or advanced math (Algebra III, Precalculus, Calculus) as a function of sex. Source: U.S. Department of Education, National Center for Educational Statistics. Education Longitudinal Study of 2002, the "High School Transcript Study."

one gets from this research is that much (though not all) of it is open to the charge that it is driven by a confirmatory bias on the part of some investigators. By this we mean that in the absence of an a priori, principled selection of measures that have been shown to be causally related to math and science attitudes and achievement, it is possible for researchers to focus on any behavior they coded that differentiated a teacher's response to boys and girls, claiming post hoc that this behavior may be the basis of later sex differences in math or science when it may, in fact, bear no causal relation.

For instance, had teachers' eye gaze and questioning been directed more at girls, one could take this as evidence that teachers use such behaviors to control and inhibit girls' exploratory behavior and risk taking. Clearly, even if methodological issues such as the potential for coder bias can be overcome, drawing conclusions from such research is problematic. As Beaman et al. wisely conclude, "There is clearly a need for more . . . fine-grained studies on this topic." (p. 362)

Regardless of the validity of the aforementioned claims, once again we return to the major conundrum we have repeatedly raised: *Even if maternal negative attitudes have led to girls having a lower self-assessment of their mathematical ability, and even if teachers have showered more attention on boys, and even if parents purchase more math-related toys for their sons, it has apparently not stopped girls from taking math courses at rates and levels equal to or exceeding those of boys and receiving superior grades in them (including making up nearly half of the enrollment in advanced placement physics in high school), and majoring in college mathematics approximately as often as boys, again with grades at least as good.* For these many reasons, it seems like a stretch to invoke teacher and parental behaviors as causes of the dearth of women in STEM fields.

BIAS IN THE ACADEMY?

Finally, there is some evidence that female STEM scientists are disadvantaged at multiple points along the way to attaining seniority in the field. As we will soon see in this chapter, some have claimed that women are evaluated by job search committees more harshly than comparable men. Others claim that female STEM postdoctoral fellowship applicants are cheated when they apply for grants. Still others argue that female STEM scientists face tougher obstacles getting their work accepted for publication in journals. In this section we review this evidence, beginning with the claim that, when it comes to the division of resources at their places of employment, female STEM professors are shortchanged in the resources needed to do their work once they are hired.

Claims of Unfair Division of Resources

Some have suggested that the unequal division of laboratory space and salary are causes of women's reduced success in STEM fields. These claims have been controversial. A high-profile report appearing in the March 1999 *Massachusetts Institute of Technology Faculty Newsletter* concluded that "many tenured women faculty feel marginalized and excluded from a significant role in their departments."[22] Marginalization at MIT took the form of differences in salaries, resources, and differential treatment, "despite [women having] professional accomplishments equal to those of their male colleagues."[23]

Notwithstanding the widely publicized controversy surrounding the validity of the MIT claims of sex differences in resource allocations, Hausman and Steiger[24] failed to find empirical support for the charge. They argued that sex differences in salary among MIT professors were due to differences in productivity, not gender bias. To our knowledge, MIT has refused to provide independent researchers with the data backing up their claim of gender bias. However, even if the MIT claim of bias against women faculty turns out to be unfounded, there is some other evidence of differential allocation of research resources between women and men, which some have alleged could be a source of disadvantage for senior STEM women faculty. A self-study by the University of Pennsylvania found that female full professors in biology, chemistry, and psychology had fewer square feet assigned to them, with women's space averaging only 84% of that for male full professors' space, when the net square foot of research space per $1,000 of grant income was calculated. In the Pennsylvania School of Medicine, tenured male full professors averaged 1,950 sq. ft per $500,000 of grant income, while female full professors averaged only 1,660 sq. ft per $500,000.[25] But the picture at Penn was different for more junior faculty, with women in many cases receiving more space than their equivalent male peers.

Our sense is that, although it is possible that resource allocation discrepancies may exist in some niches, at some institutions, in some fields, and at some ranks, making it possible to explain part of the differences in success of women and men in such situations, it is unlikely that such small and unsystematic differences could be an important source of variance in accounting for the reason women are so underrepresented in math-intensive careers. It would be a rare student who would opt out of a scientific career because she discerned that female faculty's lab space was 15% smaller than male faculty's. Moreover, there is no normalization in lab space studies for preexisting differences in factors that could have led to later differences in resources, such as measures of external visibility that may garner senior male faculty greater resources, not because they are male but because of their eminence.

Differences in Performance Evaluation

When STEM faculty themselves are asked why women are underrepresented, they favor more prosaic reasons—such as less interest in engineering and the physical sciences—rather than conspiracy theories, such as bias against women. The least favored reasons given for women's underrepresentation have to do with ability differences between men and women, which few endorse. Figure 5.3 depicts the reasons given by scientists in a large national survey regarding women's underrepresentation in scientific fields.

Studies have begun to examine how career-relevant performance is evaluated, providing evidence that it is sometimes evaluated differently for men and women. Conducting such research is difficult, due to the private nature of most evaluation processes (they are confidential), so there are few studies available, but these few findings are alarming, at least at first blush.

One of the most striking pieces of evidence comes from a study of the peer-review process for postdoctoral fellowships in medical fields in Sweden by Wenneras and Wold,[26] which these authors conducted after obtaining data using the Freedom of the Press Act. The authors were both denied fellowship grants themselves, so they sued to get the raw data on which their scores were based.

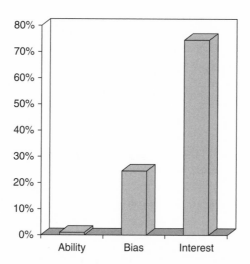

FIGURE **5.3.** Gross & Simmons (2007) surveyed 1,414 full-time professors. Only 1% support differences in ability, 25% blamed discrimination, and 74% cited sex differences in interests. (Women are twice as likely as men to blame discrimination—33.8% versus 17.1%.) Source: Gross, N. & Simmons, S. (2007). The social and political views of American professors. Working paper, Sept. 24, 2007. From author at: ngross@wjh.harvard.edu

Wenneras and Wold reported what they concluded was profound discrimination against female postdoctoral fellowship applicants in Sweden. Their conclusion is based on various analyses of the scores given to applicants by grant review committees, which the authors compared with objective data on publication records of the applicants (number of total publications, number of first-authored articles, number of citations, adjusted citation measures). Reviewers judged each application on three measures. The measure on which women lost most points relative to men was scientific competence, which is based on the number and quality of scientific publications. The authors found that the translation of objective data into subjective scores was highly biased against women, such that a female applicant had to be 2.5 times more productive than the average male applicant to receive the same competence score (see Figure 5.4).

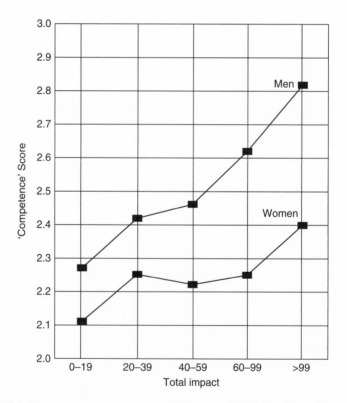

FIGURE **5.4.** The mean competence score given to male and female applicants by the MRC reviewers as a function of their scientific productivity, measured as total impact. One impact point equals one paper published in a journal with an impact factor of 1. (See text for further explanation). Source: Wenneras, C., & Wold, A. (1997). Nepotism and sexism in peer review. *Nature, 387*, p. 342. Reprinted with permission of Nature Publishing Group.

In the words of these authors, the analyses showed that "the most productive group of female applicants, containing those with 100 impact points [measure of number of publications adjusted for citation frequency] or more, was the only group of women judged to be as competent as men, although only as competent as the least productive group of male applicants (the one whose members had fewer than 20 total impact points)."[27] Given that Sweden is known for providing equal opportunities to men and women, the authors concluded that their findings of bias against women are likely to generalize to other countries, too. This study has received a great deal of attention due to the high profile of the journal in which it appeared, *Nature*, and has been cited by nearly all investigators of gender bias.

As is true with many correlational studies, however, Wenneras and Wold's 1997 conclusion of bias against female grant applicants is open to alternative interpretations. They analyzed 114 postdoctoral fellowship applications in 1995 to the Swedish Medical Research Council, 62 submitted by men and 52 by women. Sixteen of the male applications were funded (25.8%) versus only four of the women's (7.7%). When dealing with such small numbers, small adjustments can matter a great deal. For instance, what if the makeup of the review panels were disproportionately composed of biomedical professionals (not nursing or basic science) and more of the male applicants came from a medical or biomedical background? Perhaps the panelists tended to weigh publications in medical journals more heavily than publications in basic science or nursing journals—even if the latter are cited more often. Out of the 52 female applicants, only 14 came from medical backgrounds, whereas 37 of the 62 male applicants came from such backgrounds. One need not posit gender discrimination if reviewers preferred medical journals to basic science or nursing journals, even if the latter were higher cited. After all, reviewers were not given information about the impact ratings of journals, certainly not in 1995. And even if they were, they may have nevertheless favored journals they knew best. And perhaps medical panelists favored medical journals over nursing journals. If so, then the greater proportion of female applicants from nursing could have tilted the odds against them.

Consider: 12% of female applicants came from nursing backgrounds versus only 3% of males. Because the numbers are so small, the regression models would not be sensitive to sex differences, even though small differences might be sufficient to attenuate their claims of bias. Along these same lines, perhaps reviewers weighted factors such as sole-authored papers more than they did first-authored papers, and perhaps male applicants had more of these. (It is unclear from Wenneras and Wold's description if the number of sole-authored articles differed by sex, as this was not one of the measures in their six regression models.) Finally, the statistical models that these authors employed have been criticized by methodologists,[28] and the authors have not allowed independent researchers to reanalyze their data to confirm their conclusions, replying that their data were lost. None of this instills confidence in their claims of bias. Some day independent researchers will avail themselves to the Swedish data and we will discover whether Wenneras and Wold's conclusions are supported.

The point of raising these alternative explanations is not to deny that gender discrimination operates during the evaluation of grant applications. Rather, we wish to remind readers that this is a hypothesis in need of convergent empirical testing that must go beyond the small study just described. A powerful test of gender bias would be to give panelists the same curricula vitae (CVs) used in Wenneras and Wold's study, with sex of applicant systematically manipulated so ratings of male and female applicants could be assessed in response to the identical CV. Would panelists have downgraded the CV when it had a female name on it? If not, then the claim of antifemale discrimination would be misplaced, because sex would have been a proxy for unmeasured variables on which the men and women in this study differed. Perhaps gender downgrading would occur. But it strikes us as important to demonstrate this in an experimental design.

A study that meets this goal was conducted by Steinpreis et al.,[29] which we will describe later. But first, we describe two studies that bear directly on Wenneras and Wold's claims of gender bias in grant reviews. Wenneras and Wold touted a United Nations report that named Sweden as "the leading country in the world with respect to equal opportunities for men and women, so it is not too far-fetched to assume that if gender-based discrimination occurs there it may occur elsewhere. It is therefore essential that more studies are conducted in different countries and in different areas of scientific research."[30] Several studies meet this goal.

The Australian Research Council processes over 3,000 grant applications each year in all areas of science. Each of these are reviewed by 4.3 reviewers, on average. Jayasinghe et al.[31] have published several analyses of these data, using sophisticated measurement models. This is an excellent database to examine claims of bias against female applicants, because not only can one look at the fate of female applications, but one can do so as a function of many potentially confounding variables, as well as the gender of the reviewers.

Marsh et al.[32] report that although only 15.3% of the applicants for funding were women, female researchers' success was almost exactly proportional to their representation (15.2%). When gender of only the first-named investigator was considered, the success rate was 21% for both men and women. More detailed analyses on second- and third-named researchers also indicated that the success rate did not differ significantly for men and women. Supplemental analyses based on the final assessor ratings (mean of external assessor ratings) and the final panel committee ratings showed similar results.[33] Furthermore, the insignificant effect of gender did not interact with the review panel, indicating that there was no gender bias for any of the nine social science, humanities, and science disciplines they studied. Finally, because Marsh et al. knew the gender of the applicant as well as that of the reviewer, they had a unique opportunity to analyze the so-called "matching hypothesis" that female external assessors might give higher ratings to female researchers and that male external assessors might give higher ratings to male researchers. They found no evidence to support this claim. In this large grant review database, there was no evidence of a gender bias in the reviews of applications submitted by female researchers. In their words:

> Thus, proposals for which the first-named researcher was a female were not rated differently from those for which the first-named researcher was a male, and this lack of difference did not vary according to the gender of the external assessor. When these interaction effects were evaluated with the more powerful multilevel cross-classified models . . . the interaction effects remained statistically nonsignificant. In summary, there was no support for either gender bias based on applicant gender or a gender-matching bias in which female assessors gave higher ratings to female applicants and/or male assessors gave higher ratings to male applicants.

In addition, there were no significant differences between ratings of male and female external assessors for either the global researcher or project ratings. Wenneras and Wold's claim that male assessors downgraded females' grant scores finds no support in this large data set.

A second large-scale analysis was conducted by the RAND Corporation to assess gender bias in grants at three U.S. federal agencies, the National Science Foundation, the National Institutes of Health, and the Department of Agriculture. Between them, these three agencies make up the majority of funding to scientists in the United States. As was the case for the Australian Science Foundation results, the RAND study[34] concluded that there was no gender bias in the awarding of grants at the three federal agencies (as well as in two surveys), with the exception that men received more money for their grants at one agency. However, owing to a lack of data for possible controls, it is not clear what this single exception means. As far as the percentage of grants funded, there were no differences in the percentages of male and female applicants who were funded.

In view of the extensiveness of these large-scale analyses, coupled with the questions raised about the Wenneras and Wold methods and lost data, we are led to conclude that evidence for claims of this form of gender discrimination is lacking.

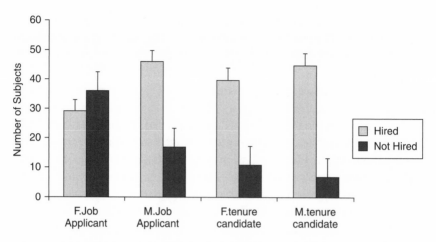

FIGURE **5.5.** Hireability of the job applicants and tenure candidates based on the quality of the curriculum vitae the participants were asked to evaluate. Source: Steinpreis, R. E., Anders, K. A., & Ritzke, D. (1999). The impact of gender on the review of the CVs of job applicants and tenure candidates: A national empirical study. *Sex Roles, 41*, 509–528.

Claims of Bias against Female Job Applicants

As mentioned previously, a study of search committee recommendations for hiring of assistant professors[35] gets closer to the claims that Wenneras and Wold made. Steinpreis et al. used a randomized experimental survey design to study possible bias in job-search committee recommendations. They asked 238 psychologists to play the role of mock search committee members, who were charged with reviewing fictitious male and female assistant professor job candidates, as well as more advanced job seekers who might be eligible for tenure. They used the same CV, but varied the sex of the applicant. As can be seen in Figure 5.5, they found that mock search committee members favored the junior-level CV when it had a male name on it. However, they did not exhibit any gender bias for the fictitious job applicants who were more senior and eligible for early tenure. Even though the male and female CVs sent to mock search committee members were identical, new PhD CVs labeled as male were given preferential ratings by mock search committee members. Interestingly, the female search committee members rated the female job seekers downward as much as the male search members did (see Figure 5.5). So, if there is bias in the system, it is not specific to male raters. In the words of the authors:

> Both men and women were more likely to vote to hire a male job applicant than a female job applicant with an identical record. Similarly, both sexes reported that the male job applicant had done adequate teaching, research, and service experience compared to the female job applicant with an identical record. In contrast, when

men and women examined the highly competitive curriculum vitae of the real-life scientist who had gotten early tenure, they were equally likely to tenure the male and female tenure candidates and there was no difference in their ratings of their teaching, research, and service experience. The results of this study indicate a gender bias for both men and women in preference for male job applicants.[36]

A similar finding emerged from a study in a completely different field, that of music performance.[37] This study found that nonblind auditions (those in which the jury could see the applicant) for coveted positions in one of eight symphony orchestras discriminated against women. In most cases, more women were picked once these orchestras shifted away from nonblind auditions, to the use of screens that obscured players' identity from judges (so-called blind auditions), even with the same sample of players. Although this study was in a completely different field, it does provide further support for the suggestion that bias in supposedly objective evaluation processes can occur.

Research has also shown that women working on tasks as part of a team receive less credit than do men, at least in a business context, even for identical work. For tasks that are seen as stereotypically male,[38] if there is ambiguity about the true quality of the woman's contribution to a joint task, the woman's contribution is downplayed. Both male and female judges rated a hypothetical worker's performance worse when they thought the individual was female, even though the description of the task and performance were identical. This study used a business context, but might easily apply to evaluation of team members' contributions to joint projects in other fields, such as lab meetings where ideas for experiments are developed.

Trix and Psenka[39] studied letters of reference written on behalf of job candidates for faculty positions in a medical school. Over 300 letters of recommendation for *successful* candidates for faculty positions were examined. They reported that letters written for female applicants differed from those written for male applicants in terms of length, in the percentages lacking basic features, in the percentages with "doubt-raising" language, and in the frequency of mention of status terms. In addition, the most common possessive phrases for female and male applicants ("her teaching" and "his research") underscored sex stereotypes regarding women as teachers and students versus men as researchers. However, because Trix and Psenka's analysis lacked the critical base-rate data on the number of unsuccessful male and female candidates, causal conclusions cannot be drawn from their analyses. We have no data on the proportions of job applicants who were female/male—for human subject reasons such information was not made available to the researchers. It is possible that proportionately equivalent numbers of women as men were hired, or that even greater numbers of women than men were hired. If either was the case, this would suggest that Trix and Psenka's scheme did not mesh with search committee members' interpretations of the letters or that letters were not given much weight in hiring decisions. Given the fact that the women were hired, one way of interpreting what happened is to say that more women were hired than deserved to be, on the basis of their lesser letters of recommendation. We cannot tell what the correct interpretation is without the missing information.

Amy Budden et al.[40] analyzed publication acceptance rates for women for the journal *Behavioral Ecology*. Their analysis followed the start of blind peer review in which the gender of the author is not known by the reviewers (the author's name on submitted manuscripts is deleted before being sent out to reviewers for appraisal). The authors found that acceptances of female first-authored papers went up 7.9% in the 4 years following the initiation of blind review, compared with the 4 years prior to its onset. Webb et al., however, argued that the increase in women's acceptances was observed in the decade *prior* to blind reviewing, as well as in other journals that never initiated it, thus arguing against Budden et al.'s claim of bias against women scientists.[41]

Finally, although several of the studies just described showed that women can be rated significantly lower than men who perform equally well (often downgraded by female raters as much as by male raters[42]), they did not concern the hiring and promotion process of women in the fields where women are the most underrepresented, the math-intensive STEM fields. This leaves open the hope that such biases are not the cause of women's underrepresentation in those fields—clearly a hope in need of empirical testing. Recent evidence suggests that the promotion process of women in academic science departments is now similar to that of men. Still, as we have noted, far fewer women with PhDs enter the tenure track, perhaps as a result of family responsibilities and career deferral discussed earlier.[43]

So, although we come down on the side that thinks claims of overt discrimination are overblown, we nevertheless recognize that even a tiny degree of discrimination or unconscious barriers can be deleterious for women's progress in the academy. The way that small biases can snowball to derail women can be counterintuitive to those not familiar with multiplicative models. For example, Martell et al.[44] used computer modeling to show how a small initial amount of sex discrimination can translate into a large difference in outcome between men and women over time. They modeled the effect on career progress of small (1% and 5% of variance-sized) differences in work performance ratings of men and women who began at parity. So, starting with a 1% or 5% gap in job ratings between women and men, as the model runs through repeated iterations representing successive promotion rounds, and assuming a pyramidal career structure and tournament model of promotion (individuals

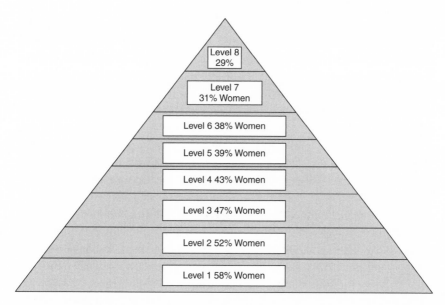

FIGURE **5.6.** Percentage of women at each level for the 5% variance. Source: Adapted from data from Martell, R. F., Lane, D. M., & Emrich, J. (1996). Male-female differences: A computer simulation. *American Psychologist, 51,* 157–158.

must make it through each level to be considered for the next), the proportion of women dropped significantly.

After the eighth round, the percentage of women was reduced to 35% and 29%, for 1% and 5% of variance differences in ratings, respectively, despite starting out with women being at parity. Thus, a very small difference can become magnified over successive rounds (see Figure 5.6). The authors conclude that small biases should therefore not be dismissed as insignificant, because, over time, they can accumulate into quite large consequences.

A Summary and an Analogy of Sorts

To recap, the evidence regarding direct discrimination against women is mixed. Steinpress et al. demonstrated that women are downrated vis-à-vis men with identical CVs, several studies demonstrated that women are downrated in various non-STEM contexts (orchestra, business), and Weneras and Wold argued that women are downrated when they apply for postdoctoral fellowship grants. Running counter to this evidence are studies and analyses suggesting little or no differences between ratings of women and men for grants and jobs. In particular, counter-evidence shows that: a) granting agencies do not appear to discriminate against females; b) certain STEM fields (engineering, physics) hire women as assistant professors on tenure track at rates that actually exceed their proportion among new PhDs; and c) Ginther and Kahn's extensive analyses demonstrating a fairly level playing field as far as hiring and promotion of women in STEM fields is concerned. So, how should we reconcile this inconsistency? Before leaving the allegation that female job and grant applicants are the victims of sexist bias, it might be interesting to consider a non-sexist, although still bias-oriented explanation–the possibility that women are not what is being discriminated against, but rather, mothers, and especially mothers with young children.

Bear in mind the finding that female search committee members downgrade women job applicants as much as male raters downgrade them in Steinpreiss et al.'s study. Thus, it might be argued that basing hiring decisions on the sex of applicant is not rooted in a desire to avoid women per se, but rather that sex is a proxy for other things that both male and female employers believe to be important. We can ask "what might applicant sex be a proxy for?". Does it signal to employers statistical associations between sex and work, such as a concern that a young female applicant might have children which, according to surveys described earlier, will reduce the number of hours she devotes to the job, lower her satisfaction with work, etc.? None of this normative statistical information is, of course, fair to those female applicants who are as careerist and work-centered as their male counterparts. Statistically, however, more women than men reduce their hours at work when they have children. In principle, no one endorses treating applicants as members of groups as opposed to as individuals. However, even though every person deserves to be treated as an individual, independent of their sex, it is understandable how statistical information about work patterns of mothers and fathers can influence employers implicitly, and still not reflect prejudice against women, per se, but rather against mothers. Some may argue that there is no difference in this distinction because both possibilities reflect bias against women. However, we believe there is merit in distinguishing between employers who discriminate on the basis of the sex of an applicant outright, and those who use sex as a proxy for the likelihood that the applicant will be unable to work as many hours or as unidimensionally and dedicatedly as someone with no children. We are currently exploring this hypothesis in a large national study that is a replication and extension of Steinpreiss et al.'s study. Until we know a great deal more about this phenomenon it seems prudent to keep alternative explanations to outright gender discrimination in play, in order to maintain as refined an understanding of the real world as possible.

STEREOTYPE THREAT AND RACIAL DIFFERENCES IN PERFORMANCE

An expanding group of researchers has begun to look at the impact of other subtle aspects of the testing situation, by manipulating the mindset of the test taker with respect to cultural beliefs associated with group membership. The most vigorous area of research in this category is on a phenomenon known as "stereotype threat." Dozens of studies have been published on this topic over the past decade. We reviewed this literature in detail elsewhere[45] and here provide the gist of our prior analysis.

Stanford University professor Claude Steele[46] used the concept of stereotype threat to explore racial and gender differences in mathematics performance. Stereotype threat (ST) encompasses both intrapersonal processes and features of the testing environment. It refers to the added pressure experienced by group members in a situation in which it might be possible to confirm a negative stereotype about them. So, a woman (or a person of color) may worry that, because women (or people of color) tend to do worse on a given type of test, she, too, may do worse—and this type of self-doubt may result in her actually doing worse on the test. The result of this extra burden of worry is lower test performance. Steele[47] theorized that individuals experience a self-evaluative threat in the presence of salient negative stereotypes about their group's intellectual ability. This threat of social devaluation generates anxiety, arousal, or task-irrelevant processing that interferes with intellectual functioning and usurps cognitive resources, leading to decreased test performance in math.[48] Although those who study ST use the more general term "stereotype," these studies actually focus on the status element of stereotypes. They claim that the belief that one category of the characteristic (for example, African Americans, or women) is less competent or capable than another (Caucasians, men) *causes* the threat.

Steele and Aronson's[49] original work showed that African Americans and women are hindered by testing instructions that make their race and gender salient. The instructions could be as simple as asking test takers to check off their race or gender at the start of an exam. As pointed out by Sackett et al.,[50] this work has sometimes been misinterpreted as showing that *removing* ST *removes* group differences in performance in aptitude tests, and thus that ST explains differences in performance. However, Steele and Aronson controlled for prior SAT scores in their analyses, and instead showed that a further difference, on top of that predicted by SAT differences, could be created or eradicated by manipulating ST, not that ST eradicated racial or gender differences.

STEREOTYPE THREAT AND GENDER DIFFERENCES IN PERFORMANCE

Some current scholars attribute the gender gap in mathematics, at least in part, to negative stereotypes that are activated when gender is made salient in the context of an examination.[51] For example, girls who marked the box corresponding to their gender *after* completing the SAT advanced placement (AP) test in calculus scored significantly higher than their counterparts who checked off their gender box at the beginning of the exam—the typical procedure. According to Davies and Spencer,[52] simply having students identify their gender *following* the AP calculus exam (rather than before it) would result in an annual increase of nearly 3,000 girls eligible to begin college with advanced credit for calculus. This is presumably because directing girls' attention to their gender at the start of the exam makes gender salient, and causes anxiety that impedes the girls' performance.

Stricker et al.,[53] however, have argued that the effect is very small and of doubtful practical significance. These researchers tested large numbers of male and female students taking the AP calculus AB exam and a computerized reading assessment. They asked about gender and race either before or after students took the tests. Stricker and Ward[54] concluded: "A clear and consistent finding in these two studies was the general absence of effects of inquiring about ethnicity and gender on performance."[55] Since these two studies were originally published, two additional point-counterpoints have been published. Danaher and Crandall[56] reanalyzed these data using less stringent effects sizes than did Stricker and Ward, and claimed such gender effects are indeed meaningful, with nearly 6% additional girls and 4.7% fewer boys achieving a passing score if gender and race were checked off after the test rather than before. The result would be nearly 4,700 more girls starting college with AP calculus credit. However, all of these claims were disputed by Stricker and Ward[57] in a rejoinder. The issue is far from settled.

A former Cornell colleague in the sociology department, Shelly Correll,[58] yoked the results of an earlier national probability sample of male and female beliefs with those of an experimental study. Her results showed that men in the ST condition who were led to believe they had more math ability (these men were told men perform better than women on the test) overestimated their test performance (they estimated they had scored higher than they actually did) compared to men in the non-ST condition who were not told men are superior. The ST men also believed they needed lower scores in order to pursue coursework and careers in the area than did their female counterparts. Correll demonstrated experimentally that beliefs about gender not only affected test performance, but also led to claims about the likelihood of taking future coursework and striving for careers. In her model, gender-status beliefs led to sex differences in the use of different standards to judge competence in evaluative situations. In such situations, she concluded that "gender differences in self-assessments of task competence will emerge and lead to gender differences in emerging aspirations for career paths and activities that require task competence."[59]

Many researchers have explored how alleviating ST can reduce or abolish female disadvantage on tests of mathematical ability, at least for some groups. Spencer et al.[60] found that in a sample of college students with equivalent math backgrounds, women did as well as men when they were told that the difficult math test they were taking did not show gender differences. However, when they were told that the test did show gender differences, women did worse than men. Interestingly, women also did worse when gender was not mentioned at all, suggesting that "the normal state of affairs is for the situation to be high in ST."[61] Unlike Steele and Aronson's 1995 work, their analyses did not control for prior SAT scores, but compared groups of men and women with similar math backgrounds (those possessing above a moderate threshold for grades, experience, SAT scores, and math self-image, reflected in questions such as, "How important is math for you?"). In addition to the women's scores increasing significantly in the "no gender difference" condition, men's scores decreased slightly (but not significantly) in this condition.

A similar finding regarding lowering of men's scores in the non-ST condition was found by Biek.[62] It is possible that any threat to performance expectations, even without a negative stereotype, may be unnerving for test takers. That is, both men and women may do better or worse depending on the expectations for their group's performance. This is why in a number of studies men actually do worse when there are no instructions given about how men are superior on math tests than when such instructions are given, so it is not only that women do worse when told the test favors men, but men themselves do better under such circumstances, so-called *stereotype lift*. In line with this, using an interesting twist in experimental design, Shih et al.[63] showed that Asian American women could be manipulated to do either better or worse than a control group on a math test by emphasizing a different aspect of their identity: They did better when their Asian identity was primed (because of the stereotype that Asians are better at math) and worse when their female identity was primed (due to the implicit stereotype of math favoring men).

Other studies have also found ST effects. Quinn and Spencer[64] report an unpublished study[65] in which they successfully used priming to manipulate women to perform worse than or equal to men. They primed with TV commercials depicting women behaving either gender stereotypically or counterstereotypically. Using another priming approach, McIntyre et al.[66] erased the ST effect in their study of math performance by priming participants with brief biographies of successful women. For women, reading more biographies produced a larger positive effect. Men's performance did not change. Biek[67] also found a priming effect. In this case ST only led to a performance decrement for girls who were primed as to their self-involvement with mathematics, in a mainstream adolescent population.

As an alternative to priming with external information, Martens et al.[68] investigated what women can do by themselves to counter ST. After establishing an ST effect by labeling the test as a "quantitative examination" on the front cover and including a space for participants to record their gender, they then demonstrated a way to eradicate its effects by self-affirmation. The self-affirmation procedure required participants to write about their most valued characteristic and why it was personally important; they did this before taking the test. In a second study focusing specifically on a mental rotation task, the stereotype of female inferiority was stated up front, and again self-affirmation boosted women's performance. Such self-affirmation did not significantly affect men's performance. The women's score following self-affirmation was between the men's scores with and without self-affirmation; their scores went up a very small amount but did not differ significantly from each other. The authors did not test whether the gender gap following self-affirmation was significant, but from visual inspection of their graph it appears that it was not.

Relatedly, Dar-Nimrod and Heine[69] gave women a Graduate Record Exam-Quantitative (GRE-Q) type of math test preceded by a reading passage that pointed out that there were sex differences in math, but that they were due to environmental causes. These women were able to escape from the deleterious effects of the stereotype, whereas peers who read a similar passage pointing out that sex differences were due to genetic causes were not.

The susceptibility of the ST effect to subtle variations in the testing situation suggests that ST may explain some of the discrepancies found between different kinds of assessment methods. Consider that classroom performance is evaluated in a situation in which girls are familiar with their history of outperforming boys on math tests, getting higher grades. On high-stakes tests such as the SAT and GRE, however, girls and women are tested amidst strangers whose abilities may be unknown to them, and the test contents are not taken from their high school curriculum, but rather are novel. These factors may be important—although they are unlikely to be a catch-all explanation for all instances of lower performance by girls and women in mathematics.

In somewhat related work, Stanford psychology professor Carol Dweck et al.[70] have provided fascinating evidence that the mathematics gap that begins to emerge in junior high school can be closed by carefully scripting the implicit messages that girls are sent.[71] Dweck's demonstrations have the advantage of taking into account any differences in mathematical scores that existed before the start of the interventions, thus excluding alternative explanations. In one of her studies, she and her colleagues followed female students at Columbia University through their calculus course.[72] At the beginning of the semester, they ascertained whether students saw math ability as an innate gift, or whether they saw it as something that could be developed through learning. Throughout the semester, students were asked about whether they experienced gender stereotyping in their math class and about their sense of belonging in math—whether they felt accepted, respected, and comfortable.

Although it turned out that many female students believed stereotyping was evident in their calculus section, this had little impact on grades for women who viewed their math ability as something that could be developed through learning. In contrast, feeling surrounded by a negative stereotype had a strong impact on women who thought of their math ability as an innate gift. Over the course of the semester, their sense of belonging declined. They no longer felt accepted and comfortable in their math environment, and as a result, many said that they did not intend to pursue math in the future. This is a short-term longitudinal[73] unfolding of what Correll[74] demonstrated experimentally in a single session—that women experiencing ST underestimated their math ability and overestimated how high it would need to be for them to pursue additional coursework or careers in the area.

The foregoing shows that belief in math as a gift can not only make women vulnerable to declining performance, but also make them susceptible to stereotypes, so that when they enter an environment that they feel denigrates their level of the gift, they may lose the desire to carry on in that field. As Carol Dweck[75] put it: "In this way, we were seeing highly able women drop before our eyes—women at an elite university who began the semester with high interest in math, and who could well have had major careers in math or science."[76] One caution seems worth mentioning: In the absence of random assignment of women to gift versus learning inductions, it is possible that preexisting differences in mathematics aptitude caused the effect. Perhaps women weaker in calculus aptitude were more prone to regard their limitations as innate, hence the flip side of "gift." As the course became more difficult for them, they fell back on their sense of having limited ability, no matter how hard they tried. The pre-experimental control of mathematics scores might have been a weak measure of calculus aptitude that may not have tapped into the actual calculus ability that success in the course required. To whatever degree this concern is valid, however, the aforementioned study by Dar-Nimrod and Heine demonstrates that female students' vulnerability to the ST effect is not invariably due to preexisting differences in math ability.

After demonstrating that ST can change performance, the next step is to explore how this happens. In the work of Dweck et al., the impact of ST was most apparent when the problems were confusing or difficult. Under such circumstances, bright women became especially hampered. Spencer et al.[77]

and others also found that the effect only applied to challenging problems that stretched the limits of participants' abilities. Easy problems showed no ST effect. Quinn and Spencer[78] explored the mechanism by which ST damages female performance, and found that reducing ST made women more able to formulate problem-solving strategies. The authors suggest that, "Taking the SAT is a tense, sometimes frustrating experience for both of them [boy and girl]. However, as the girl is taking the test she has an extra worry to contend with that the boy does not: A stereotype that she, as a girl, has inferior math skills,"[79] and "the additional anxiety and diminished cognitive capacity associated with ST interferes with their ability to strategize, a process that takes focused concentration and attentional resources."[80]

Quinn and Spencer used Gallagher and DeLisi's 1994 protocols, but added an ST manipulation—a single line addition to the instructions, stating that men and women performed equally well on these problems. Although the interaction found between gender and condition was only marginally significant for the number of correct answers, a significant interaction effect was found for the inability to formulate a strategy. This finding suggests that this may be part of the mechanism by which stereotype threat causes women to underperform on these kinds of less straightforward, challenging math tests. In their 1974 landmark volume, Maccoby and Jacklin put forward an explanation that has to do with anxiety and the Yerke-Dodson law, which postulates that performance is best on items of intermediate difficulty—because the easiest items are not challenging enough to exert focused attention, and the most difficult items lead to anxiety that interferes with test-taking strategies.

Evidence to support the hypothesis that women are more insecure about their mathematical ability, and thus more subject to ST, comes from many studies.[81] Oakes describes a sequence of events in which girls are more likely to attribute their difficulty to their own inadequacies, while comparable boys attribute their problems to the inherent difficulty of the course or to poor instruction. So although boys and girls are equally motivated to succeed, girls are less confident and give up more easily.

Murphy et al.[82] have provided intriguing evidence suggesting that even successful female science and math majors at Stanford University feel uncomfortable when asked to join events in which they are outnumbered by males. They showed videos of a fake science leadership conference to 47 Stanford undergraduate math and science majors, half of whom were women. Half of these men and women saw scenes in the video that contained an equal number of men and women, and half saw one with women outnumbered 3:1. They were told the video was going to be used to recruit for the leadership conference at Stanford the following summer and were asked to indicate how likely they would be to attend it. Students watched the video with electrodes attached to their fingers and chests to monitor their physiological responses. Women and men who saw equal numbers of each sex responded to it alike, as did men who saw the version in which men outnumbered women.

But the women who watched the version in which women were outnumbered 3:1 in the video had faster heartbeats, higher blood pressure, and more sweating. They also remembered more details about the video's physical surroundings and scientific paraphernalia (like a Periodic Table chart on the wall, and issues of the journal *Nature* on the table), which the researchers interpreted reflected their enhanced vigilance and anxiety about their environment. Later these women who watched the 3:1 asymmetric video said they felt intimidated and discouraged from participating in the conference. Even competent women felt anxious and threatened when in the minority.

Lingering Questions About ST

Many of the ST studies have targeted mathematically superior samples. This is because it is the mathematically superior group that is hypothesized to suffer most from gender stereotypes, since they care more about how they perform on such tests than do people with average math ability. This may seem counterintuitive in the sense that the very women who are most math identified and feel that math is important for them are the ones who suffer most from implicit stereotypes about math being a male domain. As Quinn and Spencer[83] state: "It is those girls and women who are the very best at math that may be most affected by stereotype threat while taking a difficult math test."[84] However, Cullen et al.[85] question this argument, pointing to evidence that underperformance of women on aptitude tests, relative to their performance on course grades, is not larger for higher-scoring women, and also questioning whether ST occurs in the real world, as opposed to only under laboratory conditions. They analyzed the relationship between SAT-M scores and English class grades for a sample of over 20,000 female college freshmen, and found a linear trend showing equivalent effects for all ability levels. And under some circumstances, other researchers have also found an ST effect with less selective samples, including less mathematically able and less mathematically identified groups.[86]

Recently, Walton and Spencer[87] demonstrated that women (and ethnic minorities) actually perform worse than expected on the prior measures correlated with performance on the stereotyped task performance, usually items from the SAT-M: Their argument is that in addition to the explicit presence of the stereotype undermining female and minority performance at the time of the experiment, the measures of their prior ability in real-world contexts also are underestimates of their true ability. These researchers contend that stereotypes are implicit in many situations and depress female and minority performance in the real world so much that when adjusted to truly equate on prior ability, women do math as well as men. They estimate in their meta-analyses that the "SAT-Math test underestimates the math ability of women like those in the present sample by 19–21 points." (p. 15) They detected this level of underestimation at all levels—among low, average, and high scorers. If true, then does this imply that all prior demonstrations of sex differences in math and spatial ability are bogus—the result of biased measures that under-predict how well girls and women are capable of doing? This is probably not an implication that Walton and Spencer would endorse, given that some of the sex differences are found among infants, long before the awareness of stereo-types. It will be interesting to examine their argument with more extensive samples, including young minority children living in segregated communities who may not harbor negative stereotypes.

ST findings may also be subject to a cohort effect due to changes in preva-lence of gender stereotypic beliefs. For example, Biek[88] found that, in an young adolescent group, the majority of boys and girls did not exhibit aware-ness of the "girls are bad at math" stereotype, and Martens et al.[89] found that a quarter of women and half of men in an undergraduate sample either were not aware of or could not articulate a clear understanding of this stereotype. If awareness of the stereotype is necessary to create a performance decre-ment in a threat situation, this source of performance differences between the sexes may be becoming less prevalent. Because the relevant analysis has not been conducted, it is not possible to know for sure whether the effect size has diminished over time. One caveat, however, deserves mention: Perhaps Biek did not find awareness of the stereotype among the adolescents in his sample because sex differences in math do not emerge until junior and senior high school, and his subjects were not yet this old. Perhaps if he follows them he will detect a stereotype awareness as they get older and girls' math perfor-mance begins to be eclipsed by boys'. (The Biek data were a small part of the Walton and Spencer meta-analyses.) As for the Martens et al. finding, even if a quarter of the women were unable to articulate awareness of the stereotype, this still leaves plenty of ones who are aware to result in group differences. We mention these caveats not because we doubt that the "males are better at math" stereotype is fading among today's students, but simply to alert readers to some possible complications that need to be addressed in future research before we can be confident about these claims.

These ST studies do not imply that all male–female differences in mathe-matical performance can be eradicated in the entire population by ST-related changes. However, they do suggest that these factors may undermine the per-formance of some women, including those who are mathematically gifted, and cause them to score lower than their capabilities would suggest on some sorts of tests. ST may be less useful in explaining the dearth of women at the top of STEM professions than in explaining why women underperform on certain kinds of challenging problems on aptitude tests such as the SAT-M, compared to their performance on other less stressful assessments. Given that female performance in high school mathematics now matches that of boys', and high school girls now take and pass as many advanced courses in mathematics and science as do male high school students—and further, given that the sex asymmetry at the extreme right tail of the math distribution has been diminishing—it is difficult to know why girls still underperform boys in the non-ST conditions,[90] or why confusing or complex problems take a greater toll on their performance. At what point should we expect gender stereotypes to fade? Or have they already, as hinted at by Biek,[91] Martens et al.,[92] and others?

Finally, a series of questions needs to be addressed before we can know the mechanisms involved in ST studies, a precondition to designing interventions to boost female math performance on high-stakes tests. Martens et al.[93] hypothesized about the mediating psychological factors that are responsible for ST (cognitive load, working memory capacity, arousal, anxiety, suppression, and so forth):

> The negative effects on performance produced by stereotype threat stem first and foremost from a threat to one's self-integrity. For example, perhaps self-affirmation, by securing the self, eases a need to push away and suppress negative stereotype-relevant thoughts (Spencer, 2003), which in turn frees cognitive resources such as working memory capabilities (Schmader & Johns, 2003) to allow for improved performance.[94]

And Correll[95] has provided some data on possible mechanisms, contrasting different theories (human capital, status characteristics, and so forth). But clearly, much more research is needed to explain why in some studies the non-ST condition leads to lower male performance along with elevated female performance, and in other studies the group advantaged by the stereotype gets a boost over its non-ST level, something like a ST bonus.[96] And more work is needed to understand why in some studies ST reduced working memory and vigilance, while in others, such as Murphy et al.'s, it actually increased women's vigilance and memory for items in the environment.

Along these lines, in which countries would one expect to find the largest ST effect? If cultural beliefs about male superiority are responsible for the ST effect, then male overrepresentation in math and science ought to be greater in countries not known for their egalitarian gender beliefs, such as Turkey and Korea, as compared to the United States and the United Kingdom. However, there are proportionately twice as many female computer scientists in Turkey as in the United States.[97] It would be interesting to examine ST in the Organization for Economic Cooperation and Development (OECD) countries that were examined by Guiso et al.[98] These researchers found very large international differences in 15-year-olds' math scores, ranging from a male superiority of 22.6 points to mean female superiority of 14.5 points (in Iceland). They reported that a country's endorsement of egalitarian views about gender (for example, refusing to give scarce jobs to men over women simply because they are men) was a powerful predictor of the sex gap in math. Are the less egalitarian countries the ones where ST is most prevalent? Are women more threatened by testing situations when they were raised in a society that considers women to be second class? Work by the University of California sociologist Andrew Penner that we described in the previous chapter raises doubts about this mechanism, as does the work of sociologists Karen Bradley and Maria Charles that we describe in a subsequent chapter.

Further, it is not clear why the baseline non-ST self-assessment of mathematics ability appears to be males' perceptions, as opposed to females' perceptions. When asked how well they would need to score on a test in order to pursue later coursework and careers in that area, males and females in the non-ST condition report similar levels of test performance needed to convince them to pursue further coursework and careers. And males in the ST condition report essentially the same level of test performance would be needed. The sole group that reports they would need to score much higher is females in the ST condition.[99] So being exposed to experimental feedback about alleged male superiority in a field does not lead males to *underestimate* how well they would need to do on a test in order to pursue future coursework or careers in that area, any more than it does males and females who were not exposed to such feedback, but it does lead females to *overestimate* the scores that they would need. Females may be more cautious overall, which an old literature often reported, and this may be a factor though there is no direct test of this hypothesis. However, in Linn and Petersen's 1985 meta-analysis of mental rotation, they opined that one possible basis for sex differences is greater cautiousness of women, resulting in their reviewing their choices, double-checking their mental transformations before selecting an answer, and so on. And it would be of interest to provide females with ST instructions that advantage females (not simply neutral messages about the test not being associated with gender differences, but affirmative messages that claim female superiority). Would this lead to males test performance plummeting below that of their peers in the non-ST condition, or would their developmental histories inure them from ST? Would males exhibit ST if the domain was reading comprehension, or some other area of female superiority?

Finally, let us consider the finding that females experience a self-evaluative threat in the presence of implicit negative stereotypes about their group's intellectual ability—often it is enough merely to ask test takers to check off their gender at the beginning of an exam, which in turn results in anxiety that interferes with performance and reduces female scores. Walton and Spencer suggest that even the absence of information about the test—merely saying it is a test of math or reading—is sufficient to activate negative stereotype awareness. The big question is: Why hasn't this same mechanism resulted in females learning less math than males? If a girl taking the SAT-M "has an extra worry to contend with that the boy does not: A stereotype that she, as a girl, has inferior math skills . . . [and] the additional anxiety and diminished cognitive capacity associated with stereotype threat interferes with their ability to strategize, a process that takes focused concentration and attentional resources,"[100] then why does this same anxiety and the resultant diminished cognitive capacity not lead to less math learning in middle school, when gender stereotypes are alleged to kick in? And why do girls and women surmount such stereotypes to the point at which they not only match boys and men on the number of advanced math courses they take, but also actually get better grades in them? Assuming that students are aware of gender stereotypes about math and spatial cognition, would girls attending all-girl schools be expected to be less affected by such stereotypes? Would same-sex testing sessions reduce the effect, as suggested by some?[101]

The lack of females in the topmost percentiles of the SAT-M and GRE-Q scores may not mean that women are innately less able to do difficult math; rather, girls and women may be less able to do difficult math tests or to do math under conditions of confusion when a male superiority stereotype is implicit. More work with extreme right-tail populations is necessary to assess the magnitude and robustness of the ST effect relative to the large magnitude of the sex difference at that level on these kinds of tests.

SOCIAL–BIOLOGICAL INTERACTIONS

Many researchers endorse what some refer to as a "biopsychosocial" view of sex differences. According to this account, the role of biological factors is enmeshed with the influence of social forces at every step, in an iterative unfolding that is more complex than "main-effects" biological models suggest.[102] This view is similar to Dickens and Flynn's[103] multiplicative account of intellectual development in which small, genetically driven differences in ability or preferences early in development can snowball into large differences in performance through genes eliciting different environmentally controlled experiences.[104]

An example of the biopsychosocial perspective is Casey and Brabeck's 1990 demonstration that the spatial skills of females with non–right-handed relatives benefit more from spatially relevant experiences as compared to females whose relatives are right-handed. This finding illustrates the interaction of biological and experiential variables in the development of spatial skills. Casey et al.[105] hypothesized that genes affect brain organization, which is reflected in handedness, and thus are reflected in children's ability to capitalize on spatial experiences to develop their spatial skills. According to this hypothesis, the hemispheric brain organization of girls from all-right-handed families is relatively poor for developing spatial skills. One source of spatial experiences is playing with male siblings, who typically engage in more spatial play. According to the authors, their results show that "Children from all right-handed families do not appear to be able to use their spatial experience with male siblings to increase their spatial skills."[106] However, this interpretation is complicated by the finding that girls from all-right-handed families who did not have brothers did just as well as girls from mixed-handedness families who did have brothers. The conclusions regarding the effect of handedness (and hence genes) on spatial skills are unclear from these intriguing findings.

Some of the evidence used as support for the role of biology in sex differences has been explained in less emphatically biological terms by researchers with more of a sociocultural bent.[107] For example, in a recent collection of chapters on sex differences,[108] the various hormone researchers (Kimura, Hines, Berenbaum, and Resnick) expressed very different opinions about the causal role of hormones. Berenbaum and Resnick,[109] for example, studied girls with the condition congenital adrenal hyperplasia, or CAH. These CAH girls have greater than normal prenatal exposure to male hormones. The authors argued that differences between girls with and without CAH might be due to factors besides androgen. Berenbaum and Resnick state that CAH girls' sex-atypical behavior and superior spatial ability could be a result of their parents treating them like boys because of their masculinized external genitals, as well as others reacting to their growing competence at participating in stereotypically male activities. However, Puts et al.[110] note that genitals are often surgically repaired and CAH girls often show feminine characteristics. These facts undermine social explanations for the CAH girls' superior spatial abilities.

In closing, the claims for outright discrimination in mentoring, hiring, awarding of grants, and pay seem exaggerated as explanations for the underrepresentation of women in math-intensive fields. The best available modern evidence is that of the economists Donna Ginther and Shulamit Kahn[111] and it suggests that biases, to the extent that they exist, are small, and sometimes favor men over women (at the full professor level) and sometimes favor women over men. Granted there are some troublesome areas where women may continue to face discrimination, but they cannot reasonably be viewed as a major reason fewer women decide to enter STEM fields that are math intensive. This is because decisions about entering a STEM field are made by girls at a fairly young age, long before they know anything about the pay and rank of women in the math-intensive sciences. Even if full professor women are earning slightly less than male full professors, which some data indicate is the case, the differential is small and not something that young girls would know about when deciding on a science career. And women studying at college would be exposed to younger women faculty who do not earn less than male faculty, and sometimes earn more. (Our oldest daughter who earned a graduate degree in engineering had exposure to several younger female faculty members who worked in the same area, and our sense is that she perceived no status differentials between these women and their male peers.) Similarly, stereotype threat probably explains a small part of the dearth of women in math-intensive fields, given the magnitudes of the typical effect size found in studies ($d \sim 0.2$) and the myriad lingering questions, such as why men do not develop feelings of inferiority given years of witnessing women's superior grades. To explain the bulk of the underrepresentation of women in these fields requires moving beyond biases and threats. We do this in a later chapter when we discuss the role of preferences and choices—both freely made and coerced—but first we review some fascinating evidence that calls into question claims about ineluctable male superiority in mathematics.

Background and trend data

"Any woman who has a career and a family automatically develops something in the way of two personalities, like two sides of a dollar bill, each different in design. . . . Her problem is to keep one from draining the life from the other."

—Ivy Baker Priest

In this chapter and the following one, we delve into further evidence that calls into question the primacy of biology in explaining sex differences in STEM career success. None of this evidence is perfect, and some of it resembles "anecdata" rather than scientific data. But, taken as a whole, this body of evidence raises doubts about the role of biology as *the* major cause, or even perhaps as an important secondary cause, of the paucity of women in STEM careers. Our sense from reading this large literature, and integrating it with the studies described in previous chapters, is that biology is best viewed as one of many factors that collectively contribute to sex differences, although not nearly as significantly as some non-biological factors we describe in Chapter 8. We have organized the current biological evidence into the following categories: changes across historical time, chronological age, cohort, country of origin, and demographic characteristics (ethnicity, race, and social class). In this chapter we discuss cohort comparisons, which are comparisons over time. Then, in Chapter 7, we discuss comparisons across societies, cultures, and developmental stages.

HISTORICAL TRENDS

As was mentioned in Chapter 4, in 1995, Larry Hedges and Amy Nowell published an analysis of sex differences in cognitive abilities. Because of the prominence of the journal in which it appeared (*Science*), it soon was viewed as *the* authoritative source on sex differences in achievement, one of the most highly cited articles on this topic (cited nearly 300 times in published scientific articles, according to Google Scholar).

In their article, Hedges and Nowell examined six studies, each of which was based on a national probability sample of adolescents and young adults, and each of which was published during the three decades preceding the publication of their article. They found that the distribution of test scores for boys and girls differed substantially. The differences were especially large at the tails of the distributions—the top and bottom 5%, and 10%, as seen in Table 6.1 (we discussed this point earlier in Chapter 1).

When the data in this table are disaggregated, we find that boys excelled over girls in science, math, spatial reasoning, and social studies, as well as

TABLE **6.1.** Distribution of Male and Female Test Scores in Six National Probability Samples.

MATHEMATICS ASSESSMENT	LOWEST-SCORING 10% MALE–FEMALE RATIO	HIGHEST-SCORING 10% MALE–FEMALE RATIO	HIGHEST-SCORING 5% MALE–FEMALE RATIO
Project talent	1.00	1.33	1.50
NLS-72	0.72	1.76	2.34
NLSY: AR	1.84	1.90	2.20
NLSY: MK	0.99	1.7	1.9
HS&B	0.77	1.67	2.06
NELS:88	0.97	1.34	1.64

The data in this table are represented as a ratio of boys to girls. For example, a ratio of 1.00 means that there is an equal number of boys and girls; a ratio of 1.5 indicates that there are three boys for every two girls.

NLS-72 = National Longitudinal Study of the high school class of 1972; NLSY: AR = National Longitudinal Study of Youth Arithmetic; NLSY: MK = National Longitudinal Study of Youth Mathematics Knowledge; NELS: 88 = National Educational Longitudinal Study of the 8th Grade Class of 1988; HS&B = High School and Beyond, 198: A longitudinal survey of students in the United States. *Source*: Adapted from Hedges, L. V., & Nowell, A. (1995). Sex differences in mental test scores, variability, and numbers of high-scoring individuals. *Science, 269*, 41–45.

in various mechanical skills (and that boys also predominated at the lower left tail on these same measures). Girls excelled over boys in verbal abilities, associative memory performance (the type of memory task in which you are provided word pairs and later given one of the words and asked to supply the word paired with it), and perceptual speed. Despite the rather modest differences at the center of the distribution (the means for boys and girls were often quite similar), the greater variability of the male scores resulted in large asymmetries at the tails of the distribution, as anticipated from arguments in prior chapters. The hypothesis that small mean differences favoring boys, coupled with a larger standard deviation (the greater dispersion of scores or greater variability) for boys for some traits such as mathematics performance, was proposed as early as the nineteenth century. It was used to explain why there were allegedly more male than female geniuses and, at the same time, more males than females among the mentally retarded. As the renowned gender researcher from the University of Wisconsin, Janet Shibley Hyde[1] has pointed out, greater male variability on the order of 0.1–0.2 standard deviations could mathematically lead to a large gender ratio favoring males in the extreme right tail of the distribution. Having said this, it is worth noting that male variability is not always greater than female, as Penner[2] has demonstrated, though in our estimation it is usually greater by around 10%–20%.

As one of Hedges and Nowell's more dramatic findings, consider that despite finding only very small differences at the average or midpoint of the distribution, and moderate differences among the top 5% of scorers (1.5:1 to 2.3:1 ratios), they estimated that *boys outnumbered girls by a ratio of 7 to 1 in the top 1% on tests of mathematics and spatial reasoning*. Hedges and Nowell concluded their analysis:

> The sex differences in mathematics and science scores...are of concern because ability and achievement in science and mathematics may be necessary to excel in scientific and technical occupations. Small mean differences combined with modest differences in variance can have a surprisingly large effect on the number of individuals who excel.... The achievement of fair representation of women in science will be much more difficult if there are only one-half to one-seventh as many women as men who excel in the relevant abilities.[3]

In the aftermath of Hedges and Nowell's[4] article, there were no strident outcries and only a few criticisms, mostly concerning the implications of the findings. By and large, their findings and interpretations were not contested because they were consistent with those of other studies that had not been based on national probability samples. As noted in the last chapter, Camilla Benbow,[5] one of the seminal and highly respected researchers of high mathematical ability, and her colleagues had reported male-to-female ratios among the top 0.01% of adolescents (1 in 10,000) on the Scholastic Assessment Test-Mathematics (SAT-M) of approximately 10 to 1 or even 13 to 1. Also, in Julian Stanley's seminal work with 450 Baltimore 12- to 14-year-olds, who were recommended by their science and math teachers to a gifted program at Johns Hopkins (the Study of Mathematically Precocious Youth, or SMPY), the highest-scoring girl's score was surpassed by 43 boys.[6] Benbow and Stanley[7] concluded, "We favor the hypothesis that sex differences in achievement in and attitude towards mathematics result from superior male ability, which may in turn be related to greater male ability in spatial tasks. This male superiority is probably an expression of a combination of both endogenous and exogenous variables. We recognize, however, that our data are consistent with numerous alternative hypotheses."[8]

Hedges and Nowell's findings fit with what was believed by many to be the true state of sex differences, and therefore caused little controversy—that is, until January 14, 2005, when former Harvard president Lawrence Summers, speaking at a meeting of the National Bureau of Economic Research (NBER), commented that on aggregate, more men than women perform at the highest levels in math and science: "If you do that calculation—and I have no reason to think that it couldn't be refined in a hundred ways—you get five to one, at the high end," remarked Summers. Given that his off-the-cuff estimate of a 5-to-1 ratio at the right tail of the distribution was not out of line with some older published studies such as Hedges and Nowell's, or with studies that preceded it (though recent studies indicate that the gap has narrowed to closer to 3 to 1 at the extreme right tail of the math distribution, 0.01%), one can only surmise why his remarks caused a national stir, while previously published analyses had not. Although there may be many answers, one that seems evident is that his remark suggested that the reason women are underrepresented at the right tail is because they are cognitively deficient. This got people's attention. Respected sex-differences researcher and past president of the 150,000 member strong American Psychological Association Diane Halpern commented: "Is the under-representation of women in the sciences and math caused by sex differences in cognitive abilities? Of course, the real question is not neutral—it is about a presumed deficiency in women—are there too few women with the cognitive abilities that are needed for careers in science and math?"[9]

In his comments, Summers mentioned "three broad hypotheses about the sources of the very substantial disparities . . . with respect to the presence of women in high-end scientific professions." The first hypothesis was something he referred to as the "high-powered job hypothesis," which we have discussed in detail in Chapter 2; the second was the central issue of the present chapter, namely, "the differential aptitude at the high end"; and the third issue had to do with different socialization experiences and patterns of discrimination. Summers stated that "in my own view, their importance probably ranks in exactly the order that I just described." So it would appear that he relegated differential cognitive aptitude to secondary status. However, the first hypothesis pertained to the underrepresentation of women in high-powered careers in non-STEM fields such as law and business, where he felt women opted for family over career. As for the underrepresentation of women in mathematically intensive fields, Summers believed it was due in large part to differential aptitude, though some of the first hypothesis was also probably involved, he felt.

Many scholars have opined that the dearth of women in STEM fields is less likely to be the result of factors external to women—such as institutional discrimination, negative stereotypes about women's ability, biased promotion practices, or early socialization factors—and more likely to be due to cognitive ability differences. When Summers offered his analysis, he acknowledged the role of personal needs of young female faculty (singling out childbearing/childcare as an obvious example), which tend to be poorly aligned with institutional promotion schedules. He also noted women's reluctance to sacrifice family life for careers, or women-unfriendly institutional policies and even stereotypes, as additional factors that could account for some, though not most, of the gender gap in STEM fields. According to a transcript of Summers's remarks at the NBER, he stated:

> To what extent is there overt discrimination? Surely there is some. Much more tellingly, to what extent are there pervasive patterns of passive discrimination and stereotyping in which people like to choose people like themselves, and the people in the previous group are disproportionately white male, and so they choose people who are like themselves, who are disproportionately white male? No one who's been in a university department or who has been involved in personnel processes can deny that this kind of taste does go on, and it is something that happens, and it is something that absolutely, vigorously needs to be combated. On the other hand, I think before regarding it as pervasive, and as the dominant explanation of the patterns we observe, there are two points that should make one hesitate.

(He proceeded to outline two alternative accounts.)

Probably the single utterance that most fanned the flames of controversy surrounding his comments was Summers's assertion that behavioral genetic studies over the past 15 years have shown that many of the differences in other areas that were once thought to be environmental are now known to have substantial biological underpinnings:

> Most of what we've learned from empirical psychology in the last fifteen years has been that people naturally attribute things to socialization that are in fact not attributable to socialization. We've been astounded by the results of separated twins studies. The confident assertions that autism was a reflection of parental characteristics that were absolutely supported and that people knew from years of observational

evidence have now been proven to be wrong. And so, the human mind has a tendency to grab to the socialization hypothesis when you can see it, and it often turns out not to be true.[10]

The debate surrounding Summers's comments has sometimes been glib and directionless and overwhelmingly underinformed by scientific evidence. And some of his supporters and critics do not appear to have read his actual remarks, relying instead on inaccurate, incomplete, or out-of-context media accounts. As we have tried to demonstrate earlier in this book, compelling evidence can be recruited by Summers' supporters for a biological basis of sex differences—but, as we also demonstrated, equally compelling evidence can be mustered to argue the opposite.

Our scientific stance is that both sides should be permitted to voice their position and present their evidence without fear of censure or job termination. Let the peer-review process and books like this one sift their arguments and, together with other research integrations, build a consensus over time. The alternative is to anoint one side in the debate as the winner, shut down discussion, and condemn the other side, leading to one-party science and ultimately to arrested progress. No one should have the hubris to imagine they know all the answers to the puzzle of women's underrepresentation in math-intensive fields, and therefore advocate that those who harbor alternative views be muzzled on grounds that allowing them to voice their data and arguments may harm women. As we noted earlier, Jean-Jaques Rousseau (1762) argued that atheists should be forbidden from expressing their views for just such a reason—that the masses hearing them could be harmed from crossing the bridge into heaven. Although that harm seemed realistic in his time, from today's perspective it certainly does not. One wonders whether the potential harm to girls and women that some see in Summers's comments will seem equally unrealistic to future generations. Perhaps broadcasting doubts about their math ability damages girls' and women's self-concepts and reduces their motivation to work in math-intensive fields. However, as the parents of three daughters, we believe this is a price society must be willing to endure, because the alternative—silencing those who dare to espouse views that call into question gender equivalence—will ultimately damage scientific progress, destroy morale, and make us forget the justification for our own views. Despite our own conclusion of sociocultural rather than biological primacy, we believe that the truth should matter, and this requires open debate until such time that there is a consensus.[11] But this is not the same as endorsing reckless or hateful language or the political application of shoddy or premature research on sex differences. Here we believe stringent checks and balances need to be in place to minimize harm. However, when you read the scientific studies on sex differences, it is hard to make a case that they contain hate speech or leads to political applications. Most of them are highly technical and cautiously worded. It would be a shame to muzzle these researchers even though we disagree with them. Refuting them has led to major progress in our understanding of the nature and extent of sex differences, and more breakthroughs in understanding will occur if we do not shut down debate on this topic before a strong consensus exists.

COHORT ISSUES

With the exception of work by a handful of sex-differences researchers— specifically, meta-analyses[12] and career studies[13]—researchers of sex differences in mathematical and spatial aptitude have overlooked so-called cohort issues. That is, are we trying to explain gender differences among those already at the peak of their careers, who were born in the 1940s and 1950s, or among those currently in the career pipeline, who as children grew up in a presumably more egalitarian world of the 1970s and 1980s? And if there are differences between these groups, can they be explained by anything other than sociocultural factors? These questions are important, not least because substantial data upon which conclusions often have been drawn about male– female differences in math ability are very old—principally from women who were in high school in the early 1960s. One wonders whether they still apply.

For example, some of the most striking findings discussed by Hedges and Nowell in their 1995 *Science* article are based on data from Project Talent, a study of children born around the end of World War II, who are now entering their mid-60s to early 70s. These individuals grew up in a world quite different from the one experienced by our own three daughters, who were born in the 1980s and 1990s. Similarly, the seminal SMPY data[14] are also quite old. Would the same results be found with today's children, who did not have to swim against the tide of sex biases and lack of female role models? After all, it wasn't until the late 1970s that Harvard/Radcliffe admitted men and women on an equal-access basis, and yet today half of all undergraduates are female at this elite institution.[15] Similarly, the University of Cambridge did not start admitting women to any of its traditionally all-male undergraduate colleges until 1972 (although women had been granted official membership of the university in 1947 and admitted to two women-only colleges with partial university rights prior to that). The proportion of women undergraduates at Cambridge has steadily risen from 11% in 1968–69 to 49% in 2004–05,[16] and it is probably over 50% by now.

In her support of an innate biological basis of sex differences, the venerable hormone researcher Doreen Kimura[17] argued that sex differences in cognitive ability are "mostly unchanged in magnitude over the past three or four decades, a period in which women's roles and access to higher education have changed substantially (Feingold, 1996; Kimura, 2002)."[18] If correct, then there would be one less environmental source of difference between men and women. However, there is some important evidence that goes against this claim: Throughout the second half of the twentieth century, spatial ability has increased faster than the gene pool can be expected to have changed. Consider that Flynn has repeatedly shown that so-called "fluid" intellectual abilities, of which those having to do with spatial skills are among the most prominent, have grown faster than all other abilities.[19] The *Raven Progressive Matrices*, a visual-spatial reasoning test, shows the largest increases over the last six decades—over twice as large as the increases for nonspatial abilities such as vocabulary and verbal reasoning. And if we examine the subtests of the major intelligence tests such as the Wechsler series, we find that three of the five subtests associated with the largest increases over the past half century entail spatial reasoning (*Block Design, Picture Arrangement*, and *Object Assembly*). Performance on each of these has escalated dramatically since 1947, often by over 1.5 standard deviations. If spatial ability is under genetic control, as implied by Kimura et al., it seems unlikely that such enormous gains could have occurred over such a brief period. In fact, Flynn presents evidence from some countries that spatial ability has escalated within the lifetime of individuals, thus ruling out genes as a cause.

Among the complexities of gender differences in cognitive abilities is the issue of what to call the abilities themselves. *Block Design* on the Wechsler series of intelligence tests is a block-building task entailing an aspect of mental rotation. It is the task that is associated with the largest sex differences, and it has been linked to mathematical differences. The *Raven Progressive Matrices* involves presenting increasingly complex visual arrays with sections missing. The challenge is to select the missing swatch from among the various choices offered, a type of visual multiple-choice reasoning test that requires holding in working memory changes along two dimensions. To an outsider, the *Raven* appears to be a measure of spatial reasoning. However, psychometric researchers consider it to be primarily a measure of general intelligence (g), and only secondarily a test of spatial visualization.[20] The same is true of other measures that have been invoked in the debate over sex differences in cognitive abilities.

The reason we find this interesting is that, although 25 years ago women performed worse than men on tests such as the *Raven*, they now appear to perform equivalently to men. If the *Raven Progressive Matrices* is mainly a measure of general intelligence and only secondarily a measure of spatial visualization, then this can be explained in terms of the Flynn effect at work for women, long after men have reached a point at which the Flynn effect reached its asymptote. The Flynn effect refers to the steady upward creep in intellectual performance over time that comes about as a consequence of better environments—including schooling, nutrition, educational television, and so on. Children today routinely answer many more questions correctly on IQ tests than did their parents, and still more than their grandparents. Flynn has shown that every year is associated with a 0.3-point gain on IQ tests, although this gain is masked when the test gets renormed every 15 years or so. So, over 50 years, the average gain in IQ, if it was not masked by renorming, would be 15 points; over a century, the gain would be 30 IQ points. If, on the other hand, the *Raven Progressive Matrices* really does tap spatial ability, then women's improvement would constitute evidence that women are as good as men on the type of spatial skills tapped by this type of test. But all of this is theoretical. Fortunately, we have much more concrete cohort evidence to inform the debate.

One such bit of concrete evidence for cohort differences in math and science was presented by Shayer et al. in 2007. They analyzed sex differences on the Science Reasoning Test II Volume & Heaviness (SRT II).[21] This subtest has been used since the 1970s throughout Britain. In Table 6.2, Shayer et al.' findings illustrate three points: *(1)* in 1975 there was a male superiority of 0.54 (0.5 effect size) in the mean scores on the test; *(2)* this male advantage had disappeared by 2004; and *(3)* although both boys and girls displayed decreases in their scores over time, the relative decrease has been greatest for boys. Shayer et al. also examined the extreme right tail of the distribution. These British researchers found substantial changes over time in average scores, but the change at the extreme right tail was much larger. Virtually no children in 2003 scored in the top 10% of the range by 1976 standards. This impressive decline calls into question Doreen Kimura's assertion that sex differences in cognitive ability are "mostly unchanged in magnitude over the past three or four decades." Instead, during this period of change in society's attitudes about women's roles and their access to higher education, there have in fact

TABLE **6.2.** Means and Effect Sizes of Change on Volume and Heaviness Test of British Students From 1975 Onward.

YEAR	**Mean level**		**Effect size *(SD)* of drop**		B/G DIFFERENCE
	BOYS	GIRLS	BOYS	GIRLS	
1975–76	**5.42**	**4.88**	—	—	**0.5**
2000–01	4.59	4.45	0.76	0.39	0.13
2001–02	4.49	4.43	0.85	0.41	0.06
2002–03	4.43	4.45	0.91	0.39	−0.02
2003–04	**4.29**	**4.28**	1.04	**0.55**	**0**

Source: Shayer, M., Ginsberg, D., & Coe, R. (2007). 30 years on—a large anti-Flynn effect? The Piagetian test *Volume and Heaviness* norms 1975–2003. *British Journal of Educational Psychology, 77*, 25–41.

been large increases in women's performance relative to men. It is worth reiterating that, on average, everyone did worse on this test today than 30 years ago—boys simply declined much more than girls, evening the score.

Shayer et al. are not alone in documenting large shifts in the male-to-female scoring ratio over the past several decades; many other researchers have provided evidence of changing sex differences over time. For example, the male advantage at the extreme right tail (1 in 10,000—those scoring 700 or more on the SAT-M before age 13), which was 13:1 in 1983,[22] has shrunk steadily over time. For example, as seen in Figure 6.1, in the United States the ratio of boys to girls in the top 0.01% of advanced math has steadily declined from 13 to 1 in the 1983, to 3.2 to 1 in 2005.[23] This translates into girls comprising only roughly 7% of the extreme right tail in 1983, but gradually improving until they now comprise approximately 24%, a tripling in just over two decades. Moreover, it appears there is no sign of this upward trend leveling off (the line shows no inflection or leveling), although we must await future reports to see if this conjecture is correct. And although boys have outperformed girls on the SAT-M for over 30 years ($d = 0.39$), the magnitude has shrunk from 40 points to 33 points, though we hesitate to press this shrinkage hard because the content of the SAT has changed over time.[24]

If sex differences in mathematics achievement are primarily the result of biological factors favoring men, we would expect greater consistency across cultures and time. As we show below, the inconsistency extends beyond historical time to include cultural inconsistency, too.

Secular trends in ratios of males to females at the high end have not been stable. In addition, Stumpf and Stanley[25] found women slightly narrowing the performance gap with men in advanced placement (AP) computer science between 1982 and 1994. Also, they found that the number of women scoring greater than 700 on the U.S. College Board's Math II Achievement

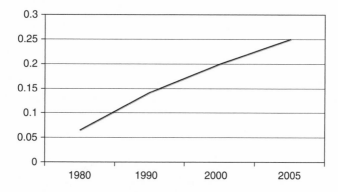

FIGURE **6.1.** Changes in female representation at the extreme right tail of mathematics score distribution for 13-year-olds (ratio of females to males).

test increased by 150%, and the number of women with high scores on the physics test increased by 142%, due to increased female participation in these generally male-dominated subjects. If such scores are a sign of the ability necessary to progress to higher levels in STEM fields, suddenly there are now many more eligible women. Furthermore, Benbow et al.[26] showed significant differences in academic attainment between two cohorts only 2 to 3 years apart, and Voyer et al.,[27] conducting an extensive review of the published literature on sex-related differences in spatial abilities, including 286 effect sizes, found most sex differences declining (though mental rotation was increasing). Finally, for mathematics, Hyde et al. in 1990 reported a mean sex effect size for studies published prior to 1973 of $d = 0:31$ (with boys superior), but only $d = 0.14$ for studies completed since 1974. Friedman[28] showed that the effect size for sex differences in mathematics shrunk from $d = 0.43$ in studies up to 1974 to $d = 0.24$ for studies between 1974 and 1988. As a rather dramatic example of historical effects, the reported 0.75 correlation between the year of publication and the effect size during the 1980s can be interpreted to indicate that sex differences have gotten steadily smaller with time.

In many cases, changes over time swamp remaining sex differences, calling into question the meaningfulness of these sex differences at the midpoint of the distribution. For example, Freeman[29] reported that the percentage of girls taking calculus courses in U.S. high schools rose from 4% in 1982 to 11% in 2000, while the percentage of boys rose from 6% to 12% over this period. Although the 1% difference that remained between the proportion of boys and girls taking calculus is statistically significant due to the large size of the sample, this difference is trivial compared with the magnitude of the change over time. This makes explanations in terms of stable genetic sex differences questionable. Even if such differences are pronounced, they are unlikely to be the primary cause of observed sex differences, given the volatility of the fluctuations we just described and others that we document below.

Cohort differences have also been found on measures of career discrimination. Consider the economist Donna Ginther's work,[30] discussed earlier, investigating career-related aspects of women in STEM fields. She found significantly lower odds of women on tenure track in scientific disciplines being promoted, controlling for demographics, productivity, and so on, in the 1972–79 cohort of PhDs (Ginther, 2004), but she found no significant sex difference in the 1980–89 cohort.

Again, we want to be clear about what we're claiming and not claiming: Although many of these findings imply environmental rather than genetic causation, they do not prove that there is not a genetic component to male–female differences in mathematical performance. They simply show that, irrespective of any genetic influence, there is substantial environmentally induced variance, and that estimates of genetic influences based on older data would lead one to higher estimates than estimates based on more recent data. More importantly, these data bring into question predictions for the future based on data from individuals who are now reaching retirement age, and who grew up in a very different world from the one children live in today.

In sum, results of the various cohort and historical trends indicate that sex differences are far from static. The gap between males and females changes in response to various factors, sometimes due to males getting worse, sometimes due to females getting better. That female math performance has increased over time is not proof that biology is irrelevant, because such increases can coexist with biologically based sex differences, much in the way gains in stature throughout the twentieth century were nevertheless consistent with very high heritabilities for height. (In other words, adult height is highly heritable, but still we have seen enormous increases in adult height over the past 100 years due to improved environment. The key is that taller parents still had the taller children throughout this period, despite all children growing much taller as a consequence of changes in nutrition, disease resistance, and stress.) These temporally influenced findings pose both a challenge and an opportunity for researchers and policy makers. The challenge is to avoid collapsing across epochs known to have very different gender gaps because the trends will cancel each other, obscuring forces at work during each separate epoch. The opportunity is to mine these secular changes in female proficiency for clues to their causes in hope that it will lead to effective interventions.

In view of the aforementioned cohort changes in sex differences, there is an unwarranted assumption that deserves to be challenged—namely, the claim that women's progress has been slow. When blue-ribbon commissions are created to study the state of women in science, they commonly bemoan the slow pace of progress and note that at the current rate women will not achieve equality in numbers of STEM scientists for many decades. Numerous recommendations have been made to speed up progress: for example, Shalala et al. in 2006 urged that universities be Title 9'd until significant gains are made in hiring women scientists, and during her presidential campaign, Hillary Clinton argued that "women comprise 43 percent of the workforce but only 23 percent of scientists and engineers," urging the government to take "diversity into account when awarding education and research grants."

All of the blue-ribbon commissions acknowledge that some strides have been made in hiring more female STEM scientists, but they argue that if society was truly committed to equality in gender representation in STEM careers, women's progress would have been swifter. After all, the solutions offered are not mysterious: Women could be mentored from junior high school onward, given preferential entrance into graduate programs in the math-intensive sciences, hired for tenure-track STEM jobs in rough proportion to their numbers obtaining PhDs, and once hired, provided with better on-the-job mentoring and progressive family-leave policies and a flexible tenure clock that enables them to keep their jobs despite taking time off to rear young children, as well as pursue other non–career-oriented goals.

Notwithstanding the above claims, women's progress has been remarkably steady and substantial during the past four decades, especially in view of the headwind into which it was running. By this we mean that large increases in women's representation in STEM careers have occurred during the same time that universities and institutes have been reducing their personnel budgets. Women have increased their representation in math-intensive fields by a factor of three in the past 40 years, while universities have been hiring far smaller proportions of tenure-track professors of either sex. Against a backdrop of very slow overall growth in the proportion of tenure-track positions, it is unreasonable to expect a reconfiguration of entire fields that were less than 10% female four decades ago into fields that are 50% female today. Such changes take a long time unless masses of male scientists are fired, something no one has proposed.

Collapsing across all fields of science and social science, by 2001 women earned 37% of the PhDs in scientific and engineering fields, up from just 8% in 1966.[31] Granted, a disproportionate number of these PhDs were earned in fields that are not math intensive, such as the social sciences. However, women have made impressive gains in math-intensive fields, too, currently obtaining 28.7% of the PhDs in mathematics, between 8% and 24% in the various subfields of engineering, nearly half in biological sciences (some subfields of which are math intensive), and 21.2% in computer sciences. And women's successes have been even greater in professional fields, obtaining 50% of the MDs, almost 75% of the DVMs from veterinary schools, and the majority of law and dental degrees. A generation ago the corresponding percentages were half or less in each of these fields.

If these rates of gain are slower than desired in being converted into tenure-track positions at colleges and universities (regarded by many as the premier and most prestigious posts) or into leadership positions in institutes and organizations, one reason is obvious. There has been a steady erosion of tenure-track positions over the past several decades—the very period of gains made by women in obtaining PhDs. As can be seen in Figure 6.2, the proportion of academic jobs classified as tenure track shrank from 56% to 31% between the 1970s and 2005. Concomitant with this shrinkage were two large expansions, the first in the proportion of jobs that are part time— growing from 30% of all academic positions to nearly 46% over this 35-year period; and the second, an expansion in the proportion of full-time jobs off tenure track, which nearly doubled, going from 12% to 20% over this same period.

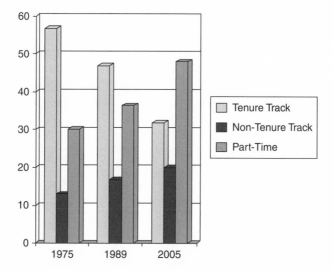

FIGURE **6.2.** Trends in faculty status over time. Source: U.S. Department of Education, IPEDS, Fall Staff Survey Compiled by the American Association of University Professors.

If viewed in light of the data in Figure 6.2, the gains in the proportion of tenure-track female STEM scientists in the last 35 years is quite remarkable, because it has occurred during a time of a diminishing proportion of tenure-track positions. An implication of these figures is that the *proportion* of tenure-track jobs filled by men has fallen significantly in recent decades. After all, how else could women have made any gains in their proportion given that the total proportion of jobs that are tenure track was declining? Doreen Kimura (2004), the eminent hormone researcher, complained that "Lest some people think that women still suffer discrimination in hiring in academia, the research, in Canada at least, shows just the opposite. Several studies have shown that women are favoured over men in university faculty hiring, including my own survey of hiring at two major British Columbia universities. Women's groups have been sadly effective at crying victim, to the point where men have become disadvantaged." (p. A13)

The bottom line is that women's advancement in STEM fields has been substantial, even if their transition from PhD to professorial positions is still not commensurate with their numbers. Trends observed in the recent past suggest further narrowing of the gender gap in the near future, as we have seen in Donna Nelson's work cited in the Introduction that some math-intensive fields have been hiring women for tenure-track positions at rates slightly in excess of their representation in the pool of new PhDs. This is not to predict that the gender gap will fully close any time soon, because it will not. Sex differences in preferences (women preferring more organic, people-oriented fields like medicine over math-intensive fields; women opting to delay tenure-track job searches to care for elderly parents, start families, or follow partners' moves) may continue to deter qualified women from competing for prestigious tenure-track posts. Only if colleges and universities make it easier to combine jobs and families and become creative by allowing tenured positions to be divided temporarily (with commensurate lengthening of the tenure clock) will the gap close precipitously. We will delve into some of these strategies in the final chapter.

Comparisons across societies, cultures, and developmental stages

"Social science affirms that a woman's place in society marks the level of civilization."

—Elizabeth Cady Stanton

As noted in Chapters 2 and 3, some researchers have offered arguments regarding evolutionary pressures that might have caused superior spatial ability in males. One example is work by David Geary, a well-respected evolutionary psychologist who specializes in mathematical achievement.[1] In two comprehensive reviews of a large animal literature, Geary suggests that evolutionarily important behaviors such as male–male competition involve greater reliance on the ability to geometrically represent three-dimensional space. Geary sees the modern legacy of this history of evolutionary selection as consisting of sex differences in spatial cognition. Similarly, others have argued that human sex differences are part of the pattern observed across the animal kingdom:

> ... parallel to certain sex differences found in nonhumans where social influences are either naturally or by virtue of a laboratory environment absent or minimal. For example, male rats are superior to female rats in learning spatial mazes, and these sex differences can be reversed by hormonal manipulation in early postnatal life (Williams & Meck, 1991).[2]

However, it is not clear what relations, if any, exist between maze-learning tasks and tests of spatial skill on which humans sexes differ—such as spatial *reasoning*, exemplified by the mental rotation task on which human males are superior, and spatial *location* memory tasks, on which human females are usually superior.[3] Intuitively, one might expect that learning the layout of a maze would be more akin to a spatial memory task than a spatial reasoning task. But, curiously, this is the opposite of the sex difference pattern found in meta-analyses of humans.

Differences have also been found in other species. Lecreuse et al.[4] at the Yerkes National Primate Research Center tested spatial memory in 90 rhesus monkeys between 10 and 30 years of age. The monkeys played a shell game, locating where food was hidden after they saw it covered in 1 of 18 identical wells on a tray. Although young adult males chose the correct food location more often (they had better spatial memory than females), they achieved their maximum performance early. The performance of the older groups revealed a sharp drop-off in performance. As a result, among the oldest monkeys, males and females had comparable spatial memory. Although the authors review human studies consistent with their findings, the direction of this effect is at odds with those concerning adult humans,[5] where women excel at spatial memory and men excel at spatial reasoning.

James Flynn, who is best known for the finding of large increases in IQ over the course of the twentieth century, has argued that Jewish Americans are not as exceptional on spatially loaded IQ test items as they are on other types of IQ items—and yet they are dominant among scientists and mathematicians.[6] Although the items reported by Flynn were not dynamic three-dimensional mental rotations, and he did not report data on ethnic differences at the extreme right tail (from which most STEM scientists hail), it is nevertheless somewhat suggestive that high spatial reasoning scores may not be the essence of success in mathematics and science. *If* this proves true, women's lower scores on spatial reasoning may not be a causal explanation for their lower numbers in scientific and technical careers.[7] Or at least one can hypothesize that low scores are not the only, or the major, reason for their underrepresentation. In the future it would be informative if overall performance on spatial subtests of IQ batteries (*Block Design, Object Assembly*) could be further studied and disaggregated, to examine the sex makeup not only at the midpoint of the distribution that was the basis of Flynn's analysis but also at the right tail.

NATIONAL AND CULTURAL DIFFERENCES

Another important dimension of sex differences is the national/cultural/ethnic or socioeconomic group under scrutiny. Environmentally driven explanations, of course, are compatible with cultural or international variability in sex differences. Genetic explanations (as will be shown) are less so, unless genetic group differences in male–female differentials in intellectual capacities are proposed. In other words, genetic explanations are unhelpful in explaining cultural variability in sex differences, unless one finds evidence showing that international variability in sex differences is the result of genetically dissimilar national groups. This is a difficult argument to make as some of the cultural contrasts have involved genetically similar, but culturally dissimilar, groups such as former east Germans and West Germans, or Chechs and Slavs.

Kimura, arguing in favor of genetically driven explanations of sex differences in STEM professions, and arguing against environmental explanations, suggested that "(cognitive sex differences) are present across cultures that vary in social pressures to conform to a gender norm. This has been documented for both mathematical reasoning and spatial ability (e.g., Geary & DeSoto, 2001)."[8] However, while this is true (Geary and DeSoto found male superiority on some mental rotation tasks in both the U.S. and China), there are other data showing that sex differences vary greatly across cultures, suggestive of specific experiential effects. For example, among some Eskimo groups in which women and men both hunt, it is alleged there is no significant spatial skill gap. Furthermore, some research has demonstrated that sex differences can be reversed, calling into question their purported intrinsic nature (Berry, 1966). For example, Icelandic high school girls are actually superior to boys on spatially loaded subtests and 15-year-olds outscore boys on math tests.[9] Also, Beller and Gafni,[10] analyzing data from representative national samples on the International Assessment of Educational Progress in mathematics and science tests for 9-year-olds, found the effect size for the male–female difference ranged from +0.28 in Korea (male superiority) to −0.06 in Ireland (female superiority). Of course, one can counter with the argument that age 9 is too soon to observe the sex differences; wait until adolescence when they begin to flourish. As we will see, waiting does not solve the quandary.

Sex trends are not always in the same direction, as we describe later. Penner (2008)[11] reports a wide range of effect sizes for high school students' sex differences in TIMSS (Third International Mathematics and Science Survey) scores across 22 countries. These range from highs of male superiority of 0.63 (Netherlands), 0.62 (Denmark), and 0.60 (Norway), to lows of 0.05 (Hungary—this indicates near parity or equivalence between the sexes) and 0.13 (United States). Penner argues that the large cross-national variation in sex differences in the TIMSS suggests that cultural rather than biological factors are involved, because the observed patterns are not explicable otherwise. In only half the countries does the magnitude of sex differences remains the same throughout all points in the distribution that Penner analyzed (favoring boys). However, several countries' sex differences are larger at the left tail (low-scoring end) of the distribution (such as Netherlands, Lithuania), while in other countries, the differences are larger at the right tail (high-scoring end, like Sweden). For some countries, girls do as well as or better than boys at the left tail, but worse at the right tail (United States, Hungary). In other countries, sex differences are most pronounced in the middle of the distribution (Russia, Austria). It is hard to come up with a compelling genetic explanation for such diversity! Of course, a persuasive environmental explanation will require careful analysis of what it is about each of these countries that tilts their sex differences in these myriad directions at different locations in the distribution. To date, we have been unpersuaded by the specific environmental explanations put forward; they seem suspiciously post hoc.

Finally, let's look at how the U.S. sex gap compares with other countries'. U.S. fifth-grade boys' average score on spatial tests was 13.1, whereas girls' was 12.4. However, Japanese and Taiwanese fifth-grade *girls* outperform U.S. *boys*, with average scores of 18.1 and 16.1, respectively.[12] Lest you imagine that this is genetic—Asians having better genes for math than Caucasians—Guiso et al.[13] found large cross-cultural differences in math achievement that could not be attributed to different gene pools. In their work, 15-year-olds' math scores on the 2003 Program for International Student Assessment, which was administered to over 250,000 students in Organization for Economic Cooperation and Development (OECD) countries, ranged from male superiority of 22.6 points (Turkey) to female superiority of 14.5 points (Iceland). Guiso et al. found much smaller sex differences in math achievement in cultures that valued egalitarianism, independently of genetic differences between them.

It appears to be the cultural mechanisms themselves rather than biology that drives these fluctuations in sex differences. But the precise cultural mechanisms remain to be decided because, as we describe later, others have not found that egalitarianism itself is a determinant even though Guiso et al. did.[14] Even within the United States, cultural differences are pronounced. Hyde et al. reported in 2008 that although average sex differences have disappeared in mathematics (at the midpoint of the ability distribution, or for the average student), Caucasian boys outnumber girls at the top 1% by a ratio of 2.06:1, while among Asian American students, girls outnumber boys 0.96:1.

To make matters even more bewildering, disaggregating the data by age group reveals further complications. As can be seen in Figure 7.1, Beller and Gafni show that, in some countries (such as Korea), the effect size for gender differences decreases between the ages of 9 and 13 (black bars higher). But in other countries (like Ireland and Spain), it increases with age (black bars lower). Another way of putting this is to say that, between the ages of 9 and 13, girls and boys come to score more similarly in Korea, but grow more different if they live in Ireland or Spain. In still other countries, there are either no sex

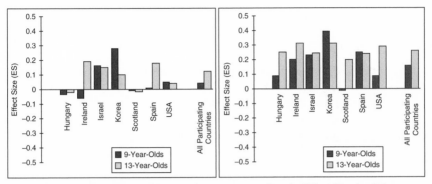

Gender Effect Size for Mathematics   Gender Effect Size for Science

FIGURE **7.1.** Age differences in effect sizes across countries. Source: Beller, M., & Gafni, N. (1996). The 1991 International Assessment of Educational Progress in mathematics and science: The gender differences perspective. *Journal of Educational Psychology, 88*, 365–377.

differences, or else differences in favor of girls. As noted earlier, in the United States, only a few gender differences in math have been found among primary school-aged children.[15] But differences do begin to accumulate around the onset of adolescence, so in this sense, effect sizes increase with age in the United States. These findings are difficult to reconcile with claims of cross-cultural invariance or with a strong genetic explanation of sex differences. It is not that we cannot possibly imagine a complex explanation that still allows genes to play an important role in producing sex differences. Rather, it is that we cannot imagine a scientifically *parsimonious* explanation involving genes. Far more compelling are explanations focusing on differing national experiences and expectations between the ages of 9 and 13.

An especially intriguing finding is that *girls* from some other nations out-perform U.S. and Canadian *boys* on mathematical aptitude tests,[16] and they often do so by greater margins than those which separate U.S. boys and U.S. girls. The cross-cultural findings are rife with examples of girls in some nations greatly outperforming American boys. For example, on one recent international math test, eighth-grade Japanese girls scored on average 569, while Japanese boys scored 571. But on this same test American girls and boys scored 502 and 507, respectively.[17] The 5-point superiority of American boys over American girls is dwarfed by the 60-plus-point superiority of Japanese girls over both. To take another example, girls in Singapore score a full standard deviation higher than Americans, and they also excel over Singaporean boys (611 for Singaporean girls; 601 for Singaporean boys).[18] This superiority of Singaporean girls is hard to discount on the basis of selective educational experiences or graduation rates, because Singaporean boys are similar on such dimensions to girls. Again, this does not rule out the possibility that genes are involved in producing sex differences in mathematics, but it does require an increasingly complex and post hoc argument. The evidence suggests that genes are likely to play a secondary role, smaller than the role played by factors that we will discuss later, such as preferences.

At a more general level, the odds of being female at the top and bottom of the ability distribution in mathematics depend significantly on which country we examine. For example, Israeli girls are twice as likely to be in the top 10% as are Canadian girls. Based on Guiso et al.' finding described earlier, one might imagine that countries known for their egalitarianism and modernity would produce greater equity in mathematics achievement between the sexes, but this is not the case. After all, Guiso et al. found that countries whose citizens tended to *disagree* with statements such as "When jobs are scarce, men should have more right to a job than women" had the smallest sex differences. In other words, more egalitarian beliefs led to smaller sex differences. However, this finding runs counter to one reported by the sociologists Karen Bradley and Maria Charles in 2006. In their analysis, there was a negative correlation between agreeing with the statement "A university education is more important for a boy than for a girl" and the ratio of women employed in computer science.[19] Countries whose citizens agreed that boys deserved greater access to a university education (such as Korea, Turkey, and Ireland) actually had more female computer scientists as a percentage of their college female population than did countries such as the United Kingdom, whose citizens harbored more egalitarian beliefs. In view of these differences, it is not clear exactly what cultural mechanisms are driving changes in sex differences across countries. But this does not gainsay the basic observation that such differences exist, and that they temper claims rooted in biology. As can be seen in Table 7.1, the chances of a girl being in the top 10% in math is far more likely in Israel, the United States, and Hungary than in Scandinavia, the Netherlands, or Canada.

TABLE **7.1.** Odds ratio of being female at the left and right tails.

	TOP 10%	BOTTOM 10%
Netherlands	0.34	6.25
Canada	0.29	2.16
Sweden	0.22	1.69
Denmark	0.25	3.27
Norway	0.22	2.65
Israel	0.63	1.35
United States	0.58	0.95
Hungary	0.54	0.74

Further calling into question a strong biological basis of sex imbalances in mathematical achievement is the lack of any consistent sex differences between kindergarten and third-grade children.[20] Similarly, there are far smaller differences between fifth-grade boys and girls in the United States ($d = 0.18$), than between U.S. boys and Japanese boys of the same age ($d = 1.42$).[21] Of course, it is possible that genes become active during adolescence, bathing the organism in hormones that are associated with the development of spatial and mathematical ability. But when we add to this finding other results we have reviewed showing large international differences among high school–aged students, and girls in some countries outperforming boys in our own, and so on, the evidence takes on a gravity that it otherwise would not. And there are other equally compelling examples in our article with Susan Barnett.[22] In sum, sex differences depend on where you look, with the gender gap in some countries being quite different from that observed in others.

Ethnic and Socioeconomic Differences

In addition to the variability in international patterns of sex differences in mathematics, as well as the variability in age cohorts and historical epochs, there is another form of variability that appears to thwart the strong biological position. We refer here to the fact that the male–female difference is not consistent across ethnic and socioeconomic groups, at least not within the United States, where such contrasts have most often been made. The gender gap in mathematics is larger for Caucasians ($d = 0.13$) than for African Americans ($d = -0.02$; slight female superiority), Hispanics ($d = 0.00$), and Asian Americans ($d = -0.09$; also female superiority).[23] That is, U.S. Caucasian males score higher than U.S. Caucasian females, whereas African American and Asian American males score slightly lower than African American and Asian American females. Among low-socioeconomic-status third graders, girls and boys do not differ notably in spatial skills; and middle-class girls are at least as good as lower-class boys on these tests.[24] Social class differences reflect many factors, including differences in the amount of time spent on homework, parents' beliefs about the importance of effort in school performance, and attitudes toward gender stereotypes, to name but a few.

Once again, our purpose in amassing these examples of inconsistent and reverse sex differences is not to claim that biology has no role in the matter. Rather, our argument is that until and unless better data are provided showing that biology is a primary cause of sex differences in math and spatial ability, biological accounts must be consigned to a secondary role in accounting for sex differences in math-intensive careers. All of the examples we described point to the noninevitability of overall gender performance gaps, at least at the center of the distribution. But what about differences at the right tail, the pre-sumed breeding grounds for future STEM scientists? Is there better evidence for the influence of biology at the extreme right tail?

Sex Differences at the Right Tail

When we talk about performance at the right tail of the distribution, the picture is just as messy as when we looked at the center. At the right tail, boys are overrepresented, but the degree of their overrepresentation depends on the measure of ability used. Although in the United States boys outnumber girls at the extremes of the mathematics and mental rotation ability spectra, there is a great deal of international inconsistency in the ratios of boys to girls at the high end. In some cultures, the ratios are much smaller than in others, and in some cultures sex differences are completely nonexistent at the right tail.[25] As stated by Spelke:

> If the genetic contribution were strong, however, then males should predominate at the upper tail of performance in all countries and at all times, and the male–female ratio should be of comparable size across different samples. Contrary to this pre-diction, the preponderance of high-scoring males is significantly smaller in some countries (e.g., Deary et al., 2003) and altogether absent in others (Feingold, 1994).[26]

Charles and Bradley[27] analyzed data compiled by OECD on higher-education degrees awarded in 2001. They examined seven fields of study, including engineering and math/physical sciences. They calculated represen-tation factors for each country by comparing male-to-female ratios, adjusted for international differences in women's enrollments in science and math majors. As expected, women predominate in traditionally female sex-typed fields such as education and health, whereas men predominate in stereo-typically masculine fields. For instance, in computer science, women are underrepresented in all 21 of the industrialized countries considered. How-ever, Charles and Bradley[28] found that male-to-female ratios varied greatly across countries. In Turkey, men were overrepresented among computer sci-ence graduates by a factor of only 1.79 to 1, while in the Czech Republic, they were overrepresented three times more, by a factor of 6.42 to 1. In the United States, the "male overrepresentation factor" is 2.10 to 1 and in the United Kingdom, 3.10 to 1.

Putting aside the question of whether there are biological sex differences that result in women aspiring to be in some fields more than others, the fact that there is so much transnational variability suggests the operation of societal stereotypes, national preferences, and cultural beliefs that influ-ence women's career preferences. Harkening back to our earlier suggestion, there has never been a strong demonstration of a link between mathematics achievement levels and entry into stereotypically male fields. We should make a distinction here between two levels of evidence. On the one hand, we disagree with the claim that two-thirds of men who enter STEM fields have SAT-M or Graduate Record Exam-Quantitative (GRE-Q) scores below 650.[29] This is almost certainly not correct. We already noted that, at our own university, graduate students in math-intensive fields have very high math aptitude, ranging from a "low" mean quantitative score of 708 to a high mean of 780, with a grand mean for all 454 graduate students in math-intensive fields equaling a GRE-Q of 759. We doubt that Cornell's graduate students are very different from those at the other top universities that together train the vast majority of STEM scientists. So, on this level we certainly do think there is a link between entry into math-intensive fields and high mathematical scores. If these schools admitted applicants randomly, those with very low scores would, as a group, have a hard time succeeding. Further support for this view comes from the work of Wise et al., based on a representative national sample that was followed over decades from ninth grade through adulthood. She and her colleagues found that high school students who entered science careers came from the top 10% of math aptitude, and probably even higher than the top 10% if the data could be further broken down into the top 5% and 1% of math ability for those who later entered math-intensive graduate careers.[30]

However, having argued that math-intensive fields are populated with high mathematical scorers, there is no evidence that having a specific score on a math test predicts who will succeed in math-intensive STEM fields. Are STEM scientists more successful if they scored 750 on the GRE-Q than if they scored 650? We do not know, nor does anyone else. Moreover, even if it was determined that a math score in the top 5% or top 1% was a prerequisite for success in a math-intensive career, there would still be an underrepresentation of women. This is because in large representative data sets, the ratio of boys to girls at the top 1% of the mathematics distribution is 2.06, meaning that approximately two-thirds of the top 1% math scorers are boys.[31] If math-intensive careers required being in the top 1% of math scorers, there ought to be one-third of engineers and physicists who are women. But less than 15% actually are, as seen in Figure 7.2. Apparently more than having a top 1% math score is at work in determining which women end up in academic careers in engineering, though it is only fair to bring up a point by critics that the top 1% may not be rarified enough if we are interested in who becomes a successful physicist or computer scientist or engineering professor. Perhaps these individuals represent the top 0.1%, top 0.01% or even the top 0.001% (i.e., 1 in a 100,000), as was the case with the Putnam fellows we described in the Preface. If so, then "merely" scoring in the top 1% may not be sufficiently gifted. Recall David Lubinski and Camilla Benbow's data showing that the top quarter of the top 1% excel over the bottom quarter of the top 1% in getting

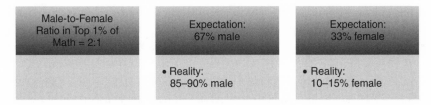

FIGURE 7.2. Sex differences in mathematics cannot explain women's underrepresentation among math and engineering faculty.

tenure-track STEM posts and publishing and being awarded patents. According to this view, if having a math score in the top 1 in a thousand (0.1%) is helpful in becoming a successful scientist, the ratio of boys to girls at the top 0.1% of the mathematics distribution is probably much higher than 2.06 to 1 ratio for the top 1%, perhaps as high as 5.0 to 1, The need for a score this rarified, however, is an empirical question for which we lack data to assess. (Once again, we note the caveat we have made elsewhere that we are not claiming that STEM scientists cannot be found who have low math scores—surely some will point to successes despite having low scores. What we are claiming is that they are statistically aberrant and there are good reasons for their success despite their low scores—reasons that do not exist for the majority of low scorers (e.g., super-high spatial ability).

Finally, lest the reader conclude that the specific causes of the underrepresentation of women in math-intensive fields are well understood, we should clarify that it is not. Just because we have challenged the biological position on the grounds that there is both international and cohort inconsistency does not mean we have identified the environmental roots of women's underrepresentation. Consider: The most economically developed countries do not produce the greatest ratios of women in computer science. In fact, depending on the culture, some of the least-advanced nations produce the highest ratios of female computer scientists. Nor is there a strong correlation between the ratio of female scientists and the proportion of women in the workforce or in high-status jobs or in higher education generally. And as far as being from a culture that is egalitarian, as Luigi Guiso and his team of economists (2008) have shown, this is related to small sex differences in math. They used the 2003 data from the Program of International Student Assessment (PISA) that was given to over 300,000 15-year-olds in 41 nations. Their analysis revealed that the boy-to-girl math gap at the top 5% and top 1% was virtually nonexistent in gender neutral countries. However, others such as the sociologist Andrew Penner have failed to find such an effect on the basis of different analyses and using a different data set. Some commentators, notably an anonymous web-based researcher known as the Griffe du Lion (see: http://www.lagriffedulion.f2s.com/math2.htm) (generally, assumed to be Johns Hopkins University sociology professor Robert A. Gordon) argue that the correlation between being in a macho culture versus a gender-emancipated one is due to a spurious correlation with national intelligence—that high IQ nations have smaller sex differences in math, regardless of their egalitarianism. One piece of evidence for this view is that if Guiso et al. had compared the 2003 PISA data on which they based their conclusions about the role of egalitarian culture to the 2006 PISA update, they would have found that even though there were no significant changes in egalitarian attitudes toward women in any of the PISA nations over this three-year period, there appears to be no relation between the gaps observed in 2003 and 2006 (r = 0.0006).

Broad national beliefs in equal opportunity for women also do not appear to be a good predictor of female entry into male fields. None of the Charles and Bradley highest-scoring nations—Turkey, South Korea, and Ireland—the authors note, is particularly known for their gender-egalitarian attitudes or practices, whereas some of the countries they outpace are far more egalitarian. Finally, a knee-jerk environmental prediction would be that girls' representation at the right tail in mathematics would increase in homes where parents stress mathematics achievement. However, Penner[32] has reported that the gap in math performance found at the right tail is actually more (not less) pronounced among girls who claim their parents value their mathematics achievement. So, problems with the strong biological position do not lead by default to a well-supported environmental position.

TRENDS OVER CHRONOLOGICAL AGE AND COUNTRY

The data in Table 7.2 are interesting to ponder. They are taken from the same report by Beller and Gafni discussed earlier, and represent the effect sizes for sex differences at different ages for different countries. Recall that these effect sizes are standardized indices of how differently boys and girls score on math and science tests.

The first thing to notice about this table is the change in effect sizes as we move from one country to another. As already noted, girls and boys differ much more in some countries than in others. For example, they differ in Korea and Israel more than they differ in Scotland. If sex differences were due to biology, then we might expect greater consistency across countries. Not only is there a great deal of inconsistency, but in Scotland, three of the four sex differences actually favor girls, that is girls do better than boys. The other thing to note about this table is the age trends. With some exceptions, as boys and girls grow older, they become more dissimilar on math and science tests. Earlier we made this same point that, with a few exceptions, effects get larger with age, and here we see the same story with a very different data set.

Some have argued that the increasing effect size with age is because hormonal changes around the time of puberty cause a spurt in male math

TABLE **7.2.** Effect sizes for sex differences in mathematics and science test scores across countries.

COUNTRY	Mathematics		Science	
	9 YEARS	13 YEARS	9 YEARS	13 YEARS
Hungary	−0.03	−0.02	0.09	0.25
Ireland	−0.06	0.19	0.20	0.31
Israel	0.16	0.15	0.23	0.24
Korea	0.28	0.10	0.39	0.31
Scotland	−0.01	−0.02	−0.01	0.20
Spain	0.01	0.18	0.25	0.24
Taiwan	0.03	0.02	0.25	0.08
United States	0.05	0.04	0.09	0.29
All countries	0.04	0.12	0.16	0.26

Source: Beller, M., & Gafni, N. (1996). The1991 International Assessment of Educational Progress in mathematics and science: The gender differences perspective. *Journal of Educational Psychology, 88*, 365–377. Table 2 and Appendix.

scores. But it is equally possible that the basis for the growing sex gap with age is the result of gender socialization, with girls becoming disaffected from math and science as they get older, viewing them as male domains. According to this latter view, there are few reliable differences between boys and girls when they begin school, but over time math becomes a gendered subject in the children's eyes, a field for men rather than women.

When we examine occupations, the picture is more complicated than the age trends above. If girls become increasingly disaffected with math and science, then we would anticipate large gaps in all fields of science. Table 7.3

TABLE **7.3.** Percentages of women in select STEM careers.

OCCUPATION	% WOMEN
Chemical Engineer	14.3
Civil Engineer	13.2
Computer Engineer	10.8
Electrical and Electronics Engineer	7.1
Industrial Engineer	14.9
Mechanical Engineer	5.8
Architect	24.4
Biologist	48.7
Psychologist	67.3
Physicians	32.3
Veterinarian	38.7

Source: U.S. Department of Labor, Bureau of Labor Statistics. (2005). Current population survey. Retrieved on June 20, 2008, from http://www.bls.gov/cps/wlf-table11-2006.pdf

shows this is not uniformly true. As we've noted throughout this book, according to recent population surveys, women are faring far better in some scientific fields (as physicians, veterinarians, biologists, and so on) than others (for example, as engineers), even though all of the fields in this table rely on science and math training to some degree. And these percentages belie a surge of women in recent graduating classes (one-half to two-thirds of recent classes of MDs and veterinarians are composed of women—so as older men retire, we can expect the proportions in such fields to shift in favor of women).

TRENDS ACROSS THE AGE SPAN

We turn now to a discussion of changes within individuals across the lifespan. The older an individual is when we assess her or his mental rotation ability, the more difficult it is to unravel biological and socialization factors. Researchers have been interested in early sex differences in spatial cognition to determine whether sex differences are observed before gender socialization makes inroads. Preschoolers are too young to have been exposed to a long developmental progression of differential societal stereotypes and differential teacher treatment; however, depending on how young they are, it may still be possible for toy use and differential parental attitudes, to affect boys and girls differently. Sex differences in spatial cognition appear to emerge quite early, according to some research. In their seminal book, Maccoby and Jacklin[33] reported that sex differences in spatial skills do not become evident around the onset of adolescence. However, since the publication of their book a great deal of research has documented earlier sex differences. Levine et al. provided an updated literature review in 1999 showing that a number of studies have documented spatial skill gaps among preschool-aged boys and girls. These researchers concluded:

> Boys as young as 4 years of age performed better than girls on a task that involved replicating spatiotemporal patterns tapped out by the experimenter on a set of blocks, [and] the size of this sex difference remained constant across the 4- to 10-year age range (Grossi, Orsini, Monetti, & De Michele, 1979; Orsini, Schiappa, & Grossi, 1981). . . . Uttal et al. (2001) found that 5-year-old boys were better at interpreting a map of a space than 5-year-old girls, particularly when the map was rotated with respect to the space it represented. Although 3-year-old girls had higher average performance than 3-year-old boys on the nonrotated map task—the only condition administered to this age group—Uttal et al. reported that the 3-year-old boys did not appear to be as engaged in the task as 3-year-old girls.[34]

Other studies searching for evidence of early sex differences on spatial tasks have also reported inconsistent results. Some studies have shown early male superiority on two-dimensional spatial rotation tasks, while others have found differences only on three-dimensional mental rotation tasks, not on two-dimensional tasks. A very early study reported by Cronin in 1967 required kindergarten and first-grade children to match triangles with their mirror images. Boys scored higher than girls on this task. Somewhat more recently, Levine et al.[35] investigated early male superiority on another two-dimensional spatial transformation task, using children of similar age (4 years to 6 years 11 months). In this task, the children were required to recognize various two-dimensional spatial transformations of shapes. Boys and girls scored equally well in the youngest age group, but a significant sex difference in favor of boys developed later. However, a 15-minute testing session on another day had a positive effect on performance for most of the age groups, and the magnitude of this effect was roughly the same size as the difference between the sexes, for both boys and girls. This suggests that it might not require a particularly large preexisting difference in experience to create observed sex differences in performance. But perhaps the observed sex gap can readily be narrowed with experience. On the other hand, the fact that a 15-minute experience on one day can, on another day, elevate *both* sexes' scores by an amount equal to their original difference says nothing about the cause of those sex differences among preschoolers.

Finally, Siegel and Schadler in 1977 reported on the results of a study in which 5-year-olds were asked to place 40 items in a three-dimensional model of their kindergarten classroom. On all three measures of spatial accuracy (local, global, and relational accuracy), boys' performance exceeded that of girls by very large amounts. In contrast to these findings, others have failed to find sex differences on two-dimensional tasks with similar age groups. McGuinness and Morley[36] found no difference on a jigsaw completion task with 3-, 4-, and 5-year-olds. However, the same authors did find a sex difference in favor of boys on a three-dimensional Lego block-building task, for some ages. Boys aged 4–5 years were 1 year more advanced than girls on this task. Girls caught up by kindergarten, which the authors suggest is probably due to a ceiling effect. (This means that the test may not have been sensitive enough to reveal male superiority among kindergartners, because everyone was getting nearly all of the items correct.)

Unfortunately, none of these studies with young children specifically focused on three-dimensional mental rotation, the skill often claimed to be key in explaining adult math skill sex differences, and none focused on infants. Instead, they focused on two-dimensional rotations of maps, puzzles, and photographs or three-dimensional nonrotational tasks. However, the Levine et al. study did compare rotation and nonrotation tasks. In this case, there was no difference found in the size of the male advantage between these types of tasks, a finding that is at variance with the adult literature, which shows the former to be a much larger cognitive sex difference. Recently, two independent labs working with infants reported sex differences on mental rotation favoring boys. David Moore and Scott Johnson reported in 2008 that 5-month-old boys displayed mental rotation, but girls did not. In their study, an object was shown revolving through a 240-degree angle many times until infants recognized it and got bored looking at it. Later, infants saw the object or its mirror image revolving through a previously unseen 120-degree angle. Only the male infants seemed to recognize the familiar object from the new perspective, which depends on mental rotation. Using static drawings of a two-dimensional object rotated in a two-dimensional (frontal) plane, Paul Quinn and Lynn Liben[37] also found mental rotation in 3- to 4-month-old male infants but not in female infants. These two studies are the best data yet indicating the existence of sex differences in infancy, long before gender socialization via differential toy use or even parental attitudes could plausibly have influenced the results.

So, what is the bottom line as far as very young children's spatial ability is concerned? Notwithstanding the positive findings of early male superiority on rotation tasks, there are some notable failures to find sex differences among somewhat older preschool-aged children. Even though the Uttal et al. study has been described in the literature[38] as demonstrating early sex differences, this does not appear to be the case from an examination of their raw data. In all four of Uttal et al.'s experiments (Uttal, Gregg, Chamberline, Sines, 2001) there is no evidence of reliable sex differences. (We were perplexed by the divergence between the description of their findings we have read and our own scrutiny of their findings, so we contacted the lead author for a clarification. Our interpretation was confirmed by David Uttal in an e-mail exchange; the discrepancy apparently was the result of other investigators citing his study in its preliminary stage when the data did seem to indicate spatial differences between very young boys and girls. But these sex differences failed to reach significance as more data became available, and the final study that was eventually published reported no reliable sex differences among preschoolers.)

As compelling as the early infancy studies by Moore and Johnson and Quinn and Liben are, they raise intriguing but unanswered questions, such as: Do girls who were less adept at mental rotation at 4 and 5 months of age catch up with boys by 8 months? If so, have boys gone on to acquire more complex forms of mental rotation that girls have yet to acquire, such that there is perpetually a sex gap? One thing that we know with confidence is that there is a well-documented male advantage on 3-D mental rotation later, but we are not sure whether it results from playing with blocks, Legos, erector sets, and the like, or is driven more by a disproportionately male biological propensity that is actualized in response to an environmental trigger. We just do not know, even though it is clear, as we show later, that female mental rotation performance can be significantly enhanced by various interventions. It is interesting to juxtapose this research with the finding by Walton and Spencer that we discussed earlier, showing that girls did as well as boys on math tests when stereotype threat (ST) was fully taken into consideration. It would be hard to argue that ST had anything to do with male babies' superiority on the mental rotation tasks of Moore and Johnson and Quinn and Liben.

Shifting our focus to slightly older children, consider once more the meta-analysis of spatial ability conducted by Linn and Petersen.[39] Although they found sex differences favoring boys, there were no changes in the magnitude of the sex differences with age—the differences did not get larger or smaller between the ages of 10 and 60 years. Linn and Petersen hypothesized several potential causes of sex differences, including girls being more cautious than boys, and taking much longer to report their mental rotations because they may have double-checked them. The authors concluded, "Males tend to outperform females on mental rotation at any age where measurement is possible. The sex differences may result from differential rate of rotation, differential efficiency in strategy application, differential use of analytic processes, or differential caution."[40] This last possibility—that girls are more cautious and double-check their rotations before answering—is one that there are recent data to support. However, it cannot explain all of the sex differences observed. Given the enormity of the literature on sex differences on mental rotation from around the world and at all ages, there is little doubt that true differences exist, and the magnitude is fairly large. The cause, as we noted, is unclear, as is its relationship to later mathematical performance, and its malleability seems possible, as we show later.

There are several studies, some with rhesus monkeys and some with humans, that report sex differences on some forms of spatial cognition but not on others, or differences favoring boys prior to training but not following it. For example Lacreuse et al.[41] showed that in young adulthood, simple spatial-memory training did not help male rhesus monkeys but dramatically helped females, raising their performance to the level of young adult males. Training probably focused the females' processing on the spatial features of the task, whereas the males were already processing these features, the authors suggest. Robinson et al.[42] investigated sex differences in early mathematical skill in a sample of mathematically advanced preschoolers and kindergartners. Although boys scored higher than girls on several measures, on the majority of the spatial measures there were no sex differences. Among the spatial measures, boys were significantly better only on the memory measure, which elsewhere has been shown to be an area of female superiority,[43] whereas boys are typically better at spatial reasoning tasks.

Thus, although there is a general pattern of boys scoring higher than girls on spatial tasks, results are occasionally discrepant. It is not clear what conclusions can reliably be drawn about the earliest roots of later male dominance in STEM fields. Siegel and Schadler suggested that one reason for the discrepancies in the scientific literature may be that the studies that failed to find sex differences employed relatively easier tasks that did not stress the spatial processing system. They opined that sex differences are most likely to be observed when the spatial system is taxed to its limit. Their argument is that the occasional discrepant study that fails to find male superiority on mental rotation of three-dimensional objects failed because they used tasks that were so easy that all children could do them without being pushed to the limits of their ability. When this happens, potential ability differences between the sexes can not be detected.

What about sex differences in math? In contrast to the confusion surrounding the onset and role of spatial cognition, the findings related to mathematics achievement are somewhat clearer. Throughout this book we have described the most commonly observed math pattern: no sex differences in math until early adolescence (middle school), at which point effect sizes favoring boys start growing and continue to grow throughout high school and beyond, especially among the highest-scoring students. Most studies of nonselect samples[44] reveal that girls are, if anything, more likely to excel over boys in math until third or fourth grade. Among high-scoring students, boys outperform girls on math tasks starting in third to sixth grade.[45] Leahey and Guo[46] found that sex differences in math were most pronounced among the high-scoring elementary school students through high school, and Reis and Park[47] reported that boys exceeded girls in math scores from eighth grade to post–high school. Finally, Benbow[48] found that boys and men outnumber girls and women in both the high-ability and low-ability groups in mathematics from early adolescence through adulthood, particularly in the highest scoring groups.

In contrast to the above studies, several studies have found boys excelling at math very early—upon entrance to kindergarten. Penner and Paret[49] used a nationally representative sample of children entering kindergarten who were followed through fifth grade. They found that at the right tail (top 5%) boys exceeded girls by approximately a sixth of a standard deviation on standardized math tests at the beginning of kindergarten, and maintained this advantaged (roughly) through fifth grade. Interestingly, they found the male advantage for Caucasian, African American, and Asian children but not for Latinos because Latinas actually outscored male peers. The male advantage was most pronounced among Asian children. Finally, and somewhat surprisingly, the male advantage was largest among the most educated families. Note how nonparsimonious biological explanations must be in order to explain such a complex pattern of ethnic and social class differences. It is not obvious what the driving force is, but plausibly it resides in the homes/cultures of these families rather than in genetic differences between the groups.

So, with some qualifiers, it seems safe to say that early sex differences in math achievement are neither large nor always in favor of boys. Around the onset of adolescence we see the start of a reliable male advantage, but mainly on so-called aptitude tests such as the Scholastic Assessment Test-Mathematics (SAT-M). On math grades, girls continue to do as well as or better than boys, an advantage they maintain to the end of college.

8

Conclusions and synthesis

"I'm having trouble managing the mansion. What I need is a wife."
—Ella Grasso, former governor of Connecticut

In attempting to answer the question, "Why are there so few women in mathematically intensive STEM fields?" we have waded through an unwieldy literature on sex differences that is filled with contradictions. We have analyzed evidence across many domains: the cognitive psychology of mental rotation, the social psychology of stereotypes, personal preferences, discrimination, hormonal bases of behavior, econometrics of hiring and promotion, and cultural comparisons of mathematics achievement. Readers may now ask whether a "bottom line" can be presented that does justice to the substantial and often inconsistent literature bearing on this question.

We begin by explaining why we do not endorse the strong biological position that claims hormones, brain organization and volumetric capacity, evolutionary selection pressures, or genes can account for most of the observed sex differences in math-intensive careers. Following this, we then explain why we do not endorse the specific environmental explanations that are typically touted. Finally, we describe what we think accounts for more of the sex imbalance than either of these strong positions. To foreshadow our conclusion, we believe that the entire corpus of research reduces to a single large effect coupled with a host of smaller effects. The largest effect concerns women's choices and preferences—their preference for nonmath careers over careers in engineering, physics, mathematics, operations research, computer science, and chemistry, and their choices having to do with fertility and its ramifications for work. These preferences and choices exist even among women who are highly talented in math; that is, they prefer to work in nonmath fields from an early age and they choose to start families at times that jeopardize career progress as they advance through ranks in all fields but particularly in some of the most math-intensive ones. Although the smaller effects (such as spatial and math ability, hormones, stereotype threat, biases) are nontrivial and do have an role in the sex imbalance, they are much less potent than the preference/choice factor in explaining why so few women are succeeding in math-intensive careers. Thus, our synthesis leads to a down-grading or even rejection of many of the claims that have been made. In the following pages we flesh out the justification for this conclusion.

ARE BIOLOGICAL CONSTRAINTS THE CULPRIT?

Let us take on the strong "biological constraints on cognition" position first. We do not believe the data we have presented in this book are consistent enough, at least at this time, to claim that the dearth of women in mathematically intensive STEM careers is a consequence of biological sex differences (hormones, brain organization and capacity, evolutionary selection pressures) impeding women's aptitude at math—either directly by their effects on brain functioning or through the mediation of spatial cognition, or indirectly via their influence on preferences or motivation. In our long scientific article with Susan Barnett we cite more of the evidence for this view; we stick to the most critical evidence here.

Importantly, there is too little consistency across studies and epochs to support a strong causal connection between biology and cognitive outcomes. In addition to the inconsistent demonstrations of neural and hormonal influences on mental rotation and mathematics ability reviewed in Chapter 3, the alleged role of math and spatial aptitude in the dearth of women in STEM is also problematic for a number of other reasons. There are substantial sex asymmetries at the extreme right tail on math aptitude that favor boys and men, at least as indexed by timed (often multiple-choice) tests such as the SAT-M and GRE-Q. Even though the magnitude of these gaps has shrunk often dramatically over time, they are still sizable by adolescence, despite the fact that there do not appear to be consistent sex differences among preadolescent children[1] with some notable exceptions.[2] However, it is not clear what the inconsistency, along with the lack of reliable sex differences among young children in math, means.

An assumption often implicit, but sometimes explicit, is that spatial ability underlies advanced mathematics[3]; that girls' presumed deficits in spatial skills involved in rotating three-dimensional figures constrain their ability to do well on advanced mathematics (e.g., see Friedman, 1995). This may well be true, but more and better evidence is needed to make this case. And studies specifically targeting the extreme right tail are needed. Most of the pertinent hormone and brain research has focused on the general population (all elementary school students, all college students), and is not focused on those who score at the extreme right tail. Finally, even among women who are at the extreme right tail of the mathematics distribution, far fewer go into math-intensive careers than do men with comparable math talent. Recall an earlier argument that if high math talent was responsible for the shortage of women in these careers, then we would still expect about 30% of math-intensive scientists to be women. This is because the ratio of men to women among the top 1% of the math distribution is 2.06—roughly 30% women. Nowhere near this level of representation of women is found in fields like engineering, physics, operations research, chemistry, computer science, and so forth.

What we do know is that, although there are often pronounced male advantages on rotation of three-dimensional objects even in infancy, there are no consistent sex differences among children in other types of spatial cognition, such as figural disembedding, spatial location memory, rotating two-dimensional figures, and so forth.[4] The mathematics tests that demonstrate the largest sex differences (SAT-M, GRE-Q) are mostly atheoretical, and adding or removing items from them may elevate or reduce their validity in ways we do not understand. They are quite heterogeneous in content, with boys outperforming girls on some types of problems, and the reverse being true for other types. It is possible that scoring in the top 1% or even the top 0.01% is an advantage in becoming a successful mathematical scientist, but the only relevant evidence for this is indirect. Ronald Nuttall et al.[5] showed that sex differences in various-ability groups' SAT-M scores disappeared when their mental rotation ability was statistically controlled, but the latter remained an important predictor even after their SAT-M scores were controlled. This strongly suggests that spatial cognition may play an important role in sex differences in math aptitude as indexed by the SAT-M. But the question remains as to whether there is a threshold SAT-M score needed to be a successful STEM scientist. Additionally, the question remains open as to the causal route by which spatial cognition exerts its effect. And, again, many women who do score at the right tail choose not to go into mathematical careers for reasons that seemingly have little to do with mathematical or spatial ability. So, we think that sex differences in mathematical and spatial ability may play a role in the underrepresentation of women in math-intensive fields, but a decidedly secondary one.

Wise et al.[6] studied the role of spatial ability in a sample of 1,100 high school students, following them from freshman through senior year of high school. They discovered that spatial ability in freshman year predicted participation in future math courses for boys, but not for girls. This is relevant because virtually 100% of the difference in math aptitude in twelfth grade was predicted by participation in elective math courses throughout high school. And the biggest predictors of taking elective math classes were ninth-grade mathematics aptitude and interest in math/science careers. But this was not because participation was a strong predictor of twelfth-grade math achievement—that is, it was not due to mathematically precocious students taking more math courses, and boys being more mathematically precocious. In fact, there were no sex differences in math aptitude among ninth graders. As in other studies, sex differences in math did not show up reliably before adolescence. Is this because of societal forces such as stereotypes and cultural beliefs? Is it because the math becomes more complex around this time? Or, is it because sex differences in math only are revealed when the test strains the system, as was suggested by some authors when sex differences in spatial ability failed to materialize?

It would be helpful to have direct longitudinal evidence that SAT-M scores in the top 1% or 0.1% represent a threshold for success in math-intensive careers. Doubtless some STEM scholars will be shown to have had lower SAT-M scores, but how aberrant are they? Many[7] appear to think STEM scientists with low math-aptitude scores are not aberrant. But as we argued earlier, we are doubtful that this is the case. Nevertheless, we note that girls are doing very well in advanced math courses, including geometry and calculus, even if their SAT-M scores lag behind those of boys at the right tail. And the gap between some foreign girls and U.S. and Canadian boys is sometimes larger than the domestic gender gap, suggesting that a closer look at the right tail in those cultures is warranted. Relatedly, foreign women occasionally represent much higher proportions of the STEM workforce than do American women. As we noted in an earlier chapter, only 20% of the female faculty in the top five mathematics departments are born in the United States, and they hail largely from the same countries that place a large number of girls in international math competitions (e.g., Romania). Although this does not obviate the possibility of biological differences, it more plausibly suggests that cultural mechanisms are at work.

In sum, the strong biological position is riddled with conflicting findings and claims. As alluring as the depictions of the link between male hormones and spatial ability are (e.g., demonstration of male rats' spatial superiority disappears following castration or the injection of testosterone into newborn female rats[8]), the evidence linking biology to the underrepresentation of women in mathematical fields is weak and unpersuasive. As we have noted already, it is possible that hormones and brain organization may play a secondary role, but other factors emerge as stronger candidates for a primary causal role. The key issue remains as to whether the math competencies indexed by scoring at the extreme right tail of the SAT-M or GRE-Q distribution are critical to STEM success. Finally, if biological/cognitive constraints were a major source of sex differences in math-intensive careers, it would be unclear why so many women manage to outperform men on math grades, get graduate degrees in mathematics, and so on. So, we conclude that there is enough evidence to believe that biological differences between the sexes may account for a small part of the sex imbalance in STEM careers, but to date there is no persuasive evidence that such differences are a major explanatory variable. And as will be seen, there are nonbiological explanations that appear to account for sex differences in math-intensive fields more parsimoniously.

IF BIOLOGICAL DIFFERENCES ARE NOT THE MAJOR CAUSE, ARE SEX DIFFERENCES IN SOCIALIZATION THE CULPRIT?

Here we take on the strong "sex differences are mainly the result of cultural/socialization" position. On this side, the evidence seems to range from weak to modest, with the result being that this, too, is not a very compelling explanation of sex imbalances in math-intensive careers. It asks too much of readers to accept that pervasive gender stereotypes, lack of parental encouragement, early toy use, and discriminatory teacher behaviors are a major cause of the lack of women in math-intensive STEM careers. How could such stereotypes be influential, given that *girls elect to take as many advanced math courses as boys—and get better grades in them?* And how can this position explain the fact that the pipeline leading up to receipt of PhDs in mathematics contains many women (recall that 48% of current majors in mathematics are women), if such stereotypes were operative during women's formative years?

Finally, although some evidence exists showing that parents encourage boys more than girls to achieve in math and science, other evidence, including the strongest in our view, indicate either that parental encouragement cannot explain sex differences in math achievement[9] or even that it is inversely related to it. Readers may remember that Penner[10] found that the gap at the right tail in math is greater among girls who report that math achievement is important to their parents than it is for girls who report their parents are less concerned about math. An observer from another planet, scanning the evidence, might think that boys must surmount negative stereotypes about their poor math ability that accrue from years of witnessing girls outperform them in math classes.

Also, it is not obvious that adolescents (at least not today's) are always aware of stereotypes about gender and math.[11] As we saw, cultures not known for their egalitarian attitudes toward women manage to prepare a greater ratio of women for some math-intensive fields (particularly computer science) than do cultures priding themselves on gender equity. And cultural explanations in terms of gender egalitarianism dissolving the sex gap in math are problematic as was pointed out in Chapter 7. Recently, Richard Lippa and his colleagues reported an interesting analysis of sex differences in mental rotation that we briefly mentioned in an earlier chapter, showing that males in 53 nations outperformed females. Missing from that discussion was the finding that the magnitude of the sex differences was positively associated with nations' gender equality and economic development, meaning that male advantage was greatest in those nations deemed to be the most gender egalitarian and most developed. This finding held up even after Lippa and his colleagues controlled for education levels and age. Finally, many common-sense arguments about the presumed influence of the environment turn out to be untrue. We mentioned that Penner[12] showed that sex differences at the right tail became more pronounced for girls whose parents valued math achievement, compared to those who said their parents did not value math achievement, and another finding by Penner and Paret[13] revealed that sex differences in math were greatest among educated families, a result that could be understood in terms of a gene–environment relationship but not in terms of a simple main-effects environment argument.[14]

There are many such peculiarities in the literature, and it is problematic to "cherry-pick" the findings that accord with our intuitions and beliefs and ignore the findings that do not. They pose fascinating challenges for various theories—such as stereotype threat—because one would assume that the gender egalitarian societies are those that engage in the least negative sex-typing, yet they are the ones that produce the largest sex differences on mental rotation and mathematics tasks. (We should hasten to add that there are ways to reconcile these seemingly opposite findings, but they require a host of post hoc assumptions that render them unpersuasive.) So, the bottom line is that the strong cultural/socialization position is at odds with too many forms of counterevidence to be a major contributor to sex differences in math-intensive STEM careers, although, as was the case for the biological position, there is sufficient evidence to accord it a secondary role in the shortage of women in these careers.

If neither the strong biological/cognitive position nor the strong cultural/socialization position seem compelling as major explanatory factors for the dearth women in math-intensive careers, what can explain it, short of some amalgam of a large number of weak biological and cultural mechanisms? Personal choices and preferences are the most apparent explanatory factors.

We have described much of this evidence previously, but will reprise some of it below.

A number of recent analyses show that the probabilities of landing a tenure-track job and being promoted are similar for both men and women, as are their salaries, once adjusted for observables that explain salary such as years on the job, type of university, and field. What this means is that these observable factors that affect for salary and promotion differences that are not biased against women, nevertheless tend to work *against* women. But this is not because they are women, but because women are more likely to be more recent PhDs (hence paid less than more senior PhDs), work at small colleges (which pay less than big research universities), and work in fields that are not as highly remunerated (the humanities as opposed to engineering and business). One need not invoke sex discrimination as a major cause of such salary differences because men possessing these characteristics (e.g., working at smaller colleges or having fewer years of work experience, or working in the humanities) earn the same as women with these characteristics.[15]

However, there is one intrinsic factor that works against women that is quite pronounced. It has to do with the personal career penalty associated with having children early in one's career, which is much greater for women than men. Schiebinger and others suggested that marital patterns discourage women from persisting on the road to high-level science and engineering careers, and a great deal of survey data accord with this view. However, this mechanism applies just as much to women in nonmath fields as to those in math-intensive ones. Women have babies and defer their careers to their partners' careers in all fields, but it is in math-intensive fields where they are most underrepresented. So, what is it about these careers? Before directly delving into this question, there are some missing pieces of the puzzle that need to be mentioned.

Is the child penalty a result of personal choices women freely make—to care for children or defer their own career aspirations to those of their partners? Some argue that these are culturally coerced decisions that women—but not men—are required to make. This may be true, but if so, women are nevertheless parties to these decisions, and many women resist these pressures. Some women, after earning a doctorate, candidly admit they place greater priority on raising their families than on their careers, and are most eager to find a job that can be adapted to their family values. (This is a reason that many women enter teaching fields so they can be home when their children arrive after school and in summers.) Men are far less likely to express such values. It is beyond the scope of this book to probe the origins of these value differences, except to the extent that they bear on the question of discrimination. Although no single factor is able to account for the underrepresentation of women in STEM fields, it is the factor of *personal family-oriented choices*—as opposed to overt discrimination or enculturation of stereotypes or biologically based cognitive limitations—that seems most potent as a reason why fewer women pursue tenure-track careers in all fields, not just those that are math intensive. Timing of fertility decisions wreaks havoc on even the best-laid plans, and female doctorates in all fields run up against the ticking biological clock.

Coupled with the timing of fertility decisions is women's greater preference for careers that are more organic and socially oriented. The evidence we reviewed from several large surveys makes clear that women who have very high levels of mathematical aptitude are far more likely to state their ideal career is medicine or biology, for example, than physics or engineering. The reverse is true of males. And women who choose to enter math-intensive fields have the highest rates of attrition from their careers as they become more senior. Thus, fewer women score at the right tail of math, which probably deters many from applying to and getting accepted by fields that are math intensive; and disproportionately more of those who score at the right tail prefer nonmath careers. And finally, there is higher attrition among the subset of women who do choose math-intensive careers than is characteristic of men who choose these careers.

IS THE PROBLEM RESTRICTED TO MATH-INTENSIVE FIELDS?

As already mentioned, one problem with the argument that family-driven choices and fertility decisions are major factors in the sex imbalance in math-intensive fields is that family-oriented choices confront women in all fields. However, they take a greater toll in fields where women are underrepresented, because they whittle down a pool of potential contributors that is low to begin with. For example, even though some women choose to prioritize the needs of their families (often choosing to start families while pretenure) in the social sciences, medicine, law, and humanities fields, it takes a smaller toll on these fields because there are small or no gender gaps among new doctorates in them. Even if half the women earning doctorates in these fields opted out of tenure-track careers (an exaggeratedly high estimate), the high numbers of those that remain would still be formidable.

One can posit reasons for why women's underrepresentation in certain fields of science might be greater than in these other fields. Perhaps launching a career in a lab science requires greater rigidity in conforming to schedules? But these potential explanations are post hoc and probably wrong. Bear in mind that the gender gap in the biological sciences is much less pronounced than it is in math-intensive fields, yet the lab requirements would seem to be at least as demanding of rigid conformity as launching a career in mathematics.

However, even in fields that are not math intensive, where there is sex equivalence in new doctorates—medicine, psychology, veterinary medicine, and law, for example—women are not found in the top positions commensurate with their numbers. If 67.8% of PhDs in psychology have been awarded to women in the most recent decade, only 48.5%) of newly hired assistant professors have been women (and an even smaller proportion are full professors—29.5%), and this remains true even after adjusting for the subfields in which they earn their doctorates (mostly in clinical, developmental, and neuroscience subfields). So, perhaps there are multiple forces at work, some tilting women away from math-intensive careers even when they have the mathematical talent to succeed in them, and others tilting them toward lower rungs on the career ladders within these non math-intensive fields where they are more numerous.

In this regard, it would be interesting to know whether the abundance of female physicians translates into proportional numbers of female deans of medical schools, center directors, or high-level veterinary school administrators. As we describe below, some internal studies of the nation's leading medical training institutions reveal higher attrition among female professionals. Even among the women who remain in the field, there is some suggestion that many are stalled at lower rungs of the career ladder, while men rise to the leadership positions—even when they are numerically in the minority. For example, as noted in an earlier chapter, men are disproportionately in leadership positions in nursing and restaurant cooking, despite women being the majority in these fields.[16]

It would also be important to know whether a disproportionate number of the women who flocked to careers in medicine, law, psychology, and so on have opted to work part time because of family needs. If so, then nonmathematical fields in which women have made strides in recent years may not be that different from those that are math intensive. Even though women are entering some nonmathematical STEM science fields at very high rates, perhaps they are nevertheless affected by the "high-powered job hypothesis" in these fields, leading to greater selection of part-time work, more dropping out, and an underrepresentation of women in top leadership posts.

Consider the field of medicine, where half of all new MDs are female. Data from the University of Pennsylvania Medical School are suggestive. Readers may remember from our earlier discussion that female full professors in biology, chemistry, and psychology within the Penn Medical School had fewer square feet of research space assigned to them, with women's space averaging only 84% of that given to male full professors when the net square foot of research space per $1,000 of grant income was calculated. However, far more ominous than such space differences is the differential rate of leaving tenure-track positions for personal reasons. As we saw, within the clinical departments of the Penn Medical School, there is a collision course between work and family life that leads to more women leaving the faculty over time. Women constitute only 18% of senior faculty (full and associate professors) on the clinician educator track, and only 9% of the senior faculty on the tenure track.[17] Although pipeline issues might be responsible for some of this sex difference (smaller numbers of women getting MDs 30 years ago, hence fewer in the tenure track stream making its way to full professorship), the differential dropout rate of women versus men is also party responsible, with female assistant professors' dropout rate of 16% being much higher than men's 9%. So, of those young men and women earning doctorates who are hired by the Penn Medical School, women leave the tenure track at nearly double the rate as do men. They do not do so because of smaller space or salary, because younger women are at parity in these categories. They drop out for personal reasons, mostly family needs.

A recent history of progress in earning doctorates can be misleading. In 1960, only 5% of medical students in the United States were women, whereas today, women comprise approximately 50%. But the problem is far from being rectified. As Hamel et al. note, despite the gains, women who enter academic medicine have been less likely than men to be promoted or to serve in leadership positions. As of 2005, only 15% of full professors and 11% of department chairs were women.[18] And something similar may be true in all fields, not just the math-intensive ones. Even in the humanities, Haslanger[19] reports that only 18.7% of the tenure-track faculty in the top 20 philosophy departments are women. In cell and molecular biology, fields where women obtain nearly half of all PhDs, women are more likely to drop out of the pipeline at multiple points—as postdoctoral associates, as assistant professors, and as associate professors. Ultimately, only 17.4% of full professors are women in the biological sciences.

This indicates that when explaining the dearth of women at the very top of the fields (as opposed to the rates of newly hired women), the situation in math-intensive STEM fields may be more the norm than the exception in nonmathematical fields, as well. The situation is exacerbated in the math fields by a confluence of factors we have mentioned: (1) fewer women scoring at the right tail in math, which reduces their chances of acceptance into math-intensive graduate fields for which the GRE-Q scores are an important consideration for admission; (2) fewer women who do score at the right tail in math preferring to enter mathematical fields even though they have the mathematical aptitude to be successful, preferring instead more organic, people-oriented fields; (3) fewer women opting to compete for tenure-track posts upon receipt of their doctorates; (4) more women leaving the field for family reasons; and (5) more women leaving the field as they advance, for career changes. Note that none of these factors entails overt discrimination against women. But that possibility, although unlikely to be a major factor, may nevertheless be a small contributor to the dearth of women in math-intensive fields, because there is evidence that senior women in physics are underpromoted. Where evidence for discrimination exists, it centers not on younger women, but on senior ones, who tend to be paid less and to be overlooked for leadership positions vis-à-vis men and younger women. Below we review briefly some of the evidence for these claims.

In her 2007 presidential address to the Association for Women in Science, Phoebe Leboy reviewed 20 medical schools, pointing out that female assistant professors lagged in the PhD pool in their disciplines from a decade earlier by 10%–15%. In other words, the number of women in the PhD pipeline did not predict the proportion of women hired as assistant professors on tenure track within the next decade. For example, in 1994–96 women comprised 45% of all PhDs awarded in the biomedical sciences, but just 29% of the tenure-track assistant professors hired within the following decade. The proportion of women in senior faculty positions at Harvard still averages only 13% across all disciplines, not just math-intensive fields,[20] suggesting that women's underrepresentation in math-intensive fields is merely an exaggerated form of a problem that can be seen in nonmath fields. For instance, according to recent data from the American Institute of Physics,[21] only 5% of full professors in physics are female. However, Ginther and Kahn's 2006 analysis shows that women are currently hired and promoted, including promoted to full professor, at rates similar to men, once fertility decisions are taken into account—although as we have seen, fertility choices are a large and important source of sex differences. This leads to the conclusion that the underrepresentation of women in math-intensive STEM fields will continue well into the future, because the numbers of female PhDs in the pipeline leading into these fields does not approach parity with men, whereas in other fields mentioned (like psychology, medicine, philosophy, and biology), the female pipeline does approach or exceed parity.

So there is some evidence for the underrepresentation of women in leadership positions in non-STEM fields, but the problem is exacerbated in math-intensive fields, even at junior levels. Therefore, we are suggesting that STEM versus non-STEM women are two overlapping groups. The magnitude of the problem is greater in math-intensive STEM fields because of the confluence of factors described above. This is precisely why there has been such intense interest in women in math-intensive fields on the part of the federal government and research agencies (for example, National Science Foundation [NSF] initiatives such as ADVANCE, which has awarded tens of millions of dollars to universities to increase the representation of women across all levels, from newly hired to senior leadership).

TABLE **8.1.** Among mathematically talented students expecting to major in the sciences, the specific fields of the expected undergraduate major.

FIELD	MEN	WOMEN	d
Engineering	43.4	22.9	0.43
Mathematics	15.9	21.1	–0.13
Biological science	13.4	23.4	–0.26
Computer science	8.3	6.0	0.08
Medical science	3.6	12.9	–0.34
Physical science	8.8	1.4	0.41
Chemistry	5.0	8.0	–0.12
Earth science	1.2	2.3	0.08
Agricultural science	0.4	2.0	0.10

Source: Adapted from Webb, R. M., Lubinski, D., & Benbow, C. P. (2002). Mathematic facile adolescents with mathematics–science aspirations: New perspectives on their educational and vocational development. *Journal of Educational Psychology, 94*, 785–794

SEX DIFFERENCES IN PREFERENCES IS AN IMPORTANT PREDICTOR

Returning to the factors listed previously, personal preferences emerge in a variety of surveys as a major impediment to women from reaching parity in certain fields. One of the most robust findings has been that women at all levels of math aptitude do not prefer math-intensive careers in anywhere near the numbers that men do. As we have alluded to repeatedly, among men and women of comparably high mathematical prowess, men are far more likely to go into math-intensive careers, and women are more likely to enter biomedical careers. As can be seen in Table 8.1, female high school students who are highly math talented expect to major in biomedical fields, but also in chemistry and mathematics (fields with minus signs indicate greater female interest; fields with positive signs indicate greater male interest). This is one of the most robust findings in the literature—women's and men's differing career interests, independent of their math ability. Strenta et al. canvassed thousands of science majors at four select universities (Brown, Yale, Cornell, and Dartmouth), and found that women were significantly more likely to switch out of science majors after entering college.[22] The sole field in which there were no sex differences in dropouts from undergraduate science programs was biology. Strenta reported that, in addition to various social factors that predicted switching out of science (aggressive or competitive climate was a turn-off to many women), there were two important cognitive factors: lower grades in science courses and lower SAT-M scores. Women disproportionately dropped out of science after the first year of college due to poor grades in basic science courses.

The preference picture plays out in other ways, one of the most interesting of which is that women with high math talent often have more options than men with comparable math abilities. This is because high-math-ability women possess cognitive profiles that are more balanced. Park et al.[23] found that if two individuals have equivalent mathematics skills, but one also has high verbal skills, the individual with the high-mathematics/high-verbal profile will achieve less vocationally in STEM fields than will the high-mathematics-only individual. In other words, those who can *only* do mathematics at a very high level, end up doing mathematics—but those with multiple extreme talents may choose to do something else, such as law, business, or literature. This could also lead to a sex difference in STEM fields, independent of any difference in mathematics ability, because women with high math ability are significantly more likely to also have very high verbal skills, as David Lubinski et al. have shown.

In summary, multiple factors of unknown relative magnitude (listed here in alphabetical order) potentially contribute to the lack of women *across all fields:* biological differences (hormone), cognitive differences, discrimination, personal preferences, profile balance, social practices/cultural beliefs, and structural aspects of higher education (such as female-unfriendly timing of tenure decisions and lack of opportunities for part-time work that segues into tenure-track positions). In some situations, structural aspects that disadvantage women may be unfortunate but nevertheless justifiable, while in others they may be unnecessarily ungenerous and disadvantageous to women. In all cases, small initial differences, whether in cognitive, social, or other domains, can potentially multiply into larger effects.

Regarding the relative paucity of women at the extreme right tail of STEM fields, the popular conception of the problem may be exaggerated. This is because of cohort issues (a focus on older data that no longer are applicable) and measurement issues such as an emphasis on aptitude tests rather than other measures of performance such as grades, and it also is due to superficial factors such as stereotype threat exaggerating sex differences in scores beyond what exists when math ability is assessed in gender neutral contexts.

Moving from all fields to the most math-intensive ones, the factors that contribute the most to the dearth of women is personal preferences and fertility choices: Women express less interest in many math-intensive fields, such as engineering, computer science, and physics. Even among the women whose math ability is in the extreme right tail of the ability distribution, there is greater desire to enter more organic, social professions that impact people rather than things. The Canadian journalist and psychologist Susan Pinker[24] relates several anecdotes about her neighbors to make this point dramatically, with one tenured professor of computer science opting to leave her field to enter another that she found more exciting and people oriented. Many readers no doubt have their own anecdotes that accord with her opinion.

To some, the fact that a woman possessing extreme levels of math ability chooses not to enter a math-intensive career is a missed opportunity, a wasted gift. Federal programs seem to implicitly make this assumption, with their programs aimed at recruiting more women into these underrepresented fields and mentoring those already in them. However, often overlooked in these discussions of "wasted talent" is the fact that women who could be successful in math-intensive STEM fields, but are not, have not fallen off the face of the earth. These women are often doing other things that are worthwhile, whether in a different career or by rearing a family. There is an often-overlooked opportunity cost to getting more women to switch into math-intensive STEM fields from their other pursuits. Actively promoting an increase in the number of women in these jobs, as opposed to simply promoting equality of opportunity—without taking into account what else these women will not therefore be doing—may give a misleading impression of the value of such an effort.[25]

WOMEN'S DESIRE FOR GREATER BALANCE LEADS TO CALLS FOR CHANGE IN ACADEMY'S CULTURE

Given the enormous demands that high-level careers place on those who pursue them and the time commitment required of those women who choose to be actively involved in raising children, it may be more fruitful to take as a starting point for discussion the incompatibility for many people of the two endeavors—career and family—as they are currently structured. Next, we should ask how women have attained the remarkably high levels of success they have in some professions, such as medicine, dentistry, law, veterinary medicine, psychology, and biology which make enormous demands on time away from home. Answering this question might give society a mechanism for opening up more opportunities instead of searching only for biological, socialization, or discriminatory reasons for why there are disproportionately fewer women at the top of some fields.

One obvious difference about the careers in which women have reached or exceeded parity is that they allow women to move in and out of full-time employment with relative ease, if not without penalty. As we remarked in an earlier chapter, although women may be less likely to achieve the level of partner in law firms or associate in medical practices, or to be co-owners of veterinary or dental corporations if they opt for part-time work while their children are young, at least they do not have to abandon their careers altogether, as might be the case if they were a professor who moved from full-time, tenure-track work to part-time teaching. Leaving tenure track usually precludes returning to it, unlike the nonacademic professions that provide greater flexibility, albeit possibly at the expense of making full partner. Research shows that women are significantly more interested in the flexibility of moving between part-time and full-time work than are men. Not all women, of course, but disproportionately more so than men.

Figure 8.1 illustrates this point with survey data from Lubinski et al.[26] As can be seen, female and male graduate students both express the desire for full-time work when they finish their doctoral training, but later, twice as many women prefer permanent part-time work, and over three times more prefer part-time work for a limited period of time. Specifically, 31% of Lubinski et al.'s female graduate school respondents said a part-time option was "important" or "extremely important," compared with only 9% of graduate-student men. The same survey asked how many hours respondents would work in their ideal job, and again, women reported they would work fewer hours per week in such jobs.

Benbow et al. have reported data on the amount of time that nearly two thousand 33-year-olds, who during their adolescence were in the top 1% of quantitative ability, claim they typically devote to their current jobs and the amount they would devote to their ideal jobs. By the age of 33, roughly twice as many high-aptitude men report working at their jobs 50-plus hours per week, and approximately three times more women report working less than 40 hours. Lubinski and Benbow reported a similar sex difference in another study of several hundred profoundly gifted participants scoring in the top 1 in 10,000 on either the SAT-M or SAT-V, leading to their suggestion that "one only needs to imagine the differences in research productivity likely to accrue over a 5- to 10-year interval between two faculty members working 45- versus 65-hour weeks (other things being equal) to understand the possible impact."[27] Their findings have been replicated on two independent cohorts that are even more mathematically and verbally exceptional[28]: a group of approximately 700 top mathematics/science graduate students identified in their mid-20s and tracked for 10 years and a group of approximately 400 profoundly gifted participants identified before age 13 and tracked for 20 years.

None of this should be surprising to anyone familiar with Catherine Hakim's surveys we discussed in Chapter 2. Recall that she found that only approximately 20% of women in these surveys prefer work-centered lifestyles in which the main commitment is to career rather than family. Anecdotal evidence suggests that this 20% of work-centered women work every bit as long and hard as work-centered men, and enjoy the same level of success as men. But far more men prefer this kind of work-centered lifestyle. Approximately 60% of women prefer what Hakim refers to as "adapted work lifestyles" where employment can be meshed with family and personal goals (e.g., being a teacher allows a parent to be home when children get out of school and during their summer vacations). Both men and women with this lifestyle put in fewer hours at their jobs. Because more women are in this category they skew the number of hours worked per week for women, as does the higher percentage of men in the work-centered category skew the male hours worked per week.

One response to such findings has been to challenge the values underlying a work-centered existence—in essence, to change the very culture of the academy. Some commentators have argued that male-centered values such as competitiveness and single-minded obsession on research are inimical to family and personal values and should not be celebrated and rewarded. On October 17, 2007 when the Subcommittee on Research and Science Education of the U.S. Congress met to discuss the topic of women in science, Donna Shalala, co-author of the National Academy of Sciences report "Beyond Bias and Barriers: Fulfilling the Potential of Women in Academic Science and Engineering," testified that women in the academy faced a hostile climate, replete with male values of competiveness that "clearly calls for a transformation of academic institutions. . . . Our nation's future depends on it." Other speakers testified about the hidden sexism of the obsessive and

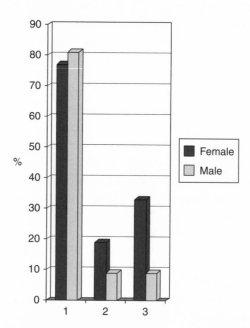

FIGURE **8.1.** Sex differences in lifecourse preferences. Code: 1 = Grad students report full-time career was important or extremely important; 2 = Subsequently report they prefer permanent part-time; 3 = Subsequently prefer part-time for limited period of time.

competitive work ethic that women find repulsive, according to one speaker. Commenting on this testimony, the philosopher Christina Sommers noted "The list of cultural norms that appear to disadvantage women...includes the favoring of disciplinary over interdisciplinary research and publications, and the only token attention given to teaching and other service during the tenure review process. Thus it seems that it is not necessarily conscious bias against women but an ingrained idea of how the academic enterprise 'should be' that presents the greatest challenge to women seeking academic [science and engineering] careers."

We end this chapter by making explicit the goal of those calling for a culture-shift in the academy. Some of the proponents of gender equity in STEM fields have gone beyond calls for removal of discriminatory treatments and better mentoring of young women, to demands to abolish the obsessive and competitive work ethic of successful scientists that universities reward. This is because women remain underrepresented in these fields even in the absence of discriminatory hiring and promotion practices, and women have flourished in fields with few female role models and mentors (women have gone from under 10% of veterinary medicine degrees in the 1960s to approximately 77% of the seats in current veterinary programs despite few female role models to foster this explosion in enrollment). Something beyond ending discrimination and providing female role models and mentors will be necessary to close the sex gap in math-intensive fields. Calls for a "culture shift" have been offered to achieve this. However, rarely is what is meant by a culture shift made explicit. Again, Sommers words: "Most scientists have no idea of the power and scope of the equity crusade. The business community and citizens at large are completely in the dark. This is a quiet revolution....intent on radically transforming society to achieve egalitarian ideals." Sommers cites several leading proponents of the culture shift who want to increase the representation of women by altering the behavior of successful scientists whose alleged 'obsessive work habits, single-minded dedication, and intense desire for achievement,' are claimed to marginalize women and even compromise good science. She quotes one proponent who wrote, "If we continue to emphasize and reward always being on the job, we will never find out whether leading a balanced life leads to equally good or better scientific work."

The point of spelling out the goals of the culture-shift position is to inform readers of the dilemma that some gender equity proponents have confronted: none of the obvious, reasonable proposals to increase the representation of women in fields such as physics, computer science, and engineering will result in the desired sea change because men and women differ on average in their desire for work-centered careers. The types of blatant sex discrimination that everyone agrees should be stamped out is no longer able to explain the dearth of women in STEM fields. For example Shalala writes in the Preface to the

NAS report of her experiences as a graduate student in the 1960s and as a young professor: in each case, a male department chair told her that she wouldn't be getting any fellowships or a shot at tenure because women were a "bad investment." Today, such behavior is rare and cannot account for the underrepresentation of women. Something more fundamental than stamping out blatant sexism is needed to increase the presence of women in math-intensive careers. Toward that end, some have concluded that the nature of work-centered careers must be changed so that those who are rewarded and promoted for the single-minded obsessive pursuit of research at the expense of greater balance be prohibited from such pursuit. However, as Sommers puts it: "A world where women (and resocialized men) earn Nobel Prizes on flextime has no relation to reality."

What next? Research and policy recommendations

"A science career for women is now almost as acceptable as being a cheerleader."

—Myra Barker

Readers may recall research described in Chapter 2 showing that women biologists conduct higher-impact work than their male counterparts when assessed later in their careers (17 years post-PhD).[1] Clearly, these older biologists may represent more of a select group than today's average biologist. Nevertheless, it seems justified to probe the differing life courses of women's versus men's careers, to see how the timing of the current tenure and promotion system may be denying society and science the services of some talented women. If women in STEM fields make greater impacts and do more important work later in their careers, once the bulk of childrearing is complete, and if this work can be shown to compare favorably with that of male colleagues, then at minimum our institutions should be investigating and testing potential systems for offering women part-time tenure-track jobs (with concomitantly longer periods of time in which to amass a tenure portfolio) that convert to full-time tenured jobs, if they wish, once family responsibilities have lessened. Men wishing to experience day-to-day fatherhood rather than abdicating it to their partners might also wish to take advantage of such nontraditional career ladders. Standards for achieving tenure could be just as high; the time period to amass a portfolio would be longer and the pay reduced in proportion to effort. Maryann Mason, a leading figure in the field of economics, family, work, and mothers, has noted that, in her surveys of graduate students, postdocs, and faculty at the University of California (conducted with Mark Goulden), fewer paid family leave policies apply to fathers. Even when they do apply to fathers, fathers (like mothers) are disinclined to take them because it is seen as a sign of a lack of commitment to one's career.

The current system provides strong disincentives for talented women to have children. This is why more women in the academy are childless than are their male colleagues, and why surveys indicate that many who have children wish they had more. According to recent demographic analyses, approximately 20% of U.S. and Japanese women born between 1956 and 1972 are childless and likely to remain so, and childlessness could reach 25% in the near future. Of most relevance to this book is the finding that childlessness increases with increasing education and income. Fully one-third of women college graduates in their late 30s have no children. And only 20% of women with MBAs have children (versus 70% of men with MBAs). Among academics, as we noted in an earlier chapter, it is more common for men to have children than for women to do so. When men have children they are more likely to be tenured than are women—a fact that is explained by the longer hours of domestic work taken on by faculty mothers compared to faculty fathers. Note that, even after statistically adjusting for the number of hours worked and chronological age, compared to male physicians, male academics are 40% less likely to have a child and female academics are 20% less likely than their female physician counterparts to be mothers.

One could argue that it is in society's interest for these men and women to have and rear offspring, if they so desire, without having to permanently sacrifice their careers. It is good for children, and it allows women to make use of their high-level skills. These skills cost society so much to develop—one might ask, why should they be lost? Additionally, we are living in a period in which America desperately needs skilled scientists and engineers—so much so that we are constantly told of the need to expand the number of foreign visas offered. Recall that Hakim[2] found that about 60% of women prefer adapted work lifestyles, in which work can be fitted in with family and personal goals. These women, including many highly trained scientists, have a great deal to contribute to their fields if provisions are made to enable them to manage their personal lives simultaneously. Until fathers assume an equal role in childcare, this will mean providing mother-friendly options that rarely exist at present, several of which we describe below.

A related issue concerns the traits our current tenure and promotion system focuses on during selection. As Hamel et al.[3] opined, to be successful and advance in academic medicine, a person must devote most waking moments to his or her career. But it is worthwhile to ask whether the people we most wish to have as intellectual leaders are the ones who are willing to give up virtually everything else in their lives to pursue their careers. If so, then the current system may make great sense. But this is a testable research question that could be informed by an examination of research accomplishments of STEM scientists working in countries where family and leisure seem more sacrosanct than in the United States.

Relatedly, one can ask why colleges and universities do not offer half-time tenure-track appointments for men and women who wish to divide their energies between career and other pursuits, whether these involve family or other interests. If our limited observations are relevant, there have been cases in which our own university allowed partners to share a single tenure line so that both could be employed at the same university. When this has occurred, both partners contributed *at least* 50%, so it seemed that the university got a good deal, and the couple was given the opportunity to be employed at a level that worked best for them and their family. (In one case, the couple segued to two full-time tenure-track appointments later, when their youngest child entered school.) Such arrangements permit a scholar to remain current in her or his field, to teach, and to do research at a reduced level, and maintain all of the accoutrements of a STEM professor (such as an office, lab, e-mail, library resources, lactation room, staff support, and graduate students, and the right to submit grants as a principal investigator rather than under the aegis of a full-time tenure-track faculty member).

Granted, these accoutrements cost the institution space and staff, but these are modest expenditures compared to the initiatives that are often implemented to launch new programs and buildings. Plus, these modest allowances hold out the promise of capitalizing on a large unassimilated talent pool awaiting better utilization. A part-time tenure-track option would allow some individuals to work their entire careers at half time—teaching half time and doing research half time—if they wished to do so. Others may want to transition to full-time positions when conditions warrant it, provided their institutions have an opening. But in principle, there does not seem to be a reason this could not be done, and it would immediately allow tens of thousands of talented women to keep their hand in the game, so to speak.

Another issue not often discussed in the current debate, but still (we believe) relevant, concerns the unintended consequences of the structure of the educational system on both women and men. At present, content taught in high school and introductory college courses in the sciences bears little resemblance to anything that practicing scientists actually do. Testing is rigorous, focused on extensive memorization, and problems of close transfer are passed off as abstract reasoning. The current system is designed to weed out most students from the pool of young people pursuing graduate school and professional school degrees. If coursework instead taught the skills needed in STEM careers, and if the course exams assessed this information, then society might gain many thousands of additional STEM scientists. But the fact is that, in many cases, schools do not teach this way. A worthwhile area for further empirical study concerns the structure and content of education in the sciences, which ideally should better reflect the ultimate skills and knowledge possessed by practicing scientists so that the people best equipped to succeed as students are the same people best equipped to succeed ultimately as professionals in the field, be they women or men.

Finally, there is a fundamental research question that has plagued us throughout the three years of working on this book; namely, what is the causal relation between spatial cognition, advanced mathematics ability, and success in STEM fields? The available evidence is circumstantial at best. And yet, the answer to this question lies at the heart of the matter. How much of the shortage of women in mathematically-intensive fields exists because women lack certain spatial skills that are directly important for success in some of these fields, such as the freshmen graphics course in engineering [4]? And, how much of the shortage of women is due to women's lacking spatial skills that form the basis of complex math, which in turn is critical to success in certain fields, as many suggest?

This issue needs to be raised, lest readers forget that the existing evidence connecting spatial reasoning, math, and career success is circumstantial. When one measure of spatial cognition (such as two-dimensional mental rotation) does not predict math, then the inclination has been to focus on another measure that does predict math (three-dimensional rotation). And when spatial reasoning fails to predict sex differences in early math proficiency, the tendency has been to argue that such a prediction should not reveal itself until puberty, when hormones surge and/or when math becomes more complex.[5] The arguments tend to become circular and endlessly unfalsifiable. And yet, there *is* some suggestive evidence for a linkage.[6] We simply need more direct evidence. The same applies to research claims about the influence of male hormones in spatial and mathematical prowess. There is a great deal of research on this topic—several hundred studies in the past decade alone—and there is substantial evidence that androgen plays a role in an average person's spatial performance. But the size of the role seems small, and the literature is plagued by contradictions, complexities, and failures to replicate, not to mention an absence of focus upon the women most relevant to this debate—those at the right tail of the math ability distribution.

Further research is also needed to ensure that the concepts tapped in gatekeeper tests such as the Scholastic Assessment Test-Mathematics (SAT-M) and Graduate Record Exam-Quantitative (GRE-Q) are indicative of future performance. For this, a theoretically grounded definition of STEM field–relevant higher math skill is needed. Do some fields rely on being in the top 0.1% in the ability to visualize n-dimensional space, rotate drawings into three-dimensional models or their mirror images, and so on, as some have suggested? Or is there little gain accrued from being in the top 0.1% over and above that from being in, say, the top 15% on such skills—a point at which the sex asymmetry is less pronounced? We do not know. Are those who succeed in fields that seem to require a heavy component of spatial ability (radiology, crystallography, architecture, engineering) in the top 1% or 0.01% of spatial ability? The list of unanswered questions is unfortunately long.

SUMMARY OF OUR CONCLUSIONS ABOUT WOMEN IN STEM

Granted that the literature is often inconsistent, and at times contradictory, readers may wonder where we stand. As we have stated before, one clearly important factor explaining women's underrepresentation is that math-capable women disproportionately *choose* nonmathematics fields, and such preferences are already visible among math-competent girls during adolescence. Added to this is the fact that, of women who do choose to enter STEM fields, twice as many leave these fields as do men.[7] In our view, evidence for a direct effect of innate hormonal differences on math and spatial ability is contradictory and inconclusive, with minimal data on right-tail samples. Notwithstanding this failure to link sex differences in mathematical and spatial ability to prenatal and postnatal hormones, there *are* persistent sex differences in spatial reasoning (see Richard Lippa et al.'s report of male advantage on mental rotation in 53 nations) and mathematical ability at the right tail (approximately two males to every one female on various gatekeeper tests such as the SAT-M and GRE-Q[8]). This finding may reflect sociocultural factors, biological factors, or some combination of the two. So, we do not dismiss either hormones or spatial ability differences between the sexes as contributors to the dearth of women in math-intensive fields. However, we do downgrade them to secondary status, as significantly less important than preferences and lifestyle choices: far more women graduate with undergraduate degrees in engineering than work as engineers.

Transnational data show inconsistent sex differences at the right tail, including data from some countries showing reverse trends[9] and some, but not all, U.S. data showing a narrowing of the sex gap at the right tail over time.[10] Given these findings, we conclude that the bases of mathematical and spatial differences are almost certainly *not* purely biological, but rather, must include a strong sociocultural component. Fewer women at the right tail in mathematical and spatial ability means that fewer women are available for some math-intensive graduate programs, due to their GRE-Q scores falling short of the scores desired by graduate admissions committees. However, although there is a strong suggestion that such abilities play some causal role in women's underrepresentation, hard data linking math and spatial abilities to STEM success are indirect.[11] As we argued earlier, if each sex's representation was primarily a function of math ability, there would be twice as many women in math-intensive careers as there now are. This is because (assuming a 2.06:1 ratio of men to women at the top 1% of math ability), women would be expected to comprise approximately 30% of the professorships in math-intensive fields such as physics and engineering. In actuality, they comprise far less–for example, only 10% of faculty in physics are women.[12] Clearly, non-ability factors such as women's preferences must play an important role—math-talented women are choosing non-math careers far more frequently than are math-talented men.

We believe that most factors concerning cultural inputs and discrimination are less important today than they were in the past—society and its women have indeed come a long way. We note that unequal representation in STEM careers is not *uniquely* affected by inequality in childrearing responsibilities between the sexes, because such inequality, although very typical, leads women with children to have less time for *all* careers, not just math-intensive STEM ones. Note that, in Mason & Goulden's surveys, faculty mothers work many more hours per week at childcare than do fathers, of necessity reducing their professional hours as a consequence. One woman who posted a comment on one of our scientific articles noted that, in the military, there are many women who make the rank of colonel, and some who make the rank of general, with one factor differentiating them. In her words:

> Speaking as a woman who has a successful career in a male dominated environment (not STEM but the military), I can say that it is possible for a woman to rise to the top, if she is willing to make one of two choices (or falls into one of two categories):
>
> 1. She has no children.
> 2. If she has children, she has a husband who has a work schedule that allows him to be the one "on call" for the children.
>
> I've seen many, many female Colonels successful with selection 2. I've only seen female Generals with selection 1. At:
>   (http://science.slashdot.org/article.pl?sid=09/03/15/0049227&from=rss)

The importance of childrearing is magnified for STEM women by the coincidence of tenure decisions with childbearing, which also affects all academic fields. The tenure structure in the academy demands that women who have children make their greatest intellectual achievements contemporaneously with their greatest physical and emotional achievements, a feat fathers are virtually never expected to accomplish. When women opt out of careers to have children (or segue to part time employment), *this is a choice men are almost never required to make.* The reasons women opt out of math-intensive fields—either when first choosing a career, or later—are complex. Reasons for preferring nonmath fields may include both free and coerced choices, which can be influenced by biological and sociocultural factors that either enable or limit women.[13] Definitive conclusions about women's underrepresentation are also thwarted because the cognitive requirements for success in mathematical fields are poorly understood, despite the importance of math and spatial skills.[14] But we do know that the number of women who intend to have a career in research declines by 30 percent over the course of their doctoral training (versus a 20 percent decline for their male counterparts). Mason (2009) notes that in explaining their decision, men are more likely to report that they are turned off by the long work hours, whereas women are turned off by their perception of the incompatibility of academic careers with having children. In Mason's words: "One male student in the survey complained that he was 'fed up with the narrow-mindedness of supposedly intelligent people who are largely workaholic and expect others to be so as well.' But most women give up on academic-research careers for family concerns. As one woman in the survey said, 'I could not have come to graduate school more motivated to be a research-oriented professor. Now I feel that can only be a career possibility if I am willing to sacrifice having children.' "

There is no question that children are a major reason for the dearth of women in all fields at senior levels. Children are also a significant reason for women's underrepresentation in math-intensive fields, where women begin in smaller numbers, meaning that any attrition is magnified compared to fields such as the humanities in which women are more prevalent, meaning that attrition still leaves many women in the pipeline.

WHERE DO WE WANT TO GO FROM HERE?

In addition to the obvious goal of ensuring that there is no overt discrimination against women in STEM fields, a second more controversial goal is to create equality of opportunity, despite the differences currently inherent in men's versus women's lives. That is, society could try to remold the pathway to top STEM jobs to make them fit with modern women's lives. Historically, this type of change happened when universities transitioned from the Oxbridge monastic system of live-in colleges designed for single male scholars to the modern system. The modern system fits the life of the traditional mid-twentieth-century breadwinner with a stay-at-home spouse to take care of him and his children. There was a time when conventional wisdom stated that scholars should not be permitted to marry and move out of college accommodations, because it would break up the intellectual community and destroy the interactions that were thought to be the key to intellectual development. Yet very few professors at research universities now live with their colleagues and students in residence halls, and even the few who do are likely to be living in residence houses with their families as house deans and residential faculty fellows. The stereotype of the male faculty breadwinner with a stay-at-home spouse to take care of him and his children has over time come to characterize fewer and fewer faculty, as the surveys reviewed in earlier chapters revealed.

Ample evidence is already available, as described earlier, to show that the current structure of the academic ladder, with its conflicts between career and family demands, causes many otherwise qualified women not to reach the top of STEM fields—and of those who do, more are likely to be single, divorced, and childless than is true of their male counterparts. What, if anything, should be done about this situation is unclear, however. Evidence is needed regarding the long-term productivity impacts of early career interruptions and part-time work. Evidence is also needed about the consequences of modifying the tenure system to avoid making long-term decisions about individuals' careers at a time when family demands render current productivity unrepresentative of future potential. The practicality of career gaps and part-time work will likely vary by field. This practicality depends on the pace of change in the knowledge base, laboratory work constraints, and multiplier effects resulting from not training doctoral students, not submitting grants, etc., earlier in one's career as opposed to later on. It is also likely that the feasibility of career interruptions will depend on the type of institution (i.e., teaching intensive versus research intensive).

McDowell[15] studied the shelf life of journal articles published by scientists to determine how often old articles were cited. He took this information on the relative cite rates for newer versus older articles as evidence that it was possible to take a childcare leave and return, without falling far behind in the knowledge needed to resume publishing new articles. He reported that research in STEM fields became obsolete particularly fast and ceased being cited. McDowell interpreted this finding to mean that a larger child penalty would exist in these fields in terms of research productivity for women who left their careers for extended childcare leaves, because these women would return to fields that might have changed course.

If, in some fields, career gaps and part-time work are shown to be inefficient, society is presented with a choice. Do we accept the disadvantage faced by individuals (women or men) wanting to devote time and energy to family responsibilities and thus "paying" for choices they make? Or, do we force change into the system regardless, despite the possible cost to national and disciplinary productivity? Both are legitimate, although potentially unpopular options; the choice is a trade-off between personal fulfillment and allocation of scarce academic resources. If enacted clumsily, forced changes can result in resentment, rivalries, and lower efficiency that comes with attempts by some to "game" the system by strategic use of part-time contracts to hide poor productivity and low commitment to the profession. Those allegedly obsessive, competitive, single-minded scientists whom gender equity proponents want to abolish are nevertheless devoted to their careers and have made enormous strides in scientific knowledge. Their discoveries have made America a magnet for the best international graduate students, who come to U.S. universities to study with these scientists (and many of these international students remain here following their training, contributing to our future success).

What about societal goals for the rearing of girls—how might goals of increasing women in STEM fields translate into different childrearing strategies? It goes without saying that a rich childhood environment should be offered to all children—but also, if certain sex-stereotyped activities (like playing with blocks or building marble runs) are found to be particularly conducive to the development of strong math skills (which so far data merely suggest might be true), efforts might be made to encourage participation in such activities by girls who might otherwise not do so. Stronger evidence regarding the benefits of such activities is required before any concrete recommendations can be made, and they would need to be weighed against the opportunity cost of what the girls might forgo, as well as their personal preferences. If forcing girls to play with erector sets and spatially oriented video games really did lead to enhancement of their mathematical development, we still must ask if the price to them is worth it.

As we have repeatedly mentioned, women currently comprise nearly half of all new MD degrees and law degrees, as well as life science doctorates.[16] And, as already noted, they also make up the vast majority of veterinary medicine, dentistry, and psychology doctorates, to name a few areas of female ascendancy. We need to distinguish between efforts to encourage more women into underrepresented fields versus shifting women already headed for professional degrees and success in other areas into fields they may find less satisfying. Everyone can agree that encouragement to enter fields in which women have strong interest and ability is important. But many fear that efforts to channel women into fields they are less interested in, merely to achieve some degree of gender representation, could lead to unsatisfied women, as Susan Pinker's (2008) revealing book, *The Gender Paradox*, suggests. One woman, upon leaving the field of engineering to teach elementary school science, lamented:

> "When I started working in engineering I said to myself, I don't like this at all. So the electrical current goes from X to Y, from here to there. Who cares? I was unhappy and didn't want to continue. I made the decision to switch as much for me as for my

family. Education corresponds better to who I am, it reflects my more human side. In engineering I never felt that human relations were valued . . . . In high school I was pushed and encouraged to go into engineering because I was good at math and science, but if it had been my choice, I would have been a nurse. I always knew what I wanted but I was discouraged from switching out of engineering by my male teachers and by my father because teaching is less valued in society. It's great that people want more women in these disciplines but the women have to want it, too." (p. 83)

As Pinker points out, women pushed into careers they did not want or enjoy were often quite successful—as gauged by promotions, earnings, tenure, etc., but ultimately these women realized that despite their career success, they were not pursuing their overall life goals.

Regardless of how important spatial ability may prove to be in a given STEM career, we have seen that spatial ability can be enhanced through direct training, if not to complete gender parity at least much of the way. That schools do not train such skills would seem to be easily remedied, *if* it turns out that spatial cognition is critically important for success in STEM professions. On this point, though, it is worth restating our earlier caveat: Some interventions may boost boys' and men's performance even more than girls' and women's, resulting in larger sex differences than existed prior to the intervention. A national dialog among training program directors, policy makers, and ethicists is long overdue on the appropriateness of targeting interventions to girls even though these interventions could elevate boys' spatial ability, too. Hyde's[17] recommendation that all college-bound students be required to take 4 years of high school math and 4 years of high school science strikes us as sensible, as this seems to be what drives greater proportions of women in other societies into STEM fields. Girls in Ireland, Korea, and Turkey are all required to take 3–4 years of high school math and science, and these countries all produce greater proportions of women in some STEM fields than do the U.S. and Canada. But such a suggestion will only work if colleges and universities require more math and science for admission. And, again, consideration needs to be given to what will *not* be studied, if more math and science are required.

Presumably, the goal is not to get more women into math-intensive STEM jobs *at any cost,* as it would not be desirable to promote incapable women any more than it is to promote incapable men. Nor would it be desirable to nudge women into fields they may not wish to enter or might not end up enjoying, as Pinker's interviews document.[18] Hence, it may not be as simple as getting the maximum number of women into these jobs who are capable of doing well at them (up to the point at which the marginal woman is as good as the marginal man). Such a strategy does not take into account the concept of "opportunity cost"—the cost, not just in monetary terms but also in terms of well-being, happiness, and other outputs, to an individual woman and society of *not* doing whatever else she would have done, whether it be nursing, teaching, or working in the humanities, law, some other STEM profession that is not math-intensive, or no profession at all. If societal changes can enable or entice women who would have become doctors, biologists, or lawyers to instead become mathematicians or computer scientists, is this necessarily a good thing? Is it inherently more valuable to encourage women to shift from their preponderance in fields of biology and medicine to mathematics, so they can end up working on a search algorithm for Google rather than on a cure for AIDS, as both David Lubinski and Susan Barnett have wondered? What if such changes enable or entice women who would have desired most of all to be full-time mothers to instead become full-time math professors (potentially having fewer children than desired or even remaining childless)? Being a professor in a research university STEM department may well be a more high-status position than being a stay-at-home mother (or, for that matter, a professor at a community college or in a humanities department saddled with a heavy teaching load and relatively poor remuneration), but is it necessarily more worthwhile and satisfying? We are supportive of our own three daughters pursuing science careers and we do much to help them achieve this. But we also watch for signs of disaffection and have agreed not to push them to become scientists if we sense their passion lies elsewhere.

If the gender imbalance at the top of STEM fields is considered a problem in its own right, irrespective of the fairness of the system that led to this imbalance, changes can be forced on the system to increase female representation. However, society will undertake this at its peril if the full opportunity costs are not taken into account. There are two classes of such costs. First, getting more capable women into STEM professions by definition must mean fewer such women doing something else. Second, the integrity of the scientific enterprise necessitates objective methods for arbitrating disagreements, including hiring the best scientists, and peer review of findings and grant proposals. Calls to "Title 9" colleges and universities until their science programs reflect the sex balance in the workforce seem ill-advised. Christine Huff Sommers describes efforts in Congress to do just this, and she quotes Senator Hillary Clinton's campaign pledge that because "women comprise 43 percent of the workforce but only 23 percent of scientists and engineers," government should take "diversity into account when awarding education and research grants." One can agree with a goal yet be wary of the proposed means of achieving it. Quotas for education and research grants run counter to the objective means scientists have evolved to determine merit. They seem to be inching dangerously toward "identity politics" within science, wherein claims for equivalence based on gender, race, ethnicity, and so forth trump scholarly merit and personal preference. STEM departments that are presently undergoing Title 9 compliance reviews tell a sad story.[19]

None of this says anything about the possible biological differences between the sexes. This is because efforts to balance gender in STEM fields can be justified irrespective of whether the causes of imbalance include innate biological differences in mathematical ability or just cultural constraints and stereotypes. Note, as stated previously, that we find biological and ability differences between the sexes to be a distinctly secondary source of influence for the lack of women in math-intensive fields, far below the effect exerted by women's fertility choices and job preferences.

Ginger's Lament

The legendary dancer Ginger Rogers is reputed to have said that she was expected to do everything Fred Astaire did on the dance floor—but to do it while wearing high heels and dancing backwards. Many women in science feel the same way. They are expected to perform like male colleagues, but to do so while birthing, nursing, and rearing children; keeping house; taking care of elderly parents; and so on, and on. We have already seen that fertility decisions have differential costs for men and women; they either do not affect men's careers or they actually help advance them. But fertility decisions exert a significant dampening effect on women's careers, especially if the children are still young before the women are tenured: a prekindergarten-aged child lowers a woman's likelihood of having a tenure-track job by 8.2% but has no effect on a man's likelihood of having a tenure-track job. In the physical sciences, having school-aged children lowers the probability of women being promoted to full professor by 9.6% while having no effect on men. As the economist Donna Ginther and her colleagues have shown, "children create a marked divergence between men and women."[20] And although econometric analyses indicate that women no longer are judged differently than men for hiring and promotion once various observables are taken into consideration (e.g., type of institution, field of study, years of service, number of children), the reality is that some of these factors are unevenly distributed. Women are far more likely to work part time or at small, teaching-intensive colleges and community colleges precisely because they deferred full-time tenure-track careers to have children. According to surveys, men do this too, but much less often than do women.

Numerous surveys of academic men and women document that household chores and childcare fall disproportionately on the shoulders of women. Academic mothers tend to devote nearly 20 hours per week more to these activities than do academic fathers. Often this extra burden comes at a time when it is crucial to publish in professional journals, write grants, and travel to conferences. It is unsurprising that some women reduce their effort, or even opt out of academia, during this period of their lives, some hoping to resume their careers once their children are older. Sadly, the current modus vivendi makes it unlikely that a woman can leave her tenure-track job for several years and get another tenure-track job at a comparable institution. It just does not happen this way in the present system.

Once an individual (regardless of sex) leaves a tenure-track post, it is difficult to reenter academia at the same level a few years later. Hiring departments look askance at such individuals, preferring newly minted PhDs who have not been out of the loop for years and, implicitly, who have not prioritized family over career. Currently, there is not a consensus that a woman can leave her demanding tenure-track job for several years and return to it at the same level of productivity as when she exited. Depending on the field, some may believe she could not keep up with published research during intensive years of childcare, or that her absence from the lab will result in missed developmental growth (see earlier discussion of McDowell's work in this chapter).

Reasonable people can disagree about whether such beliefs are correct. Intuitively, the problem would not seem as substantial in the humanities, in which writings, at least on some topics, are ageless (such as English literature, medieval history, cultural anthropology). But in STEM fields it *may* seriously undermine one's ability to do research if a hiatus occurs during a surge in new knowledge and techniques. Colleagues in neuroscience tell us that this is true in their field in recent decades, which has been a period of huge strides in theory and technology. An absence during this time might make it very difficult for someone to reenter without a prolonged period of retraining.

The question of whether scientists can be successful if they are permitted to reduce their scientific effort for a number of years early in their careers is an empirical one. Is scientific output in the first few post-PhD years predictive of future lifetime output, as assumed by the tenure system? Or does early productivity signal nothing more than a temporary spurt of activity that is unrepresentative of later productivity or impact? (Impact refers to the frequency with which one's research is cited by others, which scholars often rely on as a measure of their work's importance.) Do fields differ in the consequences of delayed start-up or part-time work to raise children, as McDowell's older research suggested? And, if they do, are there strategies for minimizing negative consequences, short of prodding women to either leave the tenure track or not compete in the first place?

Recall that according to McDowell's research, some fields could be associated with greater penalties for scholars at any age—but particularly at the beginning of their career—who took a break from or greatly reduced their time spent on research. If a field's research becomes stale fast, then taking a long-term leave from it could jeopardize one's knowledge base—unless she or he was able to keep up with reading and new technologies while on leave. Note that we are not talking about short-term leaves, such as one to two semesters.

Colleges and universities are usually willing to grant these short-term leaves for family reasons, even beyond the scope of what the federal law requires of them for family leaves. However, many STEM female scientists have opted out of full-time employment because there was no option that allowed them to go on leave for 2, 3, or more years early in their careers. This group contributes to the underrepresentation of women in the academy. As we remarked earlier, many STEM women begin their careers by opting for part-time work while having children, or delay starting tenure-track jobs for several years until their children are old enough so that these women no longer feel the need to provide intensive parenting. These women find it very difficult to compete for full-time tenure-track jobs once they enter (or reenter) the full-time job market.

Many policy makers have invoked this fact as a possible explanation for the dearth of women in math-intensive careers, including Lawrence Summers when he made his notorious remarks at the National Bureau of Economic Research in 2005: "We would like to believe that you can take a year off, or two years off, or three years off, or be half-time for five years, and it affects your productivity during the time, but that it really doesn't have any fundamental effect on the career path. And a whole set of conclusions would follow from that in terms of flexible work arrangements and so forth. The question is, in what areas of academic life and in what ways is it actually true?"[21]

Comparison with STEM Women in Industry

In our effort to focus this book on STEM women in the academy, we have resisted delving into the issues facing STEM women in the private sector, except where comparisons illuminated the situation with academic STEM women. STEM women work in a wide range of industries (pharmaceuticals, chemical companies, engineering firms, etc.), spanning public and private sectors, in positions with varying levels of business/management tasks. This makes it somewhat more difficult to draw generalizations. However, in this closing section we note some similarities and differences between STEM women working inside and outside academia.

The economist Sylvia Ann Hewlett and her colleagues at the Center for Work-Life Policy (2008), in conjunction with the *Harvard Business Review*, conducted an extensive survey of over 3,000 women working at science and engineering firms (for related reports and commentary see www.BrainDrain.hbr.org). They report that, although on the lower rungs of corporate career ladders, 41% of scientists, engineers, and technologists are women, and their drop-out rate is surprisingly high. Fully 52% of these highly qualified women quit their jobs, most often in their mid-to-late thirties. Several of the main reasons given by these women for quitting resemble those offered by academic STEM women, though some are quite different. The number one reason given by women quitting corporate STEM jobs was a hostile, macho workplace with high incidence of sexual harassment, and an aggressive and competitive atmosphere. In the academy, sexual harassment is rarely offered as a reason for leaving the field. But a competitive, aggressive atmosphere and 60-plus-hour work weeks that jeopardize family life are certainly familiar complaints among university women that are shared by their counterparts outside the academy. Hewlett et al. summarize the top reasons why talented women scientists quit their jobs in the private sector as follows:

> "the hostility of the workplace culture drives them out. If machismo is on the run in most U.S. corporate settings, then this is its Alamo – a last holdout of redoubled intensity. Second is the dispiriting sense of isolation that comes when a woman is the only female on her team or at her rank – a problem exacerbated for others when she in turn leaves. Third, there is a strong disconnect between women's preferred work rhythms and the risky "diving catch" and "fire-fighting" behavior that is recognized and rewarded in these male-dominated fields. Two more factors round out the set. "Extreme jobs," with their long workweeks and punishing travel schedules, are particularly prevalent in science, engineering, and technology companies. (See "Extreme Jobs: The Dangerous Allure of the 70-Hour Workweek," HBR December 2006.) Because women in two-income families still bear the brunt of household management, few are able to sustain those pressures." (Hewlett et al., 2008, p. 23)

Like their academic counterparts, STEM women in the business world struggle with long work weeks, a culture of competition, and primary responsibility for home management and childcare. It is not surprising that the time of greatest flight from their careers is in their mid-to-late 30s—their final chance to have children. We close on this point because it extends our argument that the underrepresentation of women in science may be far more pervasive than simply in math-intensive careers. As we noted throughout, women are also in short supply in senior management posts (e.g., department chairs, full professors, center directors), and this is true in the humanities as well as in the sciences. Based on Hewlett et al.'s survey, the representation of women appears, if anything, even more discouraging in the private sector, provided we look beyond initial gender-hiring rates to see what happens as these women advance in their fields. However, according to one major survey academic women are less satisfied with their jobs than academic men whereas women in STEM industry are more satisfied than men. Clearly, the dust hasn't settled on this issue and more and better data will hopefully illuminate the positive and negative aspects of both workplaces.

Anecdata

A personal anecdote, something we have tried to minimize throughout this book is apt here. We have a colleague who, upon completion of her doctorate, decided against applying for professional jobs. She had two young children and wanted a third. She was in her 30s and chose to devote her coming years to childrearing of an intensity that would be impossible while holding a full-time job. She is a brilliant woman whose accomplishments en route to completing her PhD were sufficient to have earned her invitations to interview for tenure-track positions at top universities. It has now been 8 years since she left graduate school, and we see her a great deal. In fact, we collaborate with her often and her accomplishments have continued to grow. She is still the same brilliant woman she was in graduate school, and her publications have increased, including some in very high-profile journals. She was able to collaborate with us because the projects were ones that were flexible; they didn't require scheduled teaching or lab work, interacting with research assistants, or meetings at times when she was driving her three children to myriad after-school activities. Aware of her home needs, we invite her collaboration with us on projects that allow her to make her contribution whenever she has time to do so—after the children are asleep, while they are at school, and so forth. Her involvement on our projects has been very important and they have been improved greatly by her input.

Readers outside of the academy might be asking themselves, "What's the problem? Once her children are old enough, she can parlay her impressive vita into a first-rate STEM job." But the truth is that she probably cannot. Search committees that screen applications recommend a short list to be interviewed, and tenure-track offers would generally not extend to someone like our colleague. There are many reasons for this, and doubtless this practice might be less obvious at some institutions and in some fields than we are describing here. But the two of us have been in the academy for a combined 50 years, working at four different universities, and we have seen many such individuals bypassed for tenure-track jobs, no matter how impressive their list of accomplishments.

Why do they get overlooked? Search committees might feel that some newly minted PhD with far fewer publications than our collaborator has the potential to make a groundbreaking discovery, whereas our collaborator has already had the opportunity to do so but she has not, even though her accomplishments are substantial and comparable to those of many tenured colleagues at top institutions. Some search committee members will argue that she was only able to amass these accomplishments by virtue of being free from the onerous duties of teaching, advising, and committee work that tenure-track faculty must contend with, and that if she had to contend with such responsibilities her research accomplishments would be fewer. (Of course, she accomplished this research while doing something every bit as onerous as teaching—namely, intensive childrearing—but it is hard to objectify such conditions in a way that leads to a fair comparison, so the default seems to be to discard them altogether. Most universities would not credit childrearing.) And some search committee members probably harbor the belief that women such as our collaborator will not prioritize career, and will be less likely to devote themselves to career once hired, if it came down to a conflict between career and family life.

Finally, some colleagues probably consider anything more than a 6-month family leave excessive, given that they either bypassed having children to launch their own careers or else did have children, but placed them in infant care shortly thereafter. Our collaborator has chosen to be heavily involved in her three children's lives for many years now, taking them to three different schools each morning, chauffeuring them to various after-school activities, and sometimes assisting in their classrooms. Other collaborators of ours have not felt the need to make this level of investment, but even for them a multiyear leave was felt necessary until their child was ready for preschool (age 3). No university we know of will allow a new STEM scientist who is not yet tenured to take a 3-year leave. For that matter, it would be very rare to allow even an older, tenured faculty member to take an unpaid leave this long, unless it was part of a prestigious assignment or award—for example, if she or he had been asked by the National Science Foundation to direct one of its programs for several years, since universities regard such appointments as enhancing their external visibility and reflecting favorably upon their faculty's quality.

From Anecdata to Systematic Empirical Studies

Previously we described the analysis by McDowell,[22] who studied the cost of time away from scholarly work by classifying the shelf life of research publications in various fields to determine how often old articles continued to be cited (i.e., such articles would be regarded by the research community as still relevant for their current research). McDowell interpreted his findings as evidence that it was possible to take a childcare leave and return to work years later, without falling far behind in the knowledge one needs to publish, in some fields but not in others. He reported that research in STEM fields became obsolete particularly fast. Correspondingly, he assumed there is a greater child penalty in these fields in terms of research productivity for women than for men who were in other ways comparable.

One thing McDowell did not look at was women's ability to keep up with new reading during childrearing leaves. When he did his analyses in 1982, there was only one way to access the scientific literature—by going to the library or attending colloquia, lab meetings, and conferences. But in the past decade, it has become easy to access much of the corpus of scientific information in some fields from home, by using a university portal online. Important journals are now at one's fingertips, if women caring for young children have time to search the electronic files and read the articles. In addition, scientific work is increasingly done by teams of scientists,[23] including in some math-intensive fields. This makes it possible for some part-timers to contribute to an overall project despite being unable to bring the entire project to fruition by themselves. These part-timers can contribute online or via occasional lab visits. We have a colleague who skypes into lab meetings and we ourselves have skyped into both professional meetings and meetings with graduate students. Although not as good as being in the same room, skyping is free and works reasonably well.

Returning to our personal observations, our collaborator does use online journals heavily in our joint work, and despite devoting herself to her children, she easily finds time to keep up with the journals when her children are at school or after they are asleep. (We have witnessed this on countless occasions when we receive e-mails from her at midnight about articles she has just finished reading.) But every year or so we have to write a letter to our university administrators, asking them not to withdraw her university privileges so that she can continue to collaborate with us. Without this, privileges such as access to e-mail and library, and the ability to have documents sent to a departmental address, are terminated. These resources cost the university very little in the larger scheme, and they allow our collaborator to maintain her research at a high level. Our university has never refused to renew her privileges when we have made these requests. But there is no codified path for people like our collaborator that makes access to these resources automatic and doesn't require that she be given a subservient title, such as "visiting research associate," issued only under the aegis of our supervision.

In our case, both she and we know she is a full partner in our joint work, often the senior partner (as is reflected in some of her joint publications with us in which she is listed as the first author—which in our field designates the most significant contribution). This unfortunate state of affairs (being forced to go to great lengths to gain access to online journals, retain departmental mailing addresses, and attend colloquia) is something universities could easily rectify to allow female scholars in their communities to sustain their research activity. This is the type of issue that Shalala et al.[24] rightly referred to as "outmoded ways of thinking" on the part of institutions of higher learning. Lest readers imagine that our colleague is alone in her situation, we know of several other women with children in our hometown who have PhDs in STEM fields but have either opted not to compete for a job because of their children's needs or, in one case, have resigned from a tenure-track position at Harvard when she had twins followed 10 months later by a third child. She felt there was no way she could do justice to her three infants and fulfill the rigors of her tenure-track position. Nationally, there are many thousands of women in such situations, and to university administrators and tenured faculty they may be invisible, save on those occasions when they show up at a colloquium. Although not all of these women would desire to stay involved in research, we have no doubt that thousands of STEM scholars would, if flexible options existed for them to contribute part time, transitioning to full time when their personal situation warranted.

If, on the other hand, success in a field depends on physical presence in labs and at research team meetings, then online library services and skyping will not be the answer for STEM scientists who have opted to raise a family for a number of years. For example, in some lab-based fields, it may be important for scientists to hone their skills by working actively and in the physical presence of teams of scientists. Perhaps such needs are incompatible with leaving academia for several years, because the learning curve will be too great upon one's return. But this is surmise and there are no systematic data to test its validity. It would be interesting if fields experimented with alternative working-child-leave policies and deferred start-ups to examine the real (versus imagined) costs associated with long-term leaves and deferrals. Maybe skeptics are right and the two twains cannot be made to meet. But no one has tried, and there may be ways of retaining talented female scientists whose training was very costly and whose talent we as a nation desperately need.

Regardless of universities' willingness to implement long-term family-friendly policies, academic fields—which have autonomy when it comes to hiring experts in their areas—may require an attitude shift before they view deferred or returning scholars as being as valuable as new PhDs. Recall the statement in the *Preface* to this book, quoting a woman in the field of business, which resonates in many academic fields: "Be prepared for the realization that in the business world your stepping out time counts for less than zero . . . [and] may make potential employers think you are not as reliable as other applicants."[25]

The Question of Gender Weighting for Males

Consistent with our claim that girls exceed boys in high school grades, the gender imbalance at selective high schools is quite pronounced. This has begun to generate interest and proposals that are the flip side of proposals to increase the representation of women in math-intensive STEM fields. We refer here to proposals to increase the representation of boys in select high school programs, such as Bronx High School of Science, that prepare future scientists. Take the Chicago public schools, for example. There are 1,596 girls in the eight Chicago selective-enrollment high schools but only 933 boys; 31% of all female applicants were accepted in 2005, versus only 23% of male applicants. All but one of the selective-enrollment schools maintain at least a 60% versus 40% female-to-male student body ratio. At Brooks College Prep, the female students constitute almost 70% of the student body. Similar gender asymmetries play out in select programs across the nation (Okun, 2007).

In response to such sex imbalances, some have called for interventions designed to boost the success rate of male applicants. No one yet is arguing for preferential admission on the basis of sex, but some are proposing the creation of training programs that would teach male middle schoolers the skills needed to succeed on admission tests when they apply to elite high schools as eighth graders. But herein lies a potential problem we alluded to earlier.

When New York City created summer institutes for sixth graders to boost the selective high school admission rate of African American and Hispanic students, they did not foresee the demand this would create among Asian and Asian American families eager to give their children a leg up. These families enrolled their children in the summer institutes, which start when a child is in sixth grade. The students are taught strategies and tips to improve their scores on the standardized test used to make admission decisions among eighth graders. The result is that the groups for which the program was created— African American and Hispanic students—actually fared worse in admission to these elite high schools than they did before the summer institutes were created. Consider: During 2005–06, African American students made up 4.8% of the Bronx Science student body, down from 11.8% in 1994–95, the year before the summer institutes were created. At Brooklyn Technical High School, the proportion of African American students declined from 37.3% to 14.9%, and at Stuyvesant, African Americans today make up 2.2% of the student body, down from 4.4% in 1994–95.[26] In addition, Caucasian enrollment at two of the three select high schools has also declined. Coincident with these declines, the Asian American student body has increased in ways not anticipated. For example, it reached as high as 60.6% at Bronx Science, up from 40.8% in 1994–95.

What does all of this have to do with sex differences in admission to select high schools, colleges, and graduate programs? Any program created to increase the rate of admission of boys and men will do so only if girls and women are prevented from participating. If girls and women are allowed to participate in special institutes or training programs, they can be counted on to outperform boys and men and widen the admission gap into elite training programs even further, as the previous examples illustrate. It is a sticky wicket, indeed. The mirror dilemma occurs in areas of male strength such as when a program is shown to increase spatial ability. If boys are permitted to enroll in it, they could end up widening their advantage over girls, as some of the spatial training studies have demonstrated. Our society has much to contend with as we ponder the issues of group differences in access to and success at different careers, be they gender-group differences or racial/ethnic-group differences.

Epilogue

CODA: WOMEN IN SCIENCE AND THE NATURE OF SCIENTIFIC INQUIRY

We have three daughters, the oldest of whom completed undergraduate and graduate degrees in a math-intensive STEM field (engineering), while the younger two are in elementary school. Obviously, writing this book was animated not only by our scientific curiosity but also by our interest in our daughters' futures. We hope that further research and policy, focused on meaningful questions and issues with the potential to optimize both the gender composition and the practice of science, will be spurred by this effort. We have tried to lay out the scientific findings on both sides of the debate without taking an advocacy position, although some readers will undoubtedly feel that we occasionally have lapsed—both in being overly critical of some lines of research, and in being too generous toward others. To the extent that we have slipped, readers will take us to task. This is how scientific progress toward consensus occurs, the residue of give-and-take.

It is customary to call for more research at the end of a book like this. But what one often wants is not just any research, but rather, research that validates one's own beliefs and goals. Research with the potential to falsify pet beliefs is often avoided, disdained, and dismissed as apologia for the status quo—it is seen as unprogressive, even reactionary. We do not intend this call for more research to generate only studies aimed at debunking the status quo, endorsing favored positions, and increasing the number of options available for women who defer going on the tenure-track job market or who choose to leave it for family reasons. We believe that progress comes from free and open debate in which all sides present their best evidence and no one is excoriated for arguing the unpopular side. This means encouraging research from all corners of this issue, and being open to evidence that is antithetical to our views—for example, by arguing against more flexible options for women, if such flexible options are not supported by future research or prove impractical to implement, too costly, or detrimental to the scientific enterprise. Academics pay lip service to open-minded debate, but we too often regard "the other side" as the enemy rather than as a source of valid data that we can learn from. Thus, we reiterate that we hope in the future, scholars from all corners of this debate will come forward with their best evidence, regardless of how politically incorrect it may be perceived by others. And we hope those who attempt to refute these scholars will avoid ad hominem attacks on their presumed moral deficiencies and stick to rebutting the data.

James Flynn, whose research we alluded to earlier—showing that IQs have steadily crept upward over the twentieth century, and that women's *Raven's Progressive Matrices* scores (a type of visual abstract reasoning) are now comparable to men's—is a living testament to the value of free and open debate. He encourages rivals to put their best evidence forward without fear that they will be called sexist or racist. Consider Flynn's reaction to the work of Arthur Jensen, an ardent proponent of racial differences in genetic intelligence. Jensen has been forced to travel with a bodyguard due to fears for his personal safety. However, Flynn addressed Jensen's ideas on intellectual grounds, doing his best to refute them with empirical data while maintaining a respectful demeanor. Flynn has reported that, when he first began rebutting Jensen's hereditarian claims in the 1970s, he could not have foreseen the great strides his later research would provoke. This is because Flynn's most important discoveries were not directly motivated by Jensen's claims, but resulted from his earlier attempts to rebut them. In other words, had Jensen's contentious work not been published in the *Harvard Educational Review*, Flynn's subsequent discoveries—many of which have been truly groundbreaking and have sparked a revolution in the field of intelligence—would not have been possible. Without Jensen, Flynn has said, "I would never have made any contribution to psychology."[1] His landmark discovery of the ongoing upward rise in IQ scores from one generation to the next, known as the Flynn effect, would never have been made. Nor would his demonstration that the IQ scores of offspring of German women and World War II African American U.S. military soldiers are indistinguishable from scores of offspring of German women and Caucasian American soldiers.[2] No longer are there claims of a linear relationship between IQ and European genes. Instead, it is now recognized that cultural effects are more powerful than previously thought, and Flynn gets much of the credit, thanks to his early debates with Jensen.

In short, we urge free speech in the emerging science of sex differences. This is not a popular position; some proponents of biological or cognitive sources of sex differences have been roundly vilified, their motives and character called into question.[3] But this is not a climate in which we can expect to see all sides present their best evidence. We accept that research can have negative consequences, and that entire groups of girls and women can be hurt by careless presentation of evidence. Dweck,[4] Dar-Nimrod and Heine,[5] and others have lamented unintentional harms done to women by the publication of findings that suggest a female deficit in math. Women told that female under-achievement in mathematics is due to genetic factors perform much worse on mathematics tests than do women told that social factors are responsible. "As our research demonstrates, just hearing about that sort of idea is enough to negatively affect women's performance, and reproduce the stereotype that is out there," says one of the researchers whose work supports this claim, Steven Heine at the University of British Columbia, Canada.

As parents of three daughters, we are not insensitive to such claims, and at various times our daughters have been told by someone at school that a scientific activity was not for girls. When this occurs, we groan, and explain that this is not true, that girls can do anything they wish, and that many grow up to become great scientists. No parent of a daughter wants to think that anti-female messages are still being bandied about, more than 40 years after the first wave of the feminist revolution debunked such statements. So we are sensitive to the claim that even allowing scientists to publish and disseminate their findings can be deleterious to girls and women, and that perhaps such findings should be made to pass some higher cost-benefit threshold before being accepted for publication. But this process soon enters dangerous territory, resulting in prohibitions against publishing anything odious to one group by touting it as deleterious to girls and women.

Earlier in this book we noted that in *Emile*, Jean-Jacques Rousseau argued against allowing atheists the right to express their views because he worried that their message could bar the masses from heaven, condemning them to hell. Today, we would find prohibitions against atheists ridiculous. However, we have our own set of sacred cows, and it is often surprising that individuals who are otherwise ardent defenders of free speech come down against speech that offends some. For society to proceed to the point at which it can maximize women's talent, it will be important that we endorse free speech in science to a greater extent than has been true recently, and this means that free speech extends to published research that may offend or undermine women. This means a collective agreement that when someone argues against our pet position, we direct our refutation at their data, and not at their alleged character flaws. This is not an endorsement for hate speech or writings that advocate political applications, because surely a system of checks and balances is appropriate in such situations. But scientists who study sex differences must be free to publish their findings in journals without fear of scorn. We hope all sides enter the debate with newer and better data to help shape policies, and that policy creation is not left to politically-motivated administrators and policymakers to do by fiat, irrespective of empirical realities. After wading through many hundreds of articles, chapters, and books to prepare this document, one thing is clear: advocacy in the guise of science is a shortsighted strategy.

Notes

PREFACE

1. Sommers, 2008, p. 1
2. see Ceci et al., 2009

INTRODUCTION

1. p. A13
2. Andreescu et al., 2008
3. American Association of University Women, 1999; Pomerantz et al., 2002
4. U.S. Department of Education, 2001, Table K
5. see Ceci & Williams, 2007, for multiple different views on some of them
6. Shalala et al., 2006
7. Shalala et al., 2006
8. John Tierney, *N.Y. Times*, September 26, 2006
9. Cathy Young, *Boston Globe*, October 2, 2006
10. Singer, 2006, p. 893
11. Young, October 2, 2006, *Boston Globe*, p. 16
12. Tierney, September 26, 2006, *New York Times*, p. 23
13. for example, Halpern et al., 2007
14. Freeman, 2004
15. Freeman, 2004, p. 11
16. Lubinski & Benbow, 2007
17. for example, Lally, 2005; National Public Radio's *Science Friday*, December 2, 2005
18. for example, Muller et al., 2005 letter in *Science Magazine*, cosigned by 85 science and higher education administrators
19. Ceci & Williams, 2007; Halpern et al., 2007
20. National Academy of Science, 2005
21. see Ceci et al., 2009

CHAPTER 1

1. Gallagher & Kaufman, 2005; Xie & Shauman, 2003
2. Bridgeman & Lewis, 1996

3. 2005, p. 592
4. National Academy of Science. (2005, December 9). Convocation On Maximizing The Potential Of Women In Academe: Biological, Social, And Organizational Contributions To Science And Engineering Success. Committee on Women in Academic Science and Engineering. Washington, DC.
5. 1974
6. 2005
7. see Bushman & Anderson, 2001
8. 2005
9. for example, Fias & Fischer, 2005; Kersh et al., 2008; see Ceci et al., 2009, for additional references
10. Moore & Johnson, 2008; Quinn & Liben, 2009
11. 2001
12. 1999
13. 1991
14. 2006
15. Burnett et al., 1979; Casey et al., 1995
16. see Casey et al., 1995
17. for example, the *Kit of Factor-Referenced Cognitive Tests* by Ekstrom et al., 1976; a test based on figures produced by Vandenberg & Kuse, 1978; figures taken from Thurstone & Thurstone's 1962 *Primary Mental Abilities* test; the *Block Design* subtest from the *Wechsler Adult Intelligence Scale*, the *Purdue Visual Spatial Test-Revised*, or the *Differential Aptitude Test*
18. Peters et al., 1995

CHAPTER 2

1. 2005
2. 2006
3. 2005
4. 2003
5. Spelke & Grace, 2007
6. for example, Valian, 1998
7. for example, Hedges & Nowell, 1995; Lubinski & Benbow, 2007
8. Gallagher & Kaufman, 2005; Xie & Shauman, 2003
9. for example, Summers, 2005
10. 2007
11. 2005
12. p. 951
13. p. 952
14. Bornstein et al., 1999
15. Goldstein, 1994
16. Kenney-Benson et al., 2006
17. Duckworth & Seligman, 2006
18. p. 834
19. for example, Keach, 2003; Ferguson, 2006; Fischer, 2006
20. 1978

21. p. 481
22. Lever, 1978, p. 485
23. p. 485
24. 1999
25. 2006
26. Summers, 2005, Transcript of NBER talk
27. 2004
28. Lubinski & Benbow, 2007, pp. 90–91
29. Jacobs & Winslow, 2004, p. 117
30. 2004, p. 12
31. Hakim, 2006
32. Hakim, 2006, p. 280
33. for example, Xie & Shauman, 2003
34. Hoffer & Grigorian, 2005
35. Valian, 1998
36. from the Executive Summary
37. Pinker, 2008; Preston, 2004; Strenta et al., 1994
38. McLaughlin, 2006
39. O'Brien, 2006
40. Seid, 2006
41. Harvard University, 2005
42. 1987
43. Stanford University Report, February 9, 2005, p. 1
44. Sykes, 1988
45. McDowell, 1982
46. 1982
47. Summers, 2005
48. 1992
49. Long, 1992
50. p. 173
51. 2006
52. Mauleon & Bordons, 2006, p. 215
53. Long, 1992; Mauleon & Bordons, 2006
54. Trix & Psenka, 2005; Steinpreis et al., 1999
55. Budden et al., 2008
56. Wenneras & Wold, 1997
57. Jacobs & Winslow, 2004, p. 117
58. 2004, pp. 100–101
59. Hamel et al., 2006, p. 303
60. 2001
61. 2006
62. p. 9
63. p. 19
64. Mason & Goulden, 2004
65. Williams, 2007
66. for example, Halpern, 2007
67. Halpern, 2007, p. 129
68. Mauleon & Borden, 2006
69. Summers, 2005

70. 2008
71. Sommers, 2008, p. 7
72. p. 9
73. Ceci & Williams, 2007, p. 213
74. Eccles, 2007; Halpern, 2007; Kimura, 2007; Hyde, 2005; Hines, 2007; Lubinski & Benbow, 2007
75. see Lubinski & Benbow, 2007, for brief review
76. Achter et al., 1999; Wai et al., 2005
77. for example, Geary, 1998, 2007
78. Correll, 2004; Eccles et al., 1999
79. Ceci et al., 2009
80. Eccles, 2007

CHAPTER 3

1. Ceci & Williams, 2009; Lysenko Redux: In support of 'untouchable' science. *Nature*, p. x
2. for example, Gur et al., 2000
3. Roof et al., 1993; De Vries & Simerley, 2002
4. Lippa, 1998
5. Ceci et al., 2009; Halpern et al., 2007; Moffat & Hampson, 2005
6. Scheibinger, 1987
7. 1992a, b
8. Ankney, 1992, p. 292
9. Rushton & Ankney, 2007
10. Deary et al., 2007, p. 520
11. Haier et al., 2004, 2005
12. Haier et al., 2004
13. see also Gur & Gur, 2007
14. Haier et al., 2005
15. see Gur & Gur, 2007
16. Van Goozen et al., 1994, 1995
17. Ceci et al., 2009
18. 1996, 2000, 2002
19. Sanders et al., 2005
20. Some evidence points to sex difference in 2D:4D being related to relative concentrations of prenatal T and estrogen. This influences the female waist/hip ratio, which is negatively correlated with estradiol and positively correlated with T, and is negatively correlated with left hand preference, spatial ability, autism, and Asperger syndrome (Lutchmaya et al., 2004). Conversely, a high level of relative prenatal estrogen to T is associated with female higher verbal ability.
21. in Ceci et al., 2009
22. Ceci et al., 2009, p. xx
23. 2006
24. Baron-Cohen et al., 2004; Knickermeyer & Baron-Cohen, 2006
25. Manning, 2002; Sanders et al., 2005
26. for example, Finegan et al., 1992

27. 2008
28. 2002
29. 2001
30. 2006
31. 2006
32. 2008
33. 2005
34. see Grimshaw et al., 1995
35. 1996
36. Moffat & Hampson, 1996
37. pp. 260–261
38. Hier & Crowley, 1982
39. for example, Serbin et al., 1990
40. 2005
41. Brosnan, 2006
42. 2007
43. Kimura, 2007, p. 41
44. 2002
45. 1994
46. Berenbaum & Hines, 1992; see Hines, Fane, et al., 2003 for review
47. Hines, Ahmed, et al., 2003
48. Resnick et al., 1986; Hampson et al., 1998
49. see recent meta-analysis by Puts et al., 2008
50. 2003
51. 1996
52. Finegan et al., 1992
53. 1994, 1995
54. Ceci et al., 2009 p. xx
55. Slabbekoorn et al., 1999
56. Shute et al., 1983; McKeever, 1987
57. Hampson & Kimura, 1988
58. Hampson, 1990
59. Silverman & Phillips, 1993
60. Ho et al., 1986
61. 1986
62. 1986
63. Gordon et al., 1986; see also Slabbekoorn et al., 1999, p. 426
64. Bhasin et al., 2005, 2001
65. Bhasin et al., 2001, p. 1178
66. 2006
67. see Lecreuse et al., 2005
68. see Ceci & Williams, 2007
69. The interested reader is directed to Table 6 of Ceci et al., 2009, for a fuller description of the inconsistencies as well as a description of many additional hormone studies.
70. Brosnan, 2006
71. It is common to distinguish between organizational effects of hormones versus activational effects. The former occur primarily prenatally and shortly following birth when brain structures are undergoing organization, whereas activational effects are the result of later hormone fluctuations that influence ongoing behavior (for example, puberty, menopause, circadian rhythms, hormone administrations).

72. see Hampson & Moffat, 2005, for an excellent review
73. for example, Christiansen & Knussmann, 1987; McKeever et al., 1987; see Hogervorst et al., 2005, for a review
74. reviewed in Hogervorst et al., 2005
75. Grimshaw et al., 1995
76. for example, Neave et al., 1999
77. for review see, Bhasin et al., 2005
78. Bhasin et al., 2001, p. 1178

CHAPTER 4

1. 1991
2. for example, Geary, 2007
3. 1991
4. Irwing & Lynn, 2005; Lynn & Irwing, 2004
5. Flynn & Rossi-Case, under review
6. 2007, personal communication
7. $F(1, 286) = 0.33$, $p < 0.564$, partial eta-squared $= 0.01$
8. see Ackerman, 2006
9. Deary et al., 1999
10. 30.2 versus 27.5, respectively, $p = 0.1$ (Deary et al., 2003)
11. 2008
12. Hedges & Nowell, 1995
13. see meta-analyses by Hyde, 2005; Voyer et al., 1995
14. Hyde, 2005
15. Berger et al., 2008
16. Ceci, 1996
17. 2005
18. p. 19
19. Hugdahl et al., 2006
20. see meta-analyses by Hyde, 2007; Voyer et al., 1995
21. Spelke & Grace, 2007
22. Jardine & Martin, 1983; Watson & Kimura, 1991
23. Draganski et al., 2004; Grabner et al., 2003; 2006; Maguire et al., 2000
24. for example, Goldstein, 1994
25. Lubinski et al., 2006; Wai et al., 2005
26. Haworth et al., 2009
27. p. 15
28. Turkheimer & Halpern, 2009
29. Ceci, 1996
30. Ceci, 1996
31. 2006
32. 2008
33. see Gallagher, 1992; Lubinski & Benbow, 2007; Xie & Shaumann, 2003
34. 2007
35. Wainer & Steinberg, 1992
36. see Royer & Garofoli, 2005, for a review
37. Ceci et al., 2009
38. Sorby, 2001, 2005

39. Tendick et al., 2000
40. Carter et al., 1987; Pribyl & Bodner, 1987
41. Tartre, 1990
42. 2005
43. Spelke, 2005, p. 954
44. Ceci, 1996
45. Lubinski et al., 2006; Wai et al., 2005; Achter et al., 1999
46. Shalala et al., 2006
47. p. 24
48. see Weinberger, 2005
49. for example, Rosalyn Chiet Barnett, 2007
50. Ceci et al., 2009
51. Wise et al., 1979
52. Rosalyn Barnett speaking at a national symposium at the American Enterprise Institute, Fall 2007
53. 1995
54. Casey et al., 1997
55. 1993
56. p. 809
57. for example, Gallagher, 1992, 1992; Fennema et al., 1998
58. Barnett & Ceci, 2002
59. 1992
60. 1998
61. Fennema et al., 1998
62. Becker, 1981
63. see, for example, Ravitch, 1998
64. 1994
65. 2002
66. pp. 16–17
67. Fennema & Sherman, 1977
68. Harris & Carleton, 2006, p. 149
69. 2005
70. Spelke, 2005, p. 954
71. 1998
72. Gierl et al., 1999, p. 15
73. Correll, 2004
74. National Science Board, Division of Science Resources Statistics, 2001, Survey of Doctorate Recipients, Table H6, p. 217
75. Ceci et al., 2009
76. p. 44
77. Kolen & Brennan, 1995; Hedges & Nowell, 1998
78. 1990
79. 2003
80. Benbow & Stanley, 1983
81. Benbow, 1988; Benbow & Stanley, 1983; see also Pinker, 2002
82. 1995
83. Moore & Johnson, 2008; Quinn & Liben, 2009
84. In their extensive meta-analysis of sex differences in mental rotation performance, Linn & Peterson (1985) revealed that although sex differences were found at all ages

between 10 and 60, four common mental rotation tests did not correlate with each other as highly as would be expected if they were all tapping the same ability.
85. Barnett & Ceci, 2002
86. Voyer et al., 1995
87. see pilot study for McGuinness & Morley, 1991
88. see for example, Hyde, 2005
89. Lightdale & Prentice, 1994, in Hyde, 2005
90. Eagly & Crowley, 1986, in Hyde, 2005
91. for example, Spelke, 2005; Linn & Hyde, 1989
92. 1996
93. 1996
94. 1995
95. 1985
96. Ceci, 1996
97. see, for example, Sternberg, 2004
98. 1996
99. 2007
100. Spelke, 2005
101. 2007
102. 2005
103. see Ceci & Papierno, 2005; Papierno & Ceci, 2006

CHAPTER 5

1. 1981
2. Becker, 1981, pp. 50–51
3. Gallagher, 1990, 1992
4. Barnett & Ceci, 2002
5. Spelke, 2005
6. see Kenney-Benson et al., 2006
7. 1982
8. 1981
9. for example, Gallagher & DeLisi, 1994
10. Kenney-Benson et al., 2006, p. 22
11. Frome & Eccles, 1998
12. Hyde, Fenneman, Ryan, et al., 1990
13. 1982
14. 2008
15. American Association of University Women, 1992, p. 2
16. p. 4
17. 2005
18. pp. 29–30
19. Sanders, 2003
20. 1998
21. Kelly, 1998, p. 21
22. Massachusetts Institute of Technology Faculty Newsletter, 1999, p. 2
23. Goldberg, 1999, p. 3

24. 2001
25. Gender Equity Committee of the University of Pennsylvania, 2001, p. IV
26. 1997
27. p. 342
28. see Sommers, 2008
29. 1999
30. p. 343
31. 2003; 2006
32. 2008
33. Jayasinghe et al., 2003
34. 2005
35. Steinpreis et al., 1999
36. Steinpreis et al., 1999, p. 527
37. Goldin & Rouse, 2000
38. Heilman & Haynes, 2005
39. 2003
40. Budden, Tregenza, et al., 2008
41. Webb et al., 2008
42. see Rhode, 1997, for additional evidence
43. Ginther, 2001; Ginther & Kahn, 2006; Mason & Goulden, 2004
44. 1996
45. Ceci et al., 2009
46. 1995
47. 1997
48. Steele & Aronson, 1995
49. 1995
50. 2004
51. Lewis, 2005
52. Davies & Spencer, 2005
53. Stricker & Ward, 2004; Stricker, 2006
54. 2004
55. p. 685
56. 2008
57. 2008
58. 2004
59. p. 111
60. 1999
61. Quinn & Spencer, 2001, p. 58
62. 2006
63. 1999
64. 2001
65. Spencer et al., 1999
66. 2005
67. 2006
68. 2006
69. 2006
70. Good et al., 2005a,b
71. Dweck, 2007
72. Good et al., 2005a

73. 2006
74. 2004
75. 2007
76. p. 50
77. 1999
78. 2001
79. p. 57
80. p. 59
81. see Oakes, 1990, for a review
82. 2007
83. 2001
84. p. 59
85. 2004
86. see, for example, Martens et al., 2006; Biek, 2006
87. 2009
88. 2006
89. 2006
90. Correll, 2004
91. 2006
92. 2006
93. 2006
94. p. 239
95. 2004
96. for example, Shih et al., 1999
97. Charles & Bradley, 2006
98. 2008
99. for example, Correll, 2004
100. Quinn & Spencer, 2001, p. 59
101. for example, McGuinness & Morley, 1991; Inzlicht & Ben-Zeev, 2000
102. see Berenbaum & Resnick, 2007
103. 2001
104. Ceci et al., 2003
105. 1999
106. p. 1237
107. Hyde, 2005; Newcombe, 2007; Spelke, 2005; Vallian, 2007
108. Ceci & Williams, 2007
109. 2007
110. 2008
111. 2006

CHAPTER 6

1. 2005
2. 2008
3. p. 45
4. 1995
5. 1988

6. Stanley et al., 1974
7. 1980
8. p. 1264
9. Halpern, 2007, p. 121
10. Summers Transcript at NBER, 2005, p. 888
11. Ceci & Williams, 2009
12. Hyde, Fennema, & Lamon, 1990; Voyer et al., 1995
13. Ginther, 2001; Ginther & Kahn, 2006; Long, 1992
14. Keating et al., 1974
15. Harvard University, 2005
16. Cambridge University, 2005
17. 2007
18. Kimura, 2007, p. 41
19. Flynn, 2007
20. see Carroll, 1997
21. National Foundation for Educational Research, 1979
22. Benbow & Stanley, 1983
23. Gates, 2006
24. Royer & Garofoli, 2005
25. 1996
26. 2000
27. 1995
28. 1989
29. 2004
30. 2001
31. NAS's Committee on Science, Engineering, and Public Policy, 2005

CHAPTER 7

1. 1996, 1998
2. Kimura, 2007, p. 41
3. Voyer et al., 1995
4. 2005
5. Hyde, 2005
6. see Flynn, 1991, pp. 119–123
7. Flynn, 1998
8. Kimura, 2007, p. 41
9. Levine et al., 2005
10. 1996
11. 2007
12. Lummis & Stevenson, 1990
13. 2008
14. Charles & Bradley, 2006
15. Lachance & Mazzocco, 2006
16. for example, Valian, 1998
17. Mullis et al., 2005
18. see Valian, 2007

19. $r = -0.47$
20. Lachance & Mazzocco, 2006
21. Hyde & Linn, 2006
22. see Ceci et al., 2009
23. values from Hyde, Fennema, & Lamon, 1990
24. Levine et al., 2005
25. Feingold, 1994
26. 2005, p. 956
27. 2006
28. 2006
29. Shalala et al., 2006; Barnett, 2007
30. Wise et al., 1979
31. Hyde et al., 2008
32. 2008
33. 1974
34. Levine et al., 1999, p. 940
35. 1999
36. 1991
37. 2008
38. see above quote by Levine et al., 1999
39. 1985
40. pp. 1488–1489
41. 2005
42. 1996
43. Hyde, 2005
44. see Lachance & Mazzocco, 2006
45. Swiatek et al., 2000
46. 2001
47. 2001
48. 1992
49. 2007

CHAPTER 8

1. for example, Lachance & Mazzocco, 2006
2. Penner & Paret, 2007
3. Fias & Fischer, 2005
4. Lachance & Mazzocco, 2006
5. 2005
6. Wise, 1979
7. Shalala et al., 2006; Barnett 2007
8. Roof et al., 1993; De Vries & Simerley, 2002
9. Casambis, 2005
10. 2007
11. Biek, 2006
12. 2008
13. 2007

14. A main-effect environment argument would be that female children should flourish in the most educated homes vis-à-vis the least educated ones, because the former parents are far more likely to harbor egalitarian gender beliefs and high expectations for their daughters. But this is the opposite of what Penner and Paret found. In contrast, a gene–environment argument might be that boys have more potential for math than girls, but to bring their potential to fruition requires an environment high in resources (good schools, mathematical games, parents who push their children to excel in math, etc.). Absent such resources, the boys' potential never crystallizes and the gap between their math scores and those of girls is not nearly as wide as it is under high resources. There is a great deal of developmental data that accords with this position (Bronfenbrenner & Ceci, 1994).
15. Ginther & Kahn, 2006
16. Valian, 2007
17. Gender Equity Committee of the University of Pennsylvania, 2001, p. II
18. Hamel et al., 2006
19. Haslanger, 2007
20. Harvard University, 2005
21. Ivie & Ray, 2005
22. Strenta et al., 1994
23. 2007
24. 2008
25. see Ceci et al., 2009
26. Lubinski et al., 2001
27. Lubinski & Benbow, 2007, pp. 90–91
28. Lubinski et al., 2006, p. 198

CHAPTER 9

1. see Long, 1992
2. 2006
3. 2007
4. see Sorby & Bartmaans, 2000
5. for example, Gouchie & Kimura, 1991
6. see Kersh et al.'s 2008 review of the relationship between early spatial play behaviors and later mathematics achievements
7. Preston, 2004
8. for example, Hyde et al., 2008
9. for example, Guiso et al., 2008; Penner, 2008
10. for example, Gates, 2006
11. Humphreys et al., 1993; Shea et al., 2001
12. Gates, 2006; Ivie & Ray, 2005
13. Ceci et al., 2009
14. Park et al., 2007
15. 1982
16. Freeman, 2004
17. 2005

18. Anecdotally, we have a former student whose mother emigrated from Russia where she had been a computer scientist. Upon arriving in the United States, however, she marveled at the freedom to choose a nonmath career, saying that while growing up in Russia this was not an option. Several years later we encountered many more examples of the same thing—including in Susan Pinker's book—of Russian female STEM scientists switching careers upon emigrating to the West.
19. see Sommers's 2008 description of Columbia University's Physics Department
20. Ginther & Kahn, 2006, pp. 8–9
21. Summers, 2005
22. 1982
23. Wuchty et al., 2007
24. 2006
25. Williams, 2007, p. A13
26. Gootman, 2006

EPILOGUE

1. see http://lists.paleopsych.org/pipermail/paleopsych/2007-December/007764.html
2. Flynn, 2007
3. see Ceci & Williams, 2009
4. 2007
5. 2006

About the authors

Stephen J. Ceci holds a lifetime endowed chair in developmental psychology at Cornell University. He studies the development of intelligence and memory; is the author of approximately 350 articles, books, and chapters; and has given hundreds of invited addresses around the world (see next paragraph). Ceci's past honors and numerous scientific awards include a Senior Fulbright-Hayes fellowship and a National Institutes of Health Research Career Scientist Award. His article in *Psychological Bulletin* was awarded the 1994 Robert Chin Prize from the Society for the Psychological Study of Social Issues for the best article, and it was named one of the top 20 articles in 1994 by Hertzig and Farber. Ceci has received an IBM Supercomputing Prize, three Senior Mensa Foundation Research Prizes, and the Arthur Rickter Award. He currently serves on seven editorial boards and is past editor of several journals, including *Psychological Science in the Public Interest*, which he founded and co-edited and which is partnered with *Scientific American Mind*. Ceci is a fellow of eight divisions of the American Psychological Society and American Psychological Society. The American Academy of Forensic Psychology gave Ceci its Lifetime Distinguished Contribution Award for 2000, and the American Psychological Association gave him its 2002 Lifetime Distinguished Contribution Award for Science and Society and its 2003 Distinguished Scientific Contribution Award for the Application of Psychology (shared with Elizabeth F. Loftus). In 2005 he received the American Psychological Society's highest scientific award, the James McKeen Cattell Award (shared with E. Mavis Hetherington).

Ceci has given the keynote addresses at over 50 national and international meetings, including the British Psychological Society, the American Psychological Association, the American Psychological Society, the Midwest Psychological Association, the Eastern Psychological Association, the New England Psychological Association, the Western Psychological Association, the German Psychological Association, the Swedish Psychological Association, the Brazilian Psychological Association, the American College of Psychiatry, and the American Psychiatric Association. In 1993 Ceci was named a Master Lecturer of the American Psychological Association, and in 1995 the American Psychological Association named a book series after him (*The Ceci Series in Developmental Psychology*). He has given over 100 addresses at universities around the world, including Oxford University, Cambridge University, Oslo University, Stockholm University, Munich University, Harvard University, Yale University, Columbia University, and Princeton University. His book, *Jeopardy in the Courtroom* (with Maggie Bruck), won the

2000 William James Book Award from the American Psychological Association, and his recent edited volume (with Wendy Williams), *Why Aren't More Women in Science?* won the Independent Book Sellers Bronze Award in 2007 and was reviewed widely, including in *Science*. He has served on numerous national commissions, including the White House Task Force on Children and Families; the National Academy of Science Board of Cognitive, Sensory and Behavioral Sciences; and the National Science Foundation Advisory Board.

Wendy M. Williams is a professor in the Department of Human Development at Cornell University, where she studies the development, assessment, training, and societal implications of intelligence and related abilities. She holds PhD and master's degrees in psychology from Yale University, a master's in physical anthropology from Yale, and a BA in English and biology from Columbia University, awarded cum laude with special distinction. In the fall of 2001, Williams cofounded (and now codirects) the Cornell Institute for Research on Children (CIRC), a National Science Foundation–funded research- and outreach-based center that commissions studies on societally relevant topics and broadly disseminates its research products. She heads "Thinking Like A Scientist," a national education-outreach program designed to encourage traditionally underrepresented groups (girls, people of color, and people from disadvantaged backgrounds) to pursue science education and careers. Williams also directed the joint Harvard–Yale Practical and Creative Intelligence for School Project, and she was coprincipal investigator for a 6-year, $1.4 million Army Research Institute grant to study practical intelligence and success at leadership.

In addition to dozens of articles and chapters on her research, Williams has authored eight books and edited five volumes. They include *The Reluctant Reader* (sole authored), *How to Develop Student Creativity* (with Robert Sternberg), *Escaping the Advice Trap* (with Stephen Ceci; reviewed in *The New York Times*, *The Washington Post*, and *USA Today*), *Practical Intelligence for School* (with Howard Gardner, Robert Sternberg, Tina Blythe, Noel White, and Jin Li), and *Why Aren't More Women in Science?* (with Stephen Ceci; winner of a 2007 Independent Publisher Bronze Award). She also writes regular invited editorials for *The Chronicle of Higher Education*. Williams's research has been featured in *Nature, Newsweek, Business Week, Science, Scientific American, The New York Times, The Washington Post, USA Today, The Philadelphia Inquirer, The Chronicle of Higher Education*, and *Child Magazine*, among other media outlets. She was series editor for the Lawrence Erlbaum Educational Psychology Series and she served on the editorial review boards of the journals *Psychological Bulletin, Psychological Science in the Public Interest, Applied Developmental Psychology*, and *Psychology, Public Policy, and Law*, as well as the book publisher Magination Press (American Psychological Association Books).

Williams is a Fellow of the Association for Psychological Science and four divisions of the American Psychological Association—general psychology, developmental psychology, educational psychology, and media psychology—and she served two terms as Member-at-Large of the executive committee of the Society for General Psychology (Division 1 of the American Psychological Association). She was also program chair and dissertation award committee chair for Divisions 1 (general psychology), 3 (experimental psychology), and 15 (educational psychology) of the American Psychological Association. In 1995 and 1996 her research won first-place awards from the American Educational Research Association. Williams received the 1996 Early Career Contribution Award from Division 15 (educational psychology) of the American Psychological Association, and the 1997, 1999, and 2002 Mensa Awards for Excellence in Research to a Senior Investigator.

In 2001, the American Psychological Association named her the sole recipient of the Robert L. Fantz Award for an Early Career Contribution to Psychology in recognition of her outstanding contributions to research in the decade following receipt of the PhD. Most recently, Williams was named a 2008 G. Stanley Hall Lecturer by the American Psychological Association.

References

Achter, J. A., Lubinski, D., Benbow, C. P., & Eftekhari-Sanjani, H. (1999). Assessing vocational preferences among gifted adolescents adds incremental validity to abilities. *Journal of Educational Psychology, 91*, 777–786.

Ackerman, P. L. (2006). Cognitive sex differences and mathematics and science achievement. *American Psychologist, 61*, 722–723.

American Association of University Women. (1992). *AAUW Report: How schools short-change girls (executive summary)*. Washington, DC: Author. Retrieved December 9, 2006, from http://www.aauw.org/research/girls_education/hssg.cfm

American Association of University Women. (1999). *Gender gaps*. New York: Marlowe.

Andreescu, T., Gallian, J. A., Kane, J., & Mertz, J. E. (2008). Cross-cultural analysis of students with exceptional talent in mathematical problem solving. *Notices of the American Mathematical Society, 55*, 1248–1260.

Angoff, W. (1993). Perspective on differential item functioning methodology. In P. W. Holland & H. Wainer (Eds.), *Differential item functioning* (pp. 3–24). Hillsdale, NJ: Lawrence Erlbaum.

Ankney, C. D. (1992). Sex differences in relative brain size: The mismeasure of woman, too? *Intelligence, 16*, 329–336.

Baenninger, M. A., & Newcombe, N. (1989). The role of experience in spatial test performance: A meta-analysis. *Sex Roles, 20*, 327–344.

Barnett, S. M., & Ceci, S. J. (2002). When and where do we apply what we learn? A taxonomy for far transfer. *Psychological Bulletin, 128*(4), 612–637.

Baron-Cohen, S. (2007). Sex differences in mind: Keeping science distinct from social policy (pp. 159–172). In S. J. Ceci & W. M. Williams (Eds.), *Why aren't more women in science? Top researchers debate the evidence on a key controversy of our time*. Washington, DC: American Psychological Association Books.

Baron-Cohen, S., Lutchmaya, S., & Knickmeyer, R. C. (2004). *Prenatal testosterone in mind: Amniotic fluid studies*. Cambridge, MA: MIT Press.

Beaman, R., Wheldall, K., & Kemp, C. (2006). Differential teacher attention to boys and girls in the classroom. *Educational Review, 58*(3), 339–366.

Becker, J. R. (1981). Differential treatment of females and males in mathematics classes. *Journal for Research in Mathematics Education, 12*(1), 40–53.

Beller, M., & Gafni, N. (1996). The 1991 International Assessment of Educational Progress in mathematics and science: The gender differences perspective. *Journal of Educational Psychology, 88*, 365–377.

Benbow, C. P. (1988). Sex differences in mathematical reasoning ability in intellectually talented preadolescents: Their nature, effects, and possible causes. *Behavioral & Brain Sciences, 11*, 169–182.

Benbow, C. P., & Stanley, J. C. (1983). Sex differences in mathematical reasoning ability: More facts. *Science, 222*, 1029–1030.

Benbow, C. P., & Stanley, J. C. (1980). Sex differences in mathematical ability: Fact or artifact? *Science, 210*, 1262–1264.

Benbow, C. P., Lubinski, D., Shea, D. L., & Eftekhari-Sanjani, H. (2000). Sex differences in mathematical reasoning ability: Their status 20 years later. *Psychological Science, 11*, 474–480.

Berenbaum, S. A., & Hines, M. (1992). Early androgens are related to childhood sex-typed toy preferences. *Psychological Science, 3*, 203–206.

Berenbaum, S., & Resnick, S. (2007). The seeds of career choices: Prenatal sex hormone effects on psychological sex differences. In S. J. Ceci & W. M. Williams (Eds.), *Why aren't more women in science? Top researchers debate the evidence on a key controversy of our time* (pp. 147–158). Washington, DC: American Psychological Association Books.

Berger, R. F., Lee, S., Johnson, J., Nebgen, B., Sha, F., & Xu, J. (2008). The mystery of perpendicular 5-fold axes and the fourth dimension in intermetallic structures. *Chemistry-A European Journal, 14*, 3908–3940.

Berk, R. A. (Ed.). (1982). *Handbook of methods for detecting test bias.* Baltimore, MD: Johns Hopkins Press.

Berry, J. W. (1966). Emne and Eskimo perceptual skills. *International Journal of Psychology, 1*, 207–229.

Bhasin, S., Woodhouse, L., Casaburi, R., Singh, A. B., Mac, R. P., Lee, M., et al. (2005). Older men are as responsive as young men to the anabolic effect of graded doses of testosterone. *Journal of Clinical Endocrinology and Metabolism, 90*, 678–688.

Bhasin, S., Woodhouse, L., Casaburi, R., Singh, A. B., Bhasin, D., Berman, N., et al. (2001). Testosterone dose-response relationships in healthy young men. *American Journal of Physiology-Endocrinology and Metabolism, 281*, 1172–1181.

Biek, D. M. (2006, August). *Stereotype threat and domain identification.* Unpublished doctoral dissertation. Cornell University, Ithaca, NY.

Bornstein, M. H., Haynes, O., Pascual, L., Painter, K., & Galperin, C. (1999). Play in two societies: Pervasiveness of process, specificity of structure. *Child-Development, 70*, 317–331.

Bridgeman, B., & Lewis, C. (1996). Gender differences in college mathematics grades and SAT-M scores. *Journal of Educational Measurement, 33*, 257–270.

Bronfenbrenner, U., & Ceci, S. J. (1994). Nature-nurture in developmental perspective: A bioecological theory. *Psychological Review, 101*, 568–586.

Brosnan, M. J. (2008). Digit ratio as an indicator of numeracy relative to literacy in 7-year-old British schoolchildren. *British Journal of Psychology, 99*, 75–85.

Budden, A., Lortie, C., Tregenza, T., Aarssen, L., Koricheva, J., & Leimu, R. (2008, July). Response to Webb et al.: Double-blind review: accept with minor revisions. *Trends in Ecology and Evolution, 23*, 353–354.

Budden, A., Tregenza, T., Aarssen, L., Koricheva, J., Leimu, R., & Lortie, C. (2008, January). Double-blind review favours increased representation of female authors. *Trends in Ecology and Evolution, 23*, 4–6.

Burnett, S. A., Lane, D. L., & Dratt, L. M. (1979). Spatial visualization and sex differences in quantitative ability. *Intelligence, 3*, 345–354.

Bushman, B. J., & Anderson, C. A. (2001). Media violence and the American public: Scientific facts versus media misinformation. *American Psychologist, 56*, 477–489.

Byrnes, J. P., & Takahira, S. (1993). Explaining Gender differences on SAT-Math Items. *Developmental Psychology, 29*, 805–810.

Cambridge University. (2005). *Cambridge University Reporter Special Number 19, Vol. CXXXV, Friday 26 August 2005: Student numbers*. Cambridge, UK: Cambridge University Press.

Camilli, G., & Shepard, L. A. (1994). *Methods for identifying biased test items*. Newbury Park, CA: Sage.

Carroll, J. B. (1997). Psychometrics, intelligence and public perception. *Intelligence, 24*, 25–52.

Carter, C. S., LaRussa, M. A., & Bodner, G. M. (1987). A study of two measures of spatial ability as predictors of success in different levels of general chemistry. *Journal of Research in Science Teaching, 24*, 645–657.

Casey, M. B., & Brabeck, M. M. (1990). Women who excel on a spatial task: Proposed genetic and environmental factors. *Brain and Cognition, 12*, 73–84.

Casey, M. B., Nuttall, R., Benbow, C. P., & Pezaris, E. (1995). The influence of spatial ability on gender differences in mathematics college entrance test scores across diverse samples. *Developmental Psychology, 31*, 697–705.

Casey, M. B., Nuttall, R. L., & Pezaris, E. (1997). Mediators of gender differences in mathematics college entrance test scores: A comparison of spatial skills with internalized beliefs and anxieties. *Developmental Psychology, 33*, 669–680.

Catsambis, S. (2005). The gender gap in mathematics: Merely a step function? In A. M. Gallagher & J. C. Kaufman (Eds.), *Gender differences in mathematics: An integrative psychological approach* (pp. 222–245). Cambridge, United Kingdom: Cambridge University Press.

Ceci, S. J. (1996). *On intelligence: A bioecological treatise on intellectual development*. Cambridge, MA: Harvard University Press.

Ceci, S. J., Barnett, S. M., & Kanaya, T. (2003). Developing childhood proclivities into adult competencies: The overlooked multiplier effect. In R. J. Sternberg & E. L. Grigorenko (Eds.), *The psychology of abilities, competencies, and expertise*. UK Cambridge.

Ceci, S. J. & Konstantopoulos, S. (2009, January 30). Editorial: It's not all about class size. *The Chronicle of Higher Education*.

Ceci, S. J., & Papierno, P. B. (2005). The rhetoric and reality of gap-closing: When the "have-nots" gain, but the "haves" gain even more. *American Psychologist, 60*, 149–160.

Ceci, S. J., & Williams, W. M. (2009, February 12). Commentary: Should scientists study race and IQ? *Nature, 457*, 788–789.

Ceci, S. J., Williams, W. M., & Barnett, S. M. (2009). Women's underrepresentation in science: Sociocultural and biological considerations. *Psychological Bulletin, 135*, 218–261.

Ceci, S. J., & Williams, W. M. (Eds.). (2007). *Why aren't more women in science? Top researchers debate the evidence*. Washington, DC: American Psychological Association Books.

Charles, M., & Bradley, K. (2006). A matter of degrees: Female underrepresentation in computer science programs cross-nationally. In J. McGrath Cohoon & B. Aspray (Eds.), *Women and information technology: Research on the reasons for underrepresentation* (pp. 183–203). Cambridge, MA: MIT Press.

Christiansen, K., & Knussman, R. (1987). Sex hormones and cognitive functioning in men. *Neuropsychobiology, 18*, 27–36.

Coates, J. M., Gurnell, M., & Rustichini, A. (2009). Second-to-fourth digit ratio predicts success among high-frequency financial traders. *Proceedings of the National Academy of Sciences, 106* (2), 623–628.

Cohen, J. (1988). *Statistical power analysis for the behavioral sciences* (2nd ed.). Hillsdale, NJ: Erlbaum.

Collaer, M. L., Geffner, M. E., Kaufman, F. R., Buckingham, B., & Hines, M. (2002). Cognitive and behavioral characteristics of turner syndrome: Exploring a role for ovarian hormones in female sexual differentiation. *Hormones and Behavior, 41*, 139–155.

Connellan, J., Baron-Cohen, S., Wheelwright, S., Ba'tki, A., & Ahluwalia, J. (2001). Sex differences in human neonatal social perception. *Infant Behavior and Development, 23*, 113–118.

Correll, S. J. (2004). Constraints into preferences: Gender, status, and emerging career aspirations. *American Sociological Review, 69*, 93–114.

Cronin, V. (1967). Mirror-image reversal discrimination in kindergarten and first grade children. *Journal of Experimental Child Psychology, 5*, 577–585.

Cullen, M. J., Hardison, C. M., & Sackett, P. R. (2004). Using SAT–grade and ability–job performance relationships to test predictions derived from stereotype threat theory. *Journal of Applied Psychology, 89*, 220–230.

Danaher, K., & Crandall, C. S. (2008). Stereotype threat in applied settings re-examined. *Journal of Applied Social Psychology, 38*, 1639–1655.

Dar-Nimrod, I., & Heine, S. J. (2006). Exposure to scientific theories affects women's mathematics performance. *Science, 314*, 435.

Davies, P., & Spencer, S. (2005). The gender gap artifact: Women's underrepresentation in quantitative domains through the lens of stereotype threat. In A. M. Gallagher & J. C. Kaufman (Eds.), *Gender differences in mathematics: An integral psychological approach* (pp. 172–188). New York: Cambridge University Press.

Davison, K., & Susman, E. (2001). Are hormone levels and cognitive ability related during early adolescence? *International Journal of Behavioral Development, 25*, 416–428.

De Vries, G., & Simerley, R. B. (2002). In D. Pfaff, A. Arnold, & A. Etgen (Eds.), *Hormones, brain and behaviour: Development of hormone-dependent neuronal systems* (Vol. IV, p. 137). San Diego, CA: Academic Press.

Deary, I. J., Ferguson, K. J., Bastin, M. E., Barrow, G. W. S., Reid, L. M., Seckl, J. R., et al. (2007). Skull size and intelligence and King Robert Bruce's IQ. *Intelligence, 35*, 519–525.

Deary, I. J., Thorpe, G., Wilson, V., Starr, J. M., & Whalley, L. J. (2003). Population sex differences in IQ at age 11: The Scottish mental survey 1932. *Intelligence, 31*, 533–542.

Deary, I. J., Whalley, L., Lemmon, H., Crawford, J. R., & Starr, J. M. (1999). The stability of individual differences in mental ability from childhood to old age: Follow-up of the 1932 Scottish Mental Survey. *Intelligence, 28*, 49–55.

Dickens, W. T., & Flynn, J. R. (2001). Heritability estimates versus large environmental effects: The IQ paradox resolved. *Psychological Review, 108*, 346–369.

Draganski, B., Gaser, C., Busch, V., Schuierer, G., Bogdahn, U., & May, A. (2004). Changes in grey matter induced by training. *Nature, 427*, 311–312.

Dubb, A., Gur, R. C., Avants, B., & Gee, J. (2003). Characterization of sexual dimorphism in the human corpus callosum. *Neuroimage, 20*, 512–519.

Duckworth, A. L., & Seligman, M. E. P. (2006). Self-discipline gives girls the edge: Gender in self-discipline, grades, and achievement test scores. *Journal of Educational Psychology, 98*, 198–208.

Dweck, C. S. (2007). Is math a gift? Beliefs that put females at risk. In S. J. Ceci & W. M. Williams (Eds.), *Why aren't more women in science? Top researchers debate the evidence on a key controversy of our time* (pp. 47–56). Washington, DC: American Psychological Association.

Eccles, J. S. (2007). Where are all of the women? In S. J. Ceci & W. M. Williams (Eds.), *Why aren't more women in science? Top researchers debate the evidence* (pp. 199–210). Washington, DC: American Psychological Association.

Eccles, J. S., Barber, B., & Jozefowicz, D. (1999). Linking gender to educational, occupational, and recreational choices: Applying the Eccles et al. model of achievement-related choices. In W. B. Swann Jr., J. H. Langlois, & L. A. Gilbert (Eds.), *Sexism and stereotypes in modern society: The gender science of Janet Taylor Spence* (pp. 153–192). Washington, DC: American Psychological Association.

Ekstrom, R. B., French, J. W., & Harman, H. H. (1976). *Kit of factor-referenced cognitive tests*. Princeton, NJ: Educational Testing Service.

Englehard, G., Hansche, L., & Rutledge, K. E. (1990). Accuracy of bias review judges in identifying differential item functioning on teacher certification tests. *Applied Measurement in Education, 3*, 347–360.

Entwisle, D. R. (1997). *Children, schools, and inequality*. Boulder, CO: Westview Press.

Entwisle, D. R., Alexander, K., & Olson, L. S. (1994). The gender gap in math: Its possible origins in neighborhood effects. *American Sociological Review, 59*, 822–838.

Falter, C. M., Arroyo, M., & Davis, G. J. (2006). Testosterone: Activation or organization in spatial cognition? *Biological Psychology, 73*, 132–140.

Feingold, A. (1992). Sex differences in variability in intellectual abilities: A new look at an old controversy. *Review of Educational Research, 62*, 61–84.

Feingold, A. (1994). Gender differences in variability in intellectual abilities: A cross-cultural perspective. *Sex Roles, 30*, 81–92.

Fennema, E., Carpenter, T., Jacobs, V., Franke, M., & Levi, L. (1998). Longitudinal Study of Gender Differences in Young Children's Mathematical Thinking. *Educational Researcher, 27*, 6–11.

Fennema, E., & Sherman, J. (1977). Sex-related differences in mathematics achievement, spatial visualization and affective factors. *A mencan Educational Research Journal, 14*, 51–71.

Ferguson, R. C. (2006). *Teacher's guide: Research and benefits of chess*. Illowa Chess Club. Retrieved January 3, 2006, from http://www.quadcitychess.com/benefits_of_chess.html

Fias, W., & Fischer, M. H. (2005). Spatial representation of numbers. In J. Campbell (Ed.), *Handbook of mathematical cognition* (pp. 43–54). London: Psychology Press.

Finegan, J., Niccols, G. A., & Sitarenios, G. (1992). Relations between prenatal testosterone levels and cognitive abilities at 4 years. *Developmental Psychology, 28*, 1075–1089.

Fink, B., Brookes, H., Neave, N., Manning, J. T., & Geary, D. C. (2006) Second to fourth digit ratio and numerical competence in children. *Brain and Cognition, 61*, 211–218.

Fischer, W. (2006). *The educational value of chess*. New Horizons for Learning. Retrieved, from http://www.newhorizons.org/strategies/thinking/fischer.htm

Flynn, J. R. (1991). *Asian Americans: Achievement beyond IQ*. Hillsdale, NJ: Erlbaum.

Flynn, J. R. (1998). WAIS-III and WISC-III: IQ gains in the United States from 1972 to 1995; how to compensate for obsolete norms. *Perceptual and Motor Skillls, 86*, 1231–1239.

Flynn, J. R. (2007). *What is intelligence?* New York: Cambridge University Press.

Flynn, J. R., & Rossi-Case, L. (under review). Beyond skulls and genes: La Plata, gender, IQ gains, and Lynn's international comparisons.

Freeman, C. E. (2004). *Trends in educational equity of girls and women: 2004.* National Center for Educational Statistics. Washington DC: U.S. Department of Education.

Freeman, R., & Goroff, D. (Eds.). (2006). Improving the postdoctoral experience: An empirical approach. The science and engineering workforce in the US. Chicago, IL.: NBER/University of Chicago Press.

Friedman, L. 1995. The space factor in mathematics: gender differences. *Review of Educational Research, 65*(1), 22–50.

Frome, P., & Eccles, J. S. (1998). Parental effects on adolescents' academic self-perceptions and interests. *Journal of Personality and Social Psychology, 74*, 435–452.

Gallagher, A. M. (1992). *Sex differences in problem-solving used by high-scoring examinees on the SAT-M* (College Board Report No. 92–2, ETS RR No. 92–33). New York: College Board Publications.

Gallagher, A., & DeLisi, R. (1994). Gender differences in Scholastic Aptitude Test mathematics problem solving among high ability problem solving students. *Journal of Educational Psychology, 86*, 204–211.

Gallagher, A., Levin, J., & Cahalan, C. (2002). *Cognitive patterns of gender differences on mathematics admissions tests* (ETS Research Report 02–19 / GRE Board Professional Report No. 96–17P). Princeton, NJ: Educational Testing Service.

Gallagher, A. M., & Kaufman, J. C. (2005). *Gender differences in mathematics: An integrative psychological approach.* Cambridge, MA: Cambridge University Press.

Gates, E. (2006). A scientific point of view. *Physics Today,* 64–65 (www.physicstoday.org).

Geary, D. C. (2007). An Evolutionary Perspective on Sex Differences in Mathematics and the Sciences. In S. J. Ceci & W. M. Williams (Eds.), *Why aren't more women in science? Eminent researchers debate the evidence on a key controversy of our time* (pp. 69–72). Washington, DC: American Psychological Association.

Geary, D. C. (1996). Sexual selection and sex differences in mathematical abilities. *Behavioral and Brain Sciences, 19*, 229–284.

Geary, D. C. (1998). *Male, female: The evolution of human sex differences.* Washington, DC: American Psychological Association.

Geary D. C., & DeSoto, M. C. (2001). Sex differences in spatial abilities among adults in the United States and China. *Evolution & Cognition, 7*, 172–177.

Gender Equity Committee of the University of Pennsylvania. (2001, Dec. 4). The gender equity report. *Almanac Supplement, 48*(14).

Gierl, M., Khaliq, S., & Boughton, K. (1999). Gender differential item functioning in mathematics and science: Prevalence and policy implications. Paper presented at the symposium entitled "Improving Large-Scale Assessment in Education" at the Annual Meeting of the Canadian Society for the Study of Education Sherbrooke, Québec, Canada, June 17.

Gierl, M., & McEwen, N. (1998, May). Differential item functioning on the Alberta Education Social Studies 30 Diploma Exams. Paper presented at the annual meeting of the Canadian Society for Studies in Education, Ottawa, Ontario, Canada.

Ginther, D. K. (2001, February). Does science discriminate against women? Evidence from academia, 1973–97. *Federal Reserve Bank of Atlanta*. Working Paper, 2001–02.

Ginther, D. K. (2004, Winter). Why women earn less than men: economic explanations for the gender salary gap in science. *AWIS Magazine, 33*, 1–5.

Ginther, D. K., & Kahn, S. (2006). Does science promote women? Evidence from academia 1973–2001. Unpublished manuscript. Retrieved January 2, 2007, from http://www.nber.org/~sewp/Ginther_Kahn_revised8–06.pdf

Goldberg, C. (1999, March 23). MIT acknowledges bias against female professors. *The New York Times*, p. 1.

Goldin, C., & Rouse, C. (2000). Orchestrating impartiality: The impact of "blind" auditions on female musicians. *American Economic Review, 90*, 715–741.

Goldstein, J. H. (1994). Sex differences in toy play and use of video games In J. H. Goldstein (Ed.), *Toys, play, and child development* (pp. 110–129). New York: Cambridge University Press.

Good, C., Dweck, C. S., & Rattan, A. (2005a). *An incremental theory decreases vulnerability to stereotypes about math ability in college females*. Unpublished data, Columbia University.

Good, C., Dweck, C. S., & Rattan, A. (2005b). Portraying genius: How fixed vs. malleable portrayal of math ability affects females' motivation and performance. Unpublished data, Columbia University.

Gootman, E. (2006, August 18). In Elite N.Y. schools, a dip in Blacks and Hispanics. *New York Times*, p. 1 Education Section.

Gordon, H. W., Corbin, E. D., & Lee, P. A. (1986). Changes in specialized cognitive function following changes in hormone levels. *Cortex 22*, 399–415.

Gouchie, C., & Kimura, D. (1991). The relationship between testosterone levels and cognitive ability patterns. *Psychoneuroendocrinology, 16*, 323–334.

Grabner, R. H., Neubauer, A. C., & Stern, E. (2006). Superior performance and neural efficiency: The impact of intelligence and expertise. *Brain Research Bulletin, 69*, 422–439.

Grabner, R. H., Stern, E., & Neubauer, A. C. (2003). When intelligence loses its impact: Neural efficiency during reasoning in a familiar area. *International Journal of Psychophysiology, 49*, 89–98.

Grimshaw, G., Sitarenios, G., & Finegan, J. (1995). Mental rotation at 7 years: Relations with prenatal testosterone levels and spatial play experiences. *Brain and Cognition, 29*, 85–100.

Grossi, D., Orsini, A., Monetti, C., & De Michele, G. (1979). Sex-differences in children's spatial and verbal memory span. *Cortex, 15*, 667–670.

Guiso, L., Luigi, F. M., Sapienza, P., & Zingales, L. (2008). Diversity: Culture, gender, and math. *Science, 320*, 1164–1165.

Gur, R., & Gur, R. E. (2007). Neural substrates for sex differences in cognition. In S. J. Ceci & W. M. Williams (Eds.), *Why aren't more women in science? Top researchers debate the evidence on a key controversy of our time* (pp. 189–198). Washington, DC: American Psychological Association.

Gur, R. C., Alsop, D., Glahn, D., Petty, R., Swanson, C. L., Maldjian, J. A., et al. (2000). An fMRI study of sex differences in regional activation to a verbal and a spatial task. *Brain and Language, 74*, 157–170.

Haier, R., Jung, R. E., Yeo, R. A., Head, K., & Alkire, M. T. (2004). Structural brain variation and general intelligence. *NeuroImage, 23*(1), 425–433.

Haier, R. J., Jung, R., Yeo, R., Head, K., & Alkire, M. T. (2005). The neuroanatomy of general intelligence: Sex matters. *Neuroimage, 25*(1), 320–327.

Hakim, C. (2006). Women, careers, and work-life preferences. *British Journal of Guidance and Counseling, 34*, 279–294.

Halari, R., Sharma, T., Hines, M., Andrew, C., Simmons, A., & Kumari, V. (2006). Comparable fMRI activity with differential behavioural performance on mental rotation and overt verbal fluency tasks in healthy men and women. *Experimental Brain Research, 169*, 1–14.

Halpern, D. F. (2007). Science, sex, and good sense: Why women are underrepresented in some areas of science and math. In S. J. Ceci & W. M. Williams (Eds.), *Why aren't more women in science? Top researchers debate the evidence on a key controversy of our time* (pp. 121–130). Washington, DC: American Psychological Association Books.

Hamel, M. B., Ingelfinger, J. R., Phimister, E., & Solomon, C. (2006). EDITORIALS: Women in academic medicine—progress and challenges. *The New England Journal of Medicine, 355*, 310.

Hampson, E. (1990). Estrogen-related variations in human spatial and articulatory-motor skills. *Psychoneuroendocrinology, 15*, 97–111.

Hampson, E., & Kimura, D. (1988). Reciprocal effects of hormonal fluctuations on human motor and perceptual-spatial skills. *Behavioral Neuroscience, 102*, 456–459.

Hampson, E., & Moffat, S. D. (2005). The psychobiology of gender: The cognitive effects of reproductive hormones in the adult nervous system. In R. J. Sternberg, A. Eagley, & A. Beal (Eds.), *The psychology of gender* (2nd ed., pp. 38–64). New York: Guilford Press.

Hampson, E., Rovet, J. F., & Altmann, D. (1998). Spatial reasoning in children with congenital adrenal hyperplasia due to 21-hydroxylase deficiency. *Developmental Neuropsychology, 14*, 299–320.

Harris, A. M., & Carlton, S. (2006). Patterns of gender differences on mathematics items on the scholastic aptitude test. *Applied Measurement in Education, 6*, 136–151.

Harris, D. R. (2001). Why Are Whites and Blacks Averse to Black Neighbors? *Social Science Research 30*, 100–116.

Harvard University. (2005). *Women at Harvard University.* Retrieved January 4, 2007, from http://www.hno.harvard.edu/guide/underst/under4.html

Haslanger, S. (2007, September 10). Philosophy and sexism. *Inside Higher Education.* Retrieved October 11, 2007, from www.insidehighered.com/news/2007/09/10/philos.

Hausman, P., & Steiger, J. H. (2001, February). Confession without guilt? MIT jumped the gun to avoid a sex-discrimination controversy, but shot itself in the foot. *Independent Women's Forum*, 1–12.

Haworth, C. M. A., Dale, P. S., & Plomin, R. (2009). Sex differences and science: The etiology of science excellence. *Journal of Child Psychology and Psychiatry.*

Hedges, L. V., & Nowell, A. (1995). Sex differences in mental test scores, variability, and numbers of high-scoring individuals. *Science, 269*, 41–45.

Hedges, L. V., & Nowell, A. (1998). Changes in the Black-White gap in achievement test scores. *Sociology of Education, 72*, 111–135.

Heilman, M. E. and Haynes, M. C. (2005). No Credit Where Credit Is Due: Attributional Rationalization of Women's Success in Male–Female Teams, *Journal of Applied Psychology, 90*(5), 905–916.

Hewlett, S. A., Luce, C., & Servon, L. J. (2008, June). Stopping the exodus of women in science. *Harvard Business Review, 22–24.*

Hier, D. B., & Crowley, W. F. (1982). Spatial ability in androgen-deficient men. *New England Journal of Medicine, 306,* 1202–1205.

Hines, M. (2007). Do sex differences in cognition cause the shortage of women in science? In S. Ceci, & W. M. Williams (Eds.), *Why aren't more women in science? Top researchers debate the evidence* (pp.101–112). Washington, DC: American Psychological Asociation.

Hines, M., Ahmed, S. F., & Hughes, I. A. (2003). Psychological outcomes and gender-related development in complete androgen insensitivity syndrome. *Archives of Sexual Behavior, 32,* 93–101.

Hines, M., Fane, B. A., Pasterski, V. L., Mathews, G. A., Conway, G. S., & Brook, C. (2003). Spatial abilities following prenatal androgen abnormality: Targeting and mental rotations performance in individuals with congenital adrenal hyperplasia. *Psychoneuroendocrinology, 28,* 1010–1026.

Hines, M., & Kaufman, F. R. (1994). Androgen and the development of human sex-typical behavior—rough-and-tumble play and sex of preferred playmates in children with congenital adrenal-hyperplasia (CAH). *Child Development, 65,* 1042–1053.

Ho, H., Gilger, J. W., & Brink, T. M. (1986). Effects of menstrual cycle on spatial information processes. *Perceptual & Motor Skills, 63,* 743–751.

Hoffer, T. B., & Grigorian, K. (2005, December). *All in a week's work: Average work weeks of doctoral scientists and engineers.* National Science Foundation. NSF 06–302. Science Resources Statistics.

Hogervorst, E., Bandelow, S., & Moffat, S. D. (2005). Increasing testosterone levels and effects on cognitive functions in elderly men and women. *Drug Targets—CNS & Neurological Disorders, 4,* 531–540.

Hugdahl, K., Thomsen, T., & Ersland, L. (2006). Sex differences in visuo-spatial processing: An fMRI study of mental rotation. *Neuropsychologia, 44,* 1575–1583.

Humphreys, L., Lubinski, D., & Yao, G. (1993). Utility of predicting group membership and the role of spatial visualization in becoming an engineer, scientist, or artist. *Journal of Applied Psychology, 78,* 250–261.

Hyde, J. S. (2005). The gender similarity hypothesis. *American Psychologist, 60,* 581–592.

Hyde, J. S., Fennema, E., & Lamon, S. J. (1990). Gender differences in mathematics performance: A meta-analysis. *Psychological Bulletin, 107,* 139–155.

Hyde, J. S., Fenneman, E., Ryan, M., Frost, L. A., & Hopp, C. (1990). Gender comparisons of mathematics studies and effects: A meta-analysis. *Psychology of Women Quarterly, 14,* 299–324.

Hyde, J. S., Lindberg, S. M., Linn, M. C., Ellis, A. B., & Williams, C. C. (2008). Gender similarities characterize math performance. *Science, 321,* 494–495.

Hyde, J. S., & Linn, M. C. (2006). Gender similarities in mathematics and science. *Science, 314,* 599–600.

Inzlicht, M., & Ben-Zeev, T. (2000). A threatening intellectual environment: Why females are susceptible to experiencing problem-solving deficits in the presence of males. *Psychological Science, 11*(5), 365.

Irwing, P., & Lynn, R. (2005). Sex differences in means and variability on the Progressive Matrices in university students: A meta-analysis. *British Journal of Psychology, 96,* 505–524.

Ivie, R., & Ray, K. (2005). *Women in physics and astronomy*. College Park, MD: American Institute of Physics.

Jacobs, J. A., & Winslow, S. E. (2004). Overworked faculty: Job and stresses and family demands. *Annals of American Political and Social Scientist, 596*, 104–129.

Jacobs, J. E., & Eccles, J. S. (1985). Gender differences in math ability: The impact of media reports on parents. *Educational Researcher, 14*, 20–25.

Jacobs, J. E., & Eccles, J. S. (1992). The impact of mothers' gender-role stereotypic beliefs on mothers' and children's ability perceptions. *Journal of Personality and Social Psychology, 63*, 932–944.

Jacobs, J. A., & Winslow, S. E. (2004). Overworked faculty: job and stresses and family demands. *Annals of American Political and Social Scientist, 596*, 104–129.

Jagsi, R., Guancial, E. A., & Worobey, C. C. (2006). The "gender gap" in authorship of academic medical literature—A 35-year perspective. *The New England Journal of Medicine, 355*, 281.

Jardine, J., & Martin, N. G. (1983). Spatial ability and throwing accuracy. *Behavior Genetics, 13*, 331–340.

Jayasinghe, U. W., Marsh, H. W., & Bond, N. (2003). A multilevel cross-classified modeling approach to peer-review of grant proposals: The effects of assessor and researcher attributes on assessor ratings. *Journal of the Royal Statistical Society (A), 166*, 279–300.

Jayasinghe, U. W., Marsh, H. W., & Bond N. A. (2006). New reader trial approach to peer review in funding research grants: An Australian experiment. *Scientometics, 69*, 591–606.

Jones, C. M., Braithwaite, V. A., & Healy, S. D. (2003). The evolution of sex differences in spatial ability. *Behavioral Neuroscience, 117*, 403–411.

Keach, R. (2003). *Benefits of chess for youth. Northwest Washington Scholastic Chess*. Retrieve January 3, 2007, from http://home1.gte.net/kaech/benefits.html

Kelly, A. (1998). Gender differences in pupil-teacher interactions: A meta-analytic review. *Research in Education, 39*, 1–24.

Kenney-Benson, G. A., Pomerantz, E. M., Ryan, A. M., & Patrick, H. (2006). Sex differences in math performance: The role of children's approach to schoolwork. *Developmental Psychology, 42*, 11–26.

Kersh, J., Casey, B. M., & Young, J. M. (2008). Research on spatial skills and block building in girls and boys: The relationship to later mathematics learning. In B. Spodak & O. Saracho (Eds.), *Mathematics, science and technology in early childhood education: Contemporary perspectives on mathematics in early childhood education* (pp. 233–253). Charlotte, NC: Information Age.

Kimura, D. (1996). Sex, sexual orientation and sex hormones influence human cognitive function. *Current Opinion in Neurobiology, 6*, 259–263.

Kimura, D. (2000). *Sex and cognition*. Cambridge, MA: MIT Press.

Kimura, D. (2002). Sex hormones influence human cognitive pattern. *Neuroendocrinology Letters, 23*(Suppl. 4), 67–77.

Kimura, D. (2004). Hysteria trumps academic freedom. *Vancouver Sun*, p. A13. At: http://www.sfu.ca/~dkimura/articles/hysteria.htm

Kimura, D. (2007). Under-representation" or misrepresentation? In S. J. Ceci & W. M. Williams (Eds.), *Why aren't more women in science? Top researchers debate the evidence on a key controversy of our time* (pp. 39–46). Washington, DC: American Psychological Association Books.

Kolen, M. J., & Brennan, R. L. (1995). *Test equating*. New York: Springer Verlag.

Kucian, K., Loenneker, T., Dietrich, T., Martin, E., & von Aster, M. (2005). Gender differences in brain activation patterns during mental rotation and number related cognitive tasks. *Psychological Science, 47*, 112–131.

Kulp, M. T. (1999). Relationship between visual motor integration skill and academic performance in kindergarten through third grade. *Optometry and Vision Science, 76*, 159–163.

Kurdek, L. A., & Sinclair, R. J. (2001). Predicting reading and mathematics achievement in fourth-grade children from kindergarten readiness scores. *Journal of Educational Psychology, 93*, 451–455.

Lachance, J. A., & Mazzocco, M. M. M. (2006). A longitudinal analysis of sex differences in math and spatial skills in primary school age children. *Learning and Individual Differences, 16*, 195–216.

Lacreuse, A., Kim, C. B., Moss, M. B., Rosene, D. L., Killiany, R. J., Moore, T. L., et al. (2005). Sex, age, and training modulate spatial memory in the rhesus monkey (Macaca mulatta). *Behavioral Neuroscience, 119*, 118–126.

Lally, K. (2005, July 31). Aptitude aplenty for these young women, and their mentors, science is what comes naturally. *Washington Post*, p. W08.

Leahey, E., & Guo, G. (2001, December). Gender differences in mathematical trajectories. *Social Forces, 80*, 713–732.

Leslie, D. W. (2007, March). *The reshaping of America's academic workforce*. TIAA-CREF Institute, #87. Retrieved September 22, 2008, from www.tiaa-crefinstitute.org

Lever, J. (1976). Sex Differences in the Games Children Play. *Social Problems, 23*, 478–87.

Levine, S. C., Huttenlocher, J., Taylor, A., & Langrock, A. (1999). Early spatial differences. *Developmental Psychology, 35*, 940–949.

Levine, S. C., Vasilyeva, M., Lourenco, S. F., Newcombe, N. S., & Huttenlocher, J. (2005). Socioeconomic status modifies the sex difference in spatial skill. *Psychological Science, 16*, 841–845.

Lewis, D. (2005, June 24). Mathematics: Probing performance gaps. *Science, 308*, 1871–1872.

Linn, M. C., & Hyde, J. S. (1989). Gender, mathematics, and science. *Educational Researcher, 18*, 17–27.

Linn, M. C., & Petersen, A. C. (1985). Emergence and characterization of sex differences in spatial ability: A meta-analysis. *Child Development, 56*, 1479–1498.

Lippa, R. A. (1998). Gender-related individual differences and the structure of vocational interests on the people-things dimension. *Journal of Personality and Social Psychology, 74*, 996–1009.

Lippa, R. A. (in press). Sex differences in personality traits and gender-related occupational preferences across 53 nations: Testing evolutionary and social-environmental theories. *Archives of Sexual Behavior*.

Lippa, R. A., Collaer, M. L., & Peters, M. (in press). Sex Differences in Mental Rotation and Line Angle Judgments Are Positively Associated with Gender Equality and Economic Development across 53 Nations. Archives of Sexual Behavior.

LoBello, S. G., & Gulgoz, S. (1991). Factor analysis of the Wechsler Preschool and Primary Scale of Intelligence—Revised. *Psychological Assessment, 3*, 130–132.

Lohman, D., & Lakin, J. (2009). Consistencies in sex differences on the cognitive abilities test across countries, grades, test forms, and cohorts. *British Journal of Educational Psychology, 79*, 389–407.

Long, J. S. (1992). Measures of sex differences in scientific productivity. *Social Forces, 71*, 159–178.

Lubinski, D. (2004). Introduction to the special section on cognitive abilities: 100 years after Spearman's (1904) " 'general intelligence,' objectively determined and measured." *Journal of Personality and Social Psychology, 86*, 96–111.

Lubinski, D. S., & Benbow, C. (2007). Sex differences in personal attributes for the development of scientific expertise. In S. J. Ceci & W. M. Williams (Eds.), *Why aren't more women in science? Top researchers debate the evidence on a key controversy of our time* (pp. 79–100). Washington, DC: American Psychological Association Books.

Lubinski, D., Benbow, C. P., Shea, D. L., Eftekhari-Sanjani, H., & Halvorson, B. J. (2001). Men and women at promise for scientific excellence: Similarity not dissimilarity. *Psychological Science, 12*, 309–317.

Lubinski, D., Benbow, C. P., Webb, R. M., & Bleske-Rechek, A. (2006). Tracking exceptional human talent over two decades. *Psychological Science, 17*, 194–199.

Lutchmaya, S., Baron-Cohen, S., Raggatt, P., Knickmeyer, R., & Manning, J.T. (2004). 2nd to 4th digit ratios, fetal testosterone, and estradiol. *Early Human Development, 77*, 23–28.

Lummis, M., & Stevenson, H. W. (1990). Gender differences in beliefs and achievement: A cross-cultural study. *Developmental Psychology, 26*, 254–263.

Lynn, R. (1991). The evolution of racial differences in intelligence. *The Mankind Quarterly, 32*, 1–2, 99–121.

Lynn, R., & Irwing, P. (2004). Sex differences on the Progressive Matrices: A meta-analysis. *Intelligence, 32*, 481–498.

Maccoby, E. E., & Jacklin, C. N. (1974). *The psychology of sex differences*. Stanford, CA: Stanford University Press.

Maguire, E. A., Gadian, D. G, Johnsrude, I. S., Good, C. D., Ashburner, J., Frackowiak, R. S. J., et al. (2000). Navigation-related structural change in the hippocampi of taxi drivers. *Proceedings of the National Academy of Science, 97*, 4395–4403.

Manning, J. T. (2002). *Digit ratio: A pointer to fertility, behaviour and health*. London: Rutgers University Press.

Marsh, H., Jayasinghe, U. W., & Bond, N. W. (2008). Improving the peer-review process: Reliability, validity, bias and generalizability. *American Psychologist, 63*(3), 160–168.

Martell, R. F., Lane, D. M., & Emrich, C. (1996). Male-female differences: A computer simulation. *American Psychologist, 51*, 157–158.

Martens, A., Johns, M., Greenberg, J., & Schimel, J. (2006). Combatting stereotype threat: The effect of self-affirmation on women's intellectual performance. *Journal of Experimental Social Psychology, 42*, 236–243.

Mason, M. A. (2009). Balancing act: A bad reputation. *Chronicle of Higher Education*. At: http://chronicle.com/jobs/news/2009/01/2009012701c.htm

Mason, M. A., & Goulden, M. (2004). Marriage and baby blues: Redefining gender equity and the academy. *Annals of American Political and Social Scientist, 596*, 86–103.

Massachusetts Institute of Technology Faculty Newsletter. (1999, March), *21*(4). Retrieved, from http://web.mit.edu/fnl/women/women.html

Mauleon, E., & Bordons, M. (2006). Productivity, impact, and publication habits by gender in the area of materials science. *Scientometrics, 66*, 199–218.

McDowell, J. M. (1982). Obsolescence of knowledge and career publication profiles: Some evidence of differences among fields in costs of interrupted careers. *American Economics Review, 72*, 752–768.

McGuinness, D., & Morley, C. (1991). Sex differences in the development of visuo-spatial ability in pre-school children. *Journal of Mental Imagery, 15*, 143–150.

McIntyre, R. B., Lord, C. G., Gresky, D. M., Ten Eyck, L. L., Frye, G. D. J., & Bond, C. F. Jr. (2005). A social impact trend in the effects of role models on alleviating women's mathematics stereotype threat. *Current Research in Social Psychology, 10*(9), 116–137.

McKeever, W. F., Rich, D., Deyo, R., & Conner, R. (1987). Androgens and spatial ability: failure to find a relationship between testosterone and ability measures. *Bulletin of the Psychonomics Society, 25*, 438–440.

McLaughlin, T. (2006). *Top Wall Street jobs still elude women, minorities.* New York: Reuters. Retrieved January 3, 2007, from http://news.yahoo.com/s/nm/20061227/bs_nm/wallstreet_diversity_dc

Moffat, S. D., & Hampson, E. (1996). A curvilinear relationship between testosterone and spatial cognition in humans: possible influence of hand preference. *Psychoneuroendocrinology, 21*, 323–337.

Moffat, S. D., Zonderman, A., Metter, E., Blackman, M., Harman, S., & Resnick, S. M. (2002). Longitudinal assessment of serum free testosterone concentration predicts memory and cognitive status in men. *Journal of Clinical Endocrinology and Metabolism, 87*, 5001–5007.

Moore, D. S., & Johnson, S. P. (2008). Mental rotation in human infants: A sex difference. *Psychological Science, 19*, 1063–1066.

Muller, C. B., Ride, S. M., Fouke, J., Whitney, T., Denton, D. D., Cantor, N., et al. (2005, February 18). Gender differences and performance in science. *Science, 307*, 1043.

Mullis, I. V. S., Martin, M. O., & Foy, P. (2005). *TIMSS 2003 international report on achievement in the mathematics cognitive domains: Findings from a developmental project.* Boston, MA: TIMSS & PIRLS International Study Center. Retrieved November 24, 2005, from http://timss.bc.edu/PDF/t03_download/T03MCOGDRPT.pdf

Murphy, M. C., Steele, C., & Gross, J. J. (2007). Signaling threat: How situational cues affect women in mathematics, science, and engineering settings. *Psychological Science, 18*, 879–885.

National Academy of Science. (2005, December 9). Convocation on maximizing the potential of women in academe: Biological, social, and organizational contributions to science and engineering success. Committee on Women in Academic Science and Engineering, Washington, DC.

National Foundation for Educational Research (NFER). (1979). *Science reasoning tasks.* Windsor: Author.

National Science Board. (2006). *Science and engineering indicators 2006* (Vol. 1 and 2, NSB 06–01, 06–01A). Arlington, VA: National Science Foundation.

Neave, N., Menaged, M., & Weightman, D. (1999). Sex differences in cognition: The role of testosterone and sexual orientation. *Brain and Cognition, 41*, 245–262.

Nelson, D. J. (2007, October 31). *A national analysis of minorities in science and engineering faculties of research universities.* at: http://chem.ou.edu/~djn/diversity/Faculty_Tables_FY07/FinalReport07.html

Newcombe, N. S. (2007). Taking science seriously: Straight thinking about spatial sex differences. In S. J. Ceci & W. M. Williams (Eds.), *Why aren't more women in science? Top researchers debate the evidence on a key controversy of our time* (pp. 69–78). Washington, DC: American Psychological Association Books.

Nuttall, R. L., Casey, M. B., & Pezaris, E. (2005). Spatial ability as a mediator of gender differences on mathematics tests. In A. M. Gallagher & J. C. Kaufman (Eds.), *Gender differences in mathematics: An integrative psychological approach* (pp. 121–142). Cambridge, UK: Cambridge University Press.

O'Brien, T. (2006). Why do so few women reach the top of big law firms? *The New York Times.* Retrieved January 4, 2007, from http://www.nytimes.com/2006/ 03/19/business/yourmoney/191aw.html?ex=1300424400&en=f9b2756ce77b02bc& ei=5088&partner=rssnyt&emc=rss

Oakes, J. (1990). Opportunities, achievement, and choice: Women and minority students in science and mathematics. *Review of Research in Higher Education* 16: 153–222.

Okun, W. (2007, December 21). Disparities. *The New York Times.*

O'Neill, K. A., & McPeek, W. M. (1993). Item and test characteristics that are associated with differential item functioning. In P. W. Holland & H. Wainer (Eds.), *Differential item functioning* (pp. 255–276). Hillsdale, NJ: Lawrence Erlbaum.

Orsini, A., Schiappa, O., & Grossi, D. (1981). Sex and cultural-differences in children's spatial and verbal memory span. *Perceptual and Motor Skills, 53,* 39–42.

Papierno, P. B., & Ceci, S. J. (2006). Promoting equity or inducing disparity: The costs and benefits of widening achievement gaps through universal interventions. *The Georgetown Public Policy Review, 10,* 1–15.

Park, G., Lubinski, D., & Benbow, C. P. (2007). Contrasting intellectual patterns for creativity in the arts and sciences: Tracking intellectually precocious youth over 25 years. *Psychological Science, 18,* 948–952.

Parsons, J. E., Adler, T. F., & Kaczala, C. M. (1982). Socialization of achievement attitudes and beliefs: Parental influences. *Child Development, 53,* 310–321.

Penner, A. M. (2003). International gender × item difficulty interactions in mathematics and science achievement tests. *Journal of Educational Psychology, 95,* 650–655.

Penner, A. M. (2006). A quantile regression approach to international gender differences in mathematics. Retrieved June 12, 2008, from http://socrates.berkeley.edu/penner/

Penner, A. M. (2008). Gender differences in extreme mathematical achievement: an international perspective on biological and social factors. *American Journal of Sociology, 114,* 138–170.

Penner, A. M., & Paret, M. (2008). Gender differences in mathematics achievement: Exploring the early grades and the extremes. *Social Science Research, 37,* 239–253.

Peters, T., Laeng, B., Latham, K., Jackson, M., Zaiyouna, R., & Richardson, C. (1995). A redrawn Vandenberg and Kuse mental rotations test: Different versions and factors that affect performance. *Brain and Cognition, 28,* 39–58.

Pinker, Steven. (2002). *The blank slate.* New York: Viking.

Pinker, Susan. (2008). *The gender paradox.* New York: Harper-Collins.

Pomerantz, E. M., Altermatt, E. R., & Saxon, J. L. (2002). Making the grade but feeling distressed: Gender differences in academic performance. *Journal of Educational Psychology, 94,* 396–404.

Preston, A. (2004, Summer). Plugging leaks in the scientific workforce. *Issues in Science & Technology,* pp. 69–74.

Pribyl, J. R., & Bodner, G. M. (1987). Spatial ability and its role in organic chemistry: A study of four organic courses. *Journal of Research in Science Teaching, 24,* 229–240.

Puts, D. A., McDaniel, M. A., Jordan, C. L., & Breedlove, S. M. (2008). Spatial ability and prenatal androgens: Meta-analyses of congenital adrenal hyperplasia. *Archives of Sexual Behavior, 37,* 100–111.

Quinn, D. N., & Spencer, S. J. (2001). The interference of stereotype threat with women's generation of mathematical problem-solving strategies. *Journal of Social Issues, 57*, 55–72.

Quinn, P. C., & Liben, L. S. (2008). A sex difference in mental rotation in young infants. *Psychological Science, 19*, 1067–1070.

Ramsey, P. A. (1993). Sensitivity reviews: The ETS experience as a case study. In P. W. Holland & H. Wainer (Eds.), *Differential item functioning* (pp. 367–388). Hillsdale, NJ: Lawrence Erlbaum.

RAND. (2005). Is there gender bias in federal grant programs? Infrastructure, safety, and environment research brief. Retrieved September 17, 2008, from http://rand.org/pubs/research_briefs/RB9147/RAND_RB9147.pdf

Ravitch, D. (1998, December 17). Girls are beneficiaries of gender gap. *Wall Street Journal. Education*, p. 1.

Reis, S. M., & Park, S. (2001). Gender differences in high-achieving students in math and science. *Journal for the Education of the Gifted, 25*, 52–73.

Resnick, S. M., Berenbaum, S. A., Gottesman, I. I., & Bouchard, T. J. (1986). Early hormonal influences on cognitive functioning in congenital adrenal hyperplasia. *Developmental Psychology, 22*, 191–198.

Rhode, D. L. (1997). *Speaking of sex: The denial of gender inequality*. Cambridge, MA: Harvard University Press.

Robinson, N. M., Abbott, R. D., Berninger, V. W., & Busse, J. (1996). The structure of abilities in mathematically precocious young children: Gender similarities and differences. *Journal of Educational Psychology, 88*, 341–352.

Roof, R. L., Zhang, Q., Glasier, M. M., & Stein, D. G. (1993). Gender-specific impairment on Morris water maze task after entorhinal cortex lesion. *Behavioural Brain Research, 57*, 47–51.

Rousseau, J. J. (1762). *Emile*. NY : Basic Books. (Tr. A. Bloom, 1979.)

Royer, J. M., & Garofoli, L. M. (2005). Cognitive contributions to sex differences in math performance. In A. M. Gallagher & J. C. Kaufman (Eds.), *Gender differences in mathematics* (pp. 99–120). New York: Cambridge University Press.

Rushton, J. P. (1992a). Cranial capacity related to sex, rank, and race in a stratified random sample of 6,325 U.S. military personnel. *Intelligence, 16*, 401–413.

Rushton, J. P. (1992b). The brain size IQ debate. *Nature, 360*(6402), 292.

Rushton, J. P., & Ankney, C. D. (2007). The evolution of brain size and intelligence. In S. M. Platek & T. K. Shackelford (Eds.), *Evolutionary cognitive neuroscience* (pp. 121–161). Cambridge, MA: MIT Press.

Sackett, P., Hardison, C., & Cullen, M. (2004). On interpreting stereotype threat as accounting for African American—white differences on cognitive tests. *American Psychologist, 59*, 7–13.

Sadker, D., & Zittleman, K. (2005). Gender bias lives, for both sexes. *The Education Digest, 70*(8), 27–30.

Sanders, J. (2003). Teaching gender equity in teacher education. *The Education Digest, 68*(5), 25–29.

Sanders, G., Bereczkei, T., Csatho, A., & Manning, J. (2005). The ratio of the 2nd to 4th finger length predicts spatial ability in men but not women. *Cortex, 41*, 789–795.

Scheibinger, L. (1987). The history and philosophy of women in science: A review essay. *Journal of Women in Culture and Society, 12*(2), 305–332.

Schmader, T., & Johns, M. (2003). Converging evidence that stereotype threat reduces working memory capacity. *Journal of Personality and Social Psychology, 85,* 440–452.

Seid, J. (2006). *10 Best-paid executives: They're all men.* New York: CNN. Retrieved January 4, 2007, from http://money.cnn.com/2006/10/03/news/newsmakers/mpwpay/index.htm

Serbin, L. A., Zelkowitz, P., Doyle, A. B., Gold, D., & Wheaton, B. (1990). The socialization of sex-differentiated skills and academic performance: A mediational model. *Sex Roles, 23,* 613–628.

Shalala, D. E., Agogino, A. M., Bailyn, L., Birgeneau, R., Cauce, A. M., Deangeles, C., et al. (2006). *Beyond bias and barriers: Fulfilling the potential of women in academic science and engineering.* Washington, DC: National Academies Press.

Shayer, M., Ginsberg, D., & Coe, R. (2007). 30 years on—a large anti-Flynn effect? The Piagetian test *Volume and Heaviness* norms 1975–2003. *British Journal of Educational Psychology, 77, 25–41.*

Shea, D. L., Lubinski, D., & Benbow, C. P. (2001). Importance of assessing spatial ability in talented young adolescents: A 20-year longitudinal study. *Journal of Educational Psychology, 93,* 604–614.

Shepard, R. N., & Metzler, J. (1971). Mental rotation of three-dimensional objects. *Science, 171,* 701–703.

Shih, M., Pittinsky, T. L., & Ambady, N. (1999). Stereotype susceptibility: Identity salience and shifts in quantitative performance. *Psychological Science, 10,* 80–83.

Shute, V. J., Pellegrino, J. W., Hubert, L., & Reynolds, R. W. (1983). The relationship between androgen levels and human spatial abilities. *Bulletin of the Psychonomics Society, 21,* 465–468.

Siegel, A. W., & Schadler, M. (1977). The development of young children's spatial representations of their classroom. *Child Development, 48,* 388–394.

Sigma Xi Postdoc Survey Methods (Technical Report #2). (2006). Sigma Xi Postdoc Survey, 2005. http://postdoc.sigmaxi.org/results/tech_reports/

Silverman, I., & Phillips, K. (1993). Effects of estrogen changes during the menstrual cycle on spatial performance. *Ethology and Sociobiology, 14,* 257–270.

Singer, M. (2006). Editorial: Beyond bias and barriers. *Science, 314,* 893.

Slabbekoorn, D., van Goozen, S. H., Megens, J., Gooren, L. J. G., & Cohen-Kettenis, P. T. (1999). Activating effects of cross-sex hormones on cognitive functioning: A study of short-term and long-term hormone effects in transsexuals. *Psychoneuroendocrinology, 24,* 432–447.

Sommers, C. H. (2008, March/April). Why can't a woman be more like a man. *The American: Magazine of Ideas.* Retrieved February 1, 2009, from http://www.american.com/archive/2008/march-april-magazine-contents/why-can2019t-a-woman-be-more-like-a-man

Sorby, S. A. (2001). A course in spatial visualization and its impact on the retention of female engineering students. *Journal of Women and Minorities in Science and Engineering, 7,* 153–172.

Sorby, S. A. (2005). Impact of changes in course methodologies on improving spatial skills. *Journal of Geometry and Graphics, 9,* 99–105.

Sorby, S. A., & Bartmaans, B. J. (2000, July). The development and assessment of a course for enhancing the 3-D spatial visualization skills of first year engineering students. *Journal of Engineering Education,* 301–308.

Spelke, E. S. (2005). Sex differences in intrinsic aptitude for mathematics and science? A critical review. *American Psychologist, 60*, 950–958.

Spelke, E. S., & Grace, A. D. (2007). Sex, math, and science. In S. J. Ceci & W. M. Williams (Eds.), *Why aren't more women in science? Eminent researchers debate the evidence on a key controversy of our time* (pp. 57–68). Washington, DC: American Psychological Association.

Spencer, S. J., Steele, C. M., & Quinn, D. M. (1999). Stereotype threat and women's math performance. *Journal of Experimental Social Psychology, 35*, 4–28.

Spinath, F., Spinath, B., & Plomin, R. (2008). The nature and nurture of intelligence and motivation in the origins of sex differences in elementary school achievement. *European Journal of Personality, 22*, 211–229.

Stanford University Report. (2005, February 9). No evidence of innate gender differences in math and science, scholars assert. Stanford University.

Stanley, J., Keating, D. P., & Fox, L. H. (1974). *Mathematical talent: Discovery, description, and development*. Baltimore, MD: The Johns Hopkins University Press.

Steele, C. M. (1997). A threat is in the air: How stereotypes shape intellectual identity and performance. *American Psychologist, 52*, 613–629.

Steele, C. M., & Aronson, J. (1995). C. M. Steele and J. Aronson, Stereotype threat and the intellectual test performance of African Americans, *Journal of Personality and Social Psychology, 69*, 797–811.

Steinpreis, R. E., Anders, K. A., & Ritzke, D. (1999). The impact of gender on the review of the CVs of job applicants and tenure candidates: A national empirical study. *Sex Roles, 41*, 509–528.

Sternberg, R. J. (2004). Culture and intelligence. *American Psychologist, 59*(5), 325–338.

Strand, S., Deary, I. J., & Smith, P. (2006). Sex differences in cognitive abilities test scores: A UK national picture. *British Journal of Educational Psychology, 76*, 463–480.

Strenta, A. C., Elliott, R., Adair, R. Matier, M., & Scott, J. (1994). Choosing and leaving science in highly selective institutions. *Research in Higher Education, 35*, 513–547.

Stricker, L. J. (2006). Stereotype threat: A clarification. *Science, 312*, 1310–1312.

Stricker, L. J., & Ward, W. C. (2004). Stereotype threat, inquiring about test takers' ethnicity and gender, and standardized test performance. *Journal of Applied Social Psychology, 34*, 665–693.

Stricker, L. J., & Ward, W. C. (2008). Stereotype threat in applied settings re-examined: A reply. *Journal of Applied Social Psychology, 38*, 1656–1663.

Stumpf, H., & Stanley, J. C. (1998). Stability and change in gender-related differences on the college board advanced placement and achievement tests. *Current Directions in Psychological Science, 7*, 192–196.

Summers, L. H. (2005, January 14). Remarks at NBER on diversifying the science and engineering workforce. Cambridge, MA: National Bureau of Economic Research. Retrieved June 12, 2007, from http://www.president.harvard.edu/speeches/2005/nber.html

Swiatek, M. A., Lupkowski-Shoplik, A., & O'Donoghue, C. C. (2000). Gender differences in above-level EXPLORE scores of gifted third through sixth graders. *Journal of Educational Psychology, 92*, 718–723.

Sykes, C. J. (1988). *Profscam*. Regnery Gateway.

Tartre, L. A. (1990). Spatial skills, gender, and mathematics. In E. H. Fennema & G. C. Leder (Eds.), *Mathematics and gender* (pp. 27–59). New York: Teachers College Press.

Tendick, F., Downes, M., Goktekin, T., Cavusoglu, M., Feygin, D., Wu, X., et al. (2000). A virtual environment testbed for training laparoscopic surgical skills. *Presence: Teleoperators & Virtual Environments, 9*, 236–255.

Terzian, S. G. (2006). Science world, high school girls, and the prospect of scientific careers, 1957–1963. *History of Education Quarterly, 46*, 73–99.

Thilers, P., MacDonald, S. W. S., & Herlitz, A. (2006). The association between endogenous free testosterone and cognitive performance: A population-based study in 35 to 90 year-old men and women. *Psychoneuroendocrinology, 31*, 565–576.

Thurstone, L. L., & Thurstone, T. G. (1962). *The primary mental abilities test.* Chicago: Science Research Associates.

Trix, F., & Psenka, C. (2003). Exploring the color of glass: letters of recommendation for female and male medical faculty. *Discourse & Society, 14*(2), 191–220.

Turkheimer, E., & Halpern, D. (in press). Sex differences in variability for cognitive measures: Do the ends justify the genes? *Perspectives in Psychological Science.*

U.S. Department of Education, National Center for Education Statistics, Higher Education General Information Survey (HEGIS). "Degrees and Other Formal Awards Conferred Survey"; and Integrated Postsecondary Education Data System, "Completions Survey" (IPEDS-C:01), 2000–01.

Uttal, D. H., Gregg, V. H., Tan, L. S., Chamberline, M. H., & Sines, A. (2001). Connecting the dots: Children's use of a systematic figure to facilitate mapping and search. *Developmental Psychology, 37*, 338–350.

Valian, V. (1998). *Why so slow? The advancement of women.* Cambridge, MA: MIT Press.

Valian, V. (2007). Women at the top in science—and elsewhere. In S. J. Ceci & W. M. Williams (Eds.), *Why aren't more women in science? Top researchers debate the evidence* (pp. 27–37). Washington, DC: American Psychological Association.

Van Goozen, S. H. M., Cohen-Kettenis, P. T., Gooren, L. J. G., Frijda, N. H., & Van de Poll, N. E. (1994). Activating effects of androgens on cognitive performance: Causal evidence in a group of female-to-male transsexuals. *Neuropsychologia, 32*, 1153–1157.

Van Goozen, S. H. M., Cohen-Kettenis, P. T., Gooren, L. J. G., Frijda, N. H., & Van de Poll, N. E. (1995). Gender differences in behaviour: Activating effects of cross-sex hormones. *Psychoneuroendocrinology, 20*, 343–363.

Vandenberg, S. G., & Kuse, A. R. (1978). Mental rotations, a group test of three-dimensional spatial visualization, *Perceptual and Motor Skills, 47*, 599–604.

Vasta, R., Knott, J. A., & Gaze, C. E. (1996). Can spatial training erase the gender differences on the water-level task? *Psychology-of-Women Quarterly, 20*(4), 549–567.

Voyer, D., Boyer, S., & Bryden, M. P. (1995). Magnitude of sex differences in spatial abilities: A meta-analysis and consideration of critical variables. *Psychological Bulletin, 117*, 250–270.

Wai, J., Lubinski, D., & Benbow, C. P. (2005). Creativity and occupational accomplishments among intellectually precocious youths: An age 13 to age 33 longitudinal study. *Journal of Educational Psychology, 97*, 484–492.

Wainer, H., & Steinberg L. S. (1992). Sex differences in performance on the Mathematics section of the Scholastic Aptitude Test: A bidirectional validity study. *Harvard Educational Review, 62*, 323–336.

Walton, G. M., & Spencer, S. J. (in press). Latent ability: Grades and test scores systematically underestimate the intellectual ability of negatively stereotyped students. *Psychological Science.*

Watson, N. V., & Kimura, D. (1991). Nontrivial sex differences in throwing and intercepting: Relation to psychometrically-defined spatial functions. *Personality & Individual Differences, 12*, 375–385.

Webb, R. M., Lubinski, D., & Benbow, C. P. (2002). Mathematics facile adolescents with mathematics-science aspirations: New perspectives on their educational and vocational development. *Journal of Educational Psychology, 94*, 785–794.

Webb, T. J., O'Hara, B., & Freckleton, R. (2008, July). Does double-blind review benefit female authors? *Trends in Ecology and Evolution, 23*, 351–353.

Weinberger, C. J. (2005, September). Is the science and engineering workforce drawn from the far upper tail of the math ability distribution? Paper presented at the NBER Conference on Diversity in the Science and Engineering. University of Massachusetts, Amherst, MA.

Wenneras, C., & Wold, A. (1997). Nepotism and sexism in peer review. *Nature, 387*, 341–343.

Williams, J. C. (2007, March). The opt-out revolution revisited. *American Prospect, Special Report*, A12–A15.

Williams, C. L., & Meck, W. H. (1991). The organizational effects of gonadal steroids on sexually dimorphic spatial ability. *Psychoneuroendocrinology, 16*, 155–176.

Willingham, W. W., & Cole, N. S. (1997). *Gender and fair assessment.* Hillsdale, NJ: Erlbaum.

Wise, L. L., Steel, L., & MacDonald, C. (1979). *Origins and career consequences of sex differences in high school mathematics achievement* (Report to the National Institute of Education on its Grant NIE-G-78- 001). Palo Alto, CA: American Institutes for Research.

Wuchty, S., Jones, B., & Uzzi, B. (2007). Increasing dominance of teams in production of knowledge. *Science, 316*, 1036–1038.

Zak, P. J., Stanton, A. A., Ahmadi, A. 2007. Oxytocin increases generosity in humans. PLoS ONE 2(11): e1128. [1].

Xie, Y., & Shauman, K. A. (2003). *Women in science: Career processes and outcomes.* Cambridge, MA: Harvard University Press.

Index

Note: In this index, tables are indicated by "*t*", figures by "*f*" and notes by "*n*".